The Manual

For Dads

Kids don't come with a manual. Use this instead.

Ben Gannon

Copyright © 2017 Ben Gannon.

All rights reserved. This book or parts thereof may not be reproduced in any form, stored in any retrieval system, or transmitted in any form by any means—electronic, mechanical, photocopy, recording, or otherwise—without prior written permission of the publisher, except as provided by New Zealand copyright law.

ISBN: 9781520963082

For Shelley, the love of my life.

Contents

Introduction 1
Chapter 1: Taking a Stand Against Child Abuse 4
Chapter 2: Being a Better Man 18
Chapter 3: Getting Pregnant 64
Chapter 4: Pregnancy 75
Chapter 5: The First Year 96
Chapter 6: Ages 1 – 5 138
Chapter 7: Ages 5 – 13 198
Chapter 8: The Teenage Years - Ages 13 – 18 257
Chapter 9: Into Adulthood 314

Introduction

Congratulations dad. Either you've got kids or you soon will do - there's no greater gift in life. Whether you're rich or poor, black or white, gay or straight - we're all hardwired to become totally and utterly fulfilled through the simple act of being a parent.

Make no mistake though, dad, this is some serious shit. One or more little humans are going to rely on you to not only provide the basic necessities of life, but also to guide them and nurture them through childhood and set them on a trajectory for a happy and successful adulthood.

Nothing is going to have a more profound impact on your kids' self-esteem and lifelong happiness than their childhood. The childhood that you give them.

Give them a healthy, happy and supportive childhood and chances are they'll grow into confident, secure and happy adults. Mess it up, like far too many dads do, and they're likely to carry the scars with them forever.

It's all on you.

Unfortunately we enter parenthood as hopeless beginners. Parenting can also be tedious, stressful and exhausting. If we're not careful parenting can become a grind, affecting our happiness and our relationships with others.

In this book I present a practical, values-based approach to parenting. From before the kids are born through to adulthood, this approach will help all of us to be better dads and, most important, will help us to build stronger, happier relationships with our spouses and children.

This approach has helped me to move on from my own childhood of poverty and neglect and to become a great husband to my lovely wife and father to my four wonderful children. It is the result of years of parenting, study and from seeking the advice of others. It is based on the results of academic research, some of which is very recent, but I intentionally keep the tone conversational to make this book as accessible as possible to every reader.

This book contains no secrets or magic tricks. You won't become a baby whisperer or Nanny McPhee after reading it, as these things do not exist. Kids are people, not drones. They have vibrant personalities that can often drive us crazy and this is a good thing. Imagine how boring life would be if we humans weren't constantly compelled to seek out the companionship and responses of others. If we weren't constantly compelled to test our boundaries and to understand the universe we live in.

This is all they are doing. It may sometimes feel like your kids were sent to test the limits of your patience, but all they are doing is slowly expanding the limits of their universe.

What this book *will* do is teach you how to be the lighthouse while your children are the sea. You will be their beacon and their guide, remaining grounded and centred during periods of calm and when the waves surge and the storms come. And they will come.

Just to be clear, this book isn't about religion and if you find any religious connotations then they're purely coincidental. For the record I'm an atheist, but that's irrelevant. We can share common values, and be great parents, even if we don't share the same religious beliefs.

What's important is that we become the adults that we want our children to become. Given half a chance, they will become the adults that we are, for better or worse.

Not only will we set an example that will guide our children through a happy, contented childhood and into an exciting adulthood, but one that will make us happy and more fulfilled in the process.

The Manual

The first section of this book focuses on us as adults and the things that we need to do in our lives to enable us to become great dads. The second section covers the five key phases that our kids follow into childhood, from pregnancy to adolescence, and parenting strategies for each. The third and final section of this book focuses on making the transition from parenting children to parenting adults and on maintaining and strengthening the bonds that tie us. If we're lucky we'll be parents to adults for a lot longer than we're parents to children, but handling the transition can be harder than we think.

No matter what stage of parenthood you're in, whether your kids are still a twinkle in your eye or whether your kids are parents themselves, I encourage you to read this book from cover to cover. I know for a fact that you will learn something, because I know that I'll learn something each time I go back to it, too.

You see, the parenting techniques set out in this book are as obvious as they are simple, but we all need reminders from time to time about what they are and how they're applied.

Most important, when we're stressed and harassed and being grumpy with our kids it's important to remember not to wish a single moment away. It's true what your mum and dad said - they do grow up so fast and this stressed, harassed and grumpy moment won't be repeated. One day, when they've grown up and flown the coop you'll look back and wish that you could rewind the clock and go back to a moment just like this, if even for a little while.

If you play your cards right then so will they, so don't wish this moment away.

Chapter 1: Taking a Stand Against Child Abuse

Our first and most important role as a father and as a man is to protect our families from harm, but far too many of us are the harm that our kids and spouses need protection from.

In my home country of New Zealand we have a shocking level of domestic violence and abuse in our society, including all too many cases of physical, emotional and sexual abuse. And successive governments who seem perpetually unable to do anything about it.

One of the saddest facts about domestic abuse is that most of it goes unreported. It happens behind closed doors. Not only in the poorer suburbs, but in all of our communities.

Domestic abuse often results in physical injuries but, except in the most extreme cases, these injuries heal and can have little lasting impact on our lives. All forms of abuse, however, result in emotional wounds that remain with us for a lot longer - sometimes these don't heal at all.

Abuse can take many forms and we need to be strong enough to take a stand against it, no matter what. We need to be man enough to eliminate all forms of abuse from our kids' lives.

The first step is to recognise abuse in all its forms and, most important, to recognise any propensity for abuse within ourselves.

All forms of domestic abuse have a common purpose - to allow the abuser to gain control over the abused. Although men are the most common culprits in abusive relationships, wives, mothers, grandmothers and even children can inflict abuse on family members and loved ones.

Below is a description of the various types of domestic abuse - from the physical to the emotional. No single type of abuse is any more or less damaging as the others and often multiple forms of abuse are used to allow to the abuser to gain and maintain control over the abused.

As you read through this list I want you to reflect carefully about abuse in your life. Were you subjected to domestic abuse as a child? Are you being subjected to it now? As a father do you use abuse to control your kids or other members of your family? Far too many of us have suffered abuse at some time of our life and far too many of us fail to recognise our propensity to abuse others, to continue the cycle of abuse, until it's too late.

We need to take a zero tolerance approach to all forms of abuse - physical or otherwise. Not only within our families, but in our communities. If we want to be good fathers then we must set an example that our kids will not only be proud of but that they will want to follow.

What about smacking, you say? Smacking isn't violence, it's part of good parenting. My dad smacked me and I'm fine!

Thankfully fewer and fewer of us think this way, but if this is you then let me give you a smack and you tell me that it's not violence. Let me stand over you yelling and waving my belt in your face and tell me that it's not violence.

I would never do that, because it is violence. If this is how you treat your children then you're not 'fine'. You're repeating the same cycle of violence against your own kids that you experienced and there's nothing 'fine' about it.

But doesn't smacking our kids will make them behave better? Actually, no. Smacked kids behave no better than other kids. If anything their behaviour is worse and they're much more likely than non-smacked kids to grow up and repeat the cycle of violence against their children. Then they can claim that being smacked as a kid did them no harm, oblivious to the damage that they're doing to their children, who are much more likely to grow up to smack their kids. And the cycle continues.

Remember that domestic abuse is used to control, but being a great parent isn't about controlling your child, it's about coaching and supporting your child and *correcting* their behaviour when they misbehave. Besides, humans, even little humans, can never be completely controlled. Smacked kids bristle at the constant threat of violence and they will rebel in their own little ways. This results in more challenges to dad's authority and more rattling of cage doors, poorer behaviour and, ultimately, more smacking. When more smacking doesn't 'fix' the problem then what? We're now out of options or, worse, we resort to greater and greater levels of violence to try and regain control over our increasingly difficult to manage children.

Two of the biggest challenges that we have in preventing domestic abuse are:

1. Recognising the signs of abuse, particularly when the culprit is us or a loved one. It is often the case that the more serious the abuse, the more the abuser rationalises it to himself and convinces himself that it is normal and acceptable.
2. Having the courage to put a stop to the abuse and to take steps to avoid it from happening again. It is our duty to proactively identify and prevent abuse within our families and within our communities, but doing so takes great courage and it takes *action*.

So before you go any further, please read the definitions of domestic abuse below and take a deep look inside and ask yourself 'is this me?' Ask not just 'have I done these things' but 'can I do these things' - if the answer is 'yes' to either question then do something about it. Not tomorrow or next week or the next time you remember, but now. No matter how old our kids are, it is never, never too late to take a stand against abuse and to amend our ways.

In my case the biggest challenge was recognising the nature of my abusive behaviour. I would never dream of smacking my kids, despite the frequent spankings that I received as child, so I considered myself a non-violent dad. It took me a while to realise that I was using my size, temper and voice to intimidate my children, however, particularly my son, who I found challenging at times. Things came to a head when I lost my temper one day, threw a chair at the floor, yelled at my son and thumped a wall hard enough to make a hole.

This left him, and my other three kids, afraid and in tears and it left me feeling two inches tall. I wish it hadn't happened, but it was the wake-up call that I needed and I'm taking proactive steps to make sure it doesn't happen again. Because I started by focusing on addressing the reasons behind my son's behaviour, his behaviour has also improved, making us all happier in the process.

If you do engage in abusive behaviour then it may be that the scars that you've inflicted, to others and to yourself, may never heal. But it is never too late to stop inflicting more damage and to demonstrate to your children that you can change and that you can set an example for them to live by. As you will learn in this book, we are constantly setting the example that our children will model on their way through life.

But to become that example, you must start right now.

So this is our one and only hard and fast rule as a father:

The Father's Rule: We Are Non-violent

Violence and abuse are not ok. We will live non-violent lives and we will always treat others, particularly members of our families, with compassion and respect, even when those virtues are not reflected back at us.

We are the lighthouse, not the sea. When the sea rages all around us we remain calm. When pounded by the waves we do not seek to become waves travelling in the opposite direction. We stand firm, providing our kids with the beacon that they need to find their way. We are the unyielding presence that they will rely on, time and time again, to provide guidance, comfort and reassurance as they surge toward adulthood.

Although we always retain the right to protect ourselves and our families from harm, we will be man enough to turn the other cheek and to find non-violent resolutions to every situation.

We believe in constructive discipline, but we recognise that violence and discipline are not the same thing. We recognise that emotional and physical violence is a sign of weakness, not strength. When we are violent we are not gaining control, we have lost control. When we are violent we harm ourselves while harming those around us.

We will recognise abuse in all its forms, including physical, emotional and sexual abuse, and we will take action to prevent it, particularly within our own homes.

We understand that turning the other cheek does not mean turning away from victims of violence and we take proactive measures to protect victims of violence.

Forms of Domestic Abuse

Source: Wikipedia (abbreviated)

Don't skip this section - you'll be amazed at how many people recognise signs of abuse for the first time after reading this stuff. Even if you don't recognise the propensity for domestic violence in yourself, reading this may very well help you to identify it in others. Remember that your children are much more likely to suffer abuse at the hands of someone they know, someone from within your family or circle of friends, than at the hands of a stranger, so we must remain vigilant at all times.

The 'finding help' section below will hopefully not apply to you but it may just help you to help someone else.

Physical

Physical abuse is abuse involving contact intended to cause feelings of intimidation, pain, injury, or other physical suffering or bodily harm.

Physical abuse includes hitting, slapping, punching, choking, pushing, burning and other types of contact that result in physical injury to the victim. Physical abuse can also include behaviours such as denying the victim of medical care when needed, depriving the victim of sleep or other functions necessary to live, or forcing the victim to engage in drug/alcohol use against his/her will. If a person is suffering from any physical harm then they are experiencing physical abuse. This pain can be experienced on any level. It can also include inflicting physical injury onto other targets, such as children or pets, in order to cause psychological harm to the victim.

Sexual

Sexual abuse is any situation in which force or threat is used to obtain participation in unwanted sexual activity. Coercing a person to engage in sexual activity against their will, even if that person is a spouse or intimate partner with whom consensual sex has occurred, is an act of aggression and violence.

Sexual violence is defined by World Health Organization as:

any sexual act, attempt to obtain a sexual act, unwanted sexual comments or advances, or acts to traffic, or otherwise directed, against a person's sexuality using coercion, by any person regardless of their relationship to the victim, in any setting, including but not limited to home and work.

Marital rape, also known as spousal rape, is non-consensual sex in which the perpetrator is the victim's spouse. As such, it is a form of partner rape, of domestic violence, and of sexual abuse.

Categories of sexual abuse include:

1. Use of physical force to compel a person to engage in a sexual act against his or her will, whether or not the act is completed;
2. Attempted or completed sex act involving a person who is unable to understand the nature or condition of the act, unable to decline participation, or unable to communicate unwillingness to engage in the sexual act, e.g., because of underage immaturity, illness, disability, or the influence of alcohol or other drugs, or because of intimidation or pressure.

Emotional

Emotional abuse (also called psychological abuse or mental abuse) can include humiliating the victim privately or publicly, controlling what the victim can and cannot do, withholding information from the victim, deliberately doing something to make the victim feel diminished or embarrassed, isolating the victim from friends and family, implicitly blackmailing the victim by harming others when the victim expresses independence or happiness, or denying the victim access to money or other basic resources and necessities. Degradation in any form can be considered psychological abuse.

Emotional abuse can include verbal abuse and is defined as any behaviour that threatens, intimidates, undermines the victim's self-worth or self-esteem, or controls the victim's freedom. This can include threatening the victim with injury or harm, telling the victim that they will be killed if they ever leave the relationship, and public humiliation. Constant criticism, name-calling, and making statements that damage the victim's self-esteem are also common verbal forms of emotional abuse.

Often perpetrators will attempt and often attempt and may succeed in alienating (parental alienation), a child from a parent or extended family member, and in doing so also victimize the child when the child is engaged in emotional abuse by encouraging, teaching or forcing them to harshly criticize another victim. Emotional abuse includes conflicting actions or statements which are designed to confuse and create insecurity in the victim. These behaviours also lead the victims to question themselves, causing them to believe that they are making up the abuse or that the abuse is their fault.

Emotional abuse includes forceful efforts to isolate the victim, keeping them from contacting friends or family. This is intended to eliminate those who might try to help the victim leave the relationship and to create a lack of resources for them to rely on if they were to leave. Isolation results in damaging the victim's sense of internal strength, leaving them feeling helpless and unable to escape from the situation.

People who are being emotionally abused often feel as if they do not own themselves; rather, they may feel that their significant other has nearly total control over them. Women or men undergoing emotional abuse often suffer from depression, which puts them at increased risk for suicide, eating disorders, and drug and alcohol abuse.

Verbal

Verbal abuse is a form of emotionally abusive behaviour involving the use of language. Verbal abuse can also be referred to as the act of threatening. Through threatening a person can blatantly say they will harm you in any way and will also be considered as abuse. It may include profanity but can occur with or without the use of expletives.

Verbal abuse may include aggressive actions such as name-calling, blaming, ridicule, disrespect, and criticism, but there are also less obviously aggressive forms of verbal abuse. Statements that may seem benign on the surface can be thinly veiled attempts to humiliate; falsely accuse; or manipulate others to submit to undesirable behaviour, make others feel unwanted and unloved, threaten others economically, or isolate victims from support systems.

In Jekyll and Hyde behaviours, the abuser may fluctuate between sudden rages and false joviality toward the victim; or may simply show a very different "face" to the outside world than to the victim. While oral communication is the most common form of verbal abuse, it includes abusive communication in written form.

Economic

Economic abuse is a form of abuse when one intimate partner has control over the other partner's access to economic resources. Economic abuse may involve preventing a spouse from resource acquisition, limiting the amount of resources to use by the victim, or by exploiting economic resources of the victim. The motive behind preventing a spouse from acquiring resources is to diminish victim's capacity to support his/herself, thus forcing him/her to depend on the perpetrator financially, which includes preventing the victim from obtaining education, finding employment, maintaining or advancing their careers, and acquiring assets.

In addition, the abuser may also put the victim on an allowance, closely monitor how the victim spends money, spend victim's money without his/her consent and creating debt, or completely spend victim's savings to limit available resources.

Getting Help

If you use abuse or violence then the first and most important step is to take responsibility for your behaviour. Violence doesn't 'just happen' and it's not an appropriate response to someone else's behaviour. If you aren't man enough to take responsibility for your behaviour then there's no way you're going to be able to change it.

The next step is to take action and seek help. Telling yourself that you will change your behaviour is a good start, but far too many men suffer regret after dishing out violence and tell themselves that it won't happen again, only to relapse the next time they find themselves drunk, on drugs, in a stressful situation or simply if the mood takes them.

Making a commitment to changing your behaviour requires you to face up to your behaviour in the first place. If you abuse your loved ones then they will usually be complicit in covering it up, in-part due to the shame of allowing themselves to be abused, but mainly out of a misguided loyalty to their husband or father.

Face up to your loved ones. Tell them that you have done wrong and that it is **not** their fault. Explain to them what you are going to do to prevent it from happening again. If the abuse is serious then remove them from harm's way before it happens again. Remember, the more serious the abuse the more likely it is to recur, so *if you can't be trusted then either leave or help your family get to safety until you can find help*.

Then call the cops. That's right, call the police and tell them exactly what has happened. Own up and front up and take the ultimate responsibility for your actions.

Where I'm from in New Zealand even smacking your kids is illegal, as well it should be. My kids know that domestic violence, including smacking, is illegal and they, along with the rest of my family, expect there will be consequences if one of us breaks the law.

Those same kids are likely to go to great lengths to conceal the signs of abuse if I was to raise a hand to them (or worse), which would greatly exacerbate the harm caused to them and to me. They would know that my behaviour is illegal, but they would feel powerless to tell anyone about it.

Calling the police is a big step - the greater the abuse the bigger the step that it is. Certain types of abuse could even result in a jail term, but the simple act of handing yourself in to the police and owning up to your actions will help reduce any punishment that you receive.

Calling the police is a big step, but it isn't optional. If we are going to use a values-based approach to parenting, if we are going to teach our kids by example, then we can't make them complicit in covering up our actions. We can't burden them with a dark secret that they will carry with them for the rest of their lives. Just because you stop abusing them it doesn't mean the damage you've caused will magically disappear.

We need to take responsibility for those actions and demonstrate to them the true consequences of them.

If you have abused the ones you love, either physically or otherwise, then it's almost certain that you and your family will be involved in a conspiracy to conceal the abuse. You will convince yourself that it's not as bad as it is or that the abuse was provoked or otherwise acceptable. Maybe, in your mind, the abuse is ok because you've made amends and you're working hard on making sure it doesn't happen again.

But you haven't made amends, have you? You've created this dark and violent secret, a shame that your family will carry with them, which they will stay silent about out of some misguided, twisted loyalty.

Children need fathers, but they need safety more. If your abuse is likely to result in less access to your children then that is exactly what should happen. Put them and their safety first.

If you have used violence against another then the damage is done. Reporting that action to the police is not what will cause the punishment, but the action that has already taken place. Often if you don't report it then it will come out in other ways, so avoiding prosecution is not assured, even if you're not man enough to report it yourself.

In my case my actions were thankfully not serious enough to warrant police involvement, but once I recognised my behaviour I was careful to make sure I followed my own advice. I apologised to my son and to the rest of my family for my behaviour, told them it was wrong and explained why it was wrong. I told them that it wasn't anyone's fault but my own.

I spoke about it openly with my friends and sought their support and guidance. They were shocked, particularly at hearing I had punched a hole in the wall, but they were supportive and helpful. This helped me address my feelings of guilt and to strengthen my resolve that I would remain the lighthouse, and not become the ocean, in future.

Help is often only a phone call or a Google search away, but you need to be proactive and seek it out. There are violence prevention services in every country and they are there to help the abuser as well as the abused. Find one that will help you to take action to prevent abuse and be honest with them - no one can help you unless you're man enough face up completely to your actions.

Helping Others

One of the truly heart-breaking facts about child abuse is that, in nearly every case, others have been aware of the abuse but have not taken adequate action (or any action at all) to prevent it.

Four out of five cases of child abuse (that's 80%) are perpetuated by one or more of the child's parents. Put another way, in the vast majority of child abuse cases it is a parent who is the abuser.

Those who witness the abuse are usually family, neighbours or family friends of the abuser. It is human nature for us to minimise, in our minds, the significance of negative behaviours that we observe in those who we know and love. Our minds fill with uncertainty and we are inclined to want to give the abuser the benefit of the doubt. We are also compelled to maintain the status quo, to keep the peace, so to speak, which can paralyse us and preventing us from acting on what we see or hear.

We fear that our interaction will hurt the abused more than the abuser.

We fear the ramifications of our actions if we call out abuse and act against the abuser. Sadly, these fears are often not unfounded. Many families rally around the abuser, not the abused, and taking action against abuse can impact negatively against us.

This is not our fault. It is the fault of the abuser and it is a result of their actions, not ours.

We will always remember that the welfare of the child is the only thing that is important in cases of child abuse and we will not let these fears cloud our judgement.

It is a truly shocking statistic that one in five children in Western countries will be sexually abused or sexually assaulted before the age of 13. One in five. Yet most of these assaults go unreported and most of the perpetrators are never brought to justice.

It is our jobs, as parents and as compassionate human beings, to rail against human nature and to reject the complacency that allows so many of our children to be abused and so many abusers to escape the consequences of their actions.

If you witness the signs of child abuse it is likely to be the tip of the iceberg. Most abuse happens while you are not watching and it could be happening to others, so don't minimise it in your mind - take note and take action.

Later in this book we will look at strategies for teaching your kids how to tell between 'yes' feelings and 'no' feelings. Kids know instinctively when something *feels* wrong and we will learn how to give them the confidence and vocabulary to tell others about it.

If we become aware of child abuse, including if reported by the child themselves, then we must take action. It is our moral, and often our legal, duty to do so.

Talk to a professional straight away. Don't treat it like a family matter that needs to be kept under wraps.

If the abuse is serious, even if you suspect it is serious, then phone the police. Don't sit there worrying about whether or not you're going to waste police time - it is not your job to decide whether a crime has occurred or if someone needs protection, it is theirs. Nothing is more important than the safety of the child, so pick up the phone.

There are also governmental and charitable organisations that can help and can easily be found online. Seek help to prevent abuse, but also to help abused children to deal with the effects of their abuse. Remember that these agencies, particularly governmental agencies, can be bureaucratic and ineffective at times, so you may need to be tenacious and persistent to get help. Be prepared to do so.

If you know of someone who is being abused then don't tell yourself that you can't get involved. You're already involved, so seek help and take action.

Chapter 2: Being a Better Man

It may come as a surprise, but the first and most important chapter of The Manual hardly discusses kids or parenting strategies at all. To be great dads we have to first look inward. We have to take a long hard look at ourselves and ask 'am I the dad I want my kids to have? Am I the dad that I wish I had?'

You need to identify your strengths and weaknesses and put a plan together to address any shortcomings. You need a plan for making yourself a better man.

What if you don't *need* to be a better man?

We all need to be better.

There's always room for improvement - I'm not saying we should be self-critical, but we should always be looking for opportunities to improve our lives and the lives of our families. We stop moving forward when we're dead and if we're dead then we're not about to make very good parents.

If you're not yet a dad (and you don't have a baby on the way) then it's important to assess whether you're ready to have children and whether you have the skills and resources required to give them the childhood that they deserve. It's a good opportunity to delay having kids until you know that you're ready.

Remember, nothing is going to have a bigger impact on your kids' development than the example that you set them. Nothing is going to have a bigger impact on their happiness during childhood and nothing is going to have a bigger impact on their behaviour.

This is where most parenting books fall over. In this politically correct age many authors avoid focussing on the fitness of the parent, but that's a cop-out. If we're too lazy or too stupid to work hard at being the best parents we can be then we probably won't be very good at all. If we're not willing to make an effort then it's almost certain that our kids will follow our example. Their behaviour will suffer, they'll be less motivated and they're more likely to suffer from self-esteem and relationship issues throughout their lives.

So let's not make excuses for ourselves and let's not shy away from the importance, if we're to be great dads, husbands, men, of starting with ourselves. Let's remember that it's never too late, not while we have breath in our lungs, to better ourselves and it should be our mission to continuously improve, to keep learning and to provide an example worth emulating to our children.

Are You Old Enough?

If you're considering becoming a dad then one of the most fundamental questions you need to ask yourself is whether you're old enough for this responsibility? Have you had the life experiences necessary to make you a great dad?

Far too many parents don't stop to ask themselves this and end up having children before their time. In my home country of New Zealand teenage pregnancy is at epidemic proportions. New Zealand is not alone - most developed countries face this issue.

Evolution has provided us with bodies that are capable of reproducing well before we are emotionally ready. This may have served us well when we were living in caves and dying at a young age (making early reproduction vital for the survival of our species), but in our modern, fast-paced society we're not fully equipped to be parents until well into adulthood.

As teens (and often well into our twenties) we also have a tendency to know *everything*, disdain authority and display poor decision making skills.

Have sex without protection? Fuck yeah! Dad says I should be using protection, but what does he know? Besides, I'M GOING TO HAVE SEX! I'm not going to let a lack of condoms get in the way of me getting my end in!

Kids end up having kids and it's a disaster. Children of young parents are much more likely than others to grow up in broken homes and in poverty. They are much more likely to under-achieve socially and academically and typically fail to meet their full potential as adults. Saddest of all, they are significantly more likely to become parents before their time, perpetuating the cycle throughout generations. What a gift to give your children and grandchildren!

We should be careful not to demonise young parents - we should all support each other as parents, regardless of age and background. But if you are young and sexually active (or wanting to be) then take time to ask yourself 'am I too young to become a dad?'

If you're not yet 25 then probably, so put a rubber on it and wait until you're ready.

25? But don't our teenage years end when we turn 20? Why 25?

In reality the 'right' time to become a dad is different for every one of us, but it is my strong belief that our first quarter century in life should be about us. We spend this time developing our academic, professional and social skills and figuring out what we're going to do with our lives. If we're lucky, we spend part of this time travelling and experiencing the world and broadening our horizons.

We need time to develop our earning potential and to develop our relationships. We have to find our life partner, someone who we're likely to still want to be with in 20 years, even after the ravages of parenthood, and this takes time.

It's only as we get older that we can look back at our younger selves and realise how little we knew and how much we have learned since.

If we become teenage parents then we stunt our growth and development, which stunts the future growth and development of our children. Instead of broadening our horizons during our first quarter century we narrow our horizons and constrict our own development.

It is impossible to be a well-rounded teenage parent, just as it is impossible for us to develop fully as adults until we are in our twenties, regardless of our life experiences. Developing wisdom requires time.

So step one in being a better man is asking yourself whether you're old enough to be a dad and to be strong enough to wait until your time comes. This means not only not *trying* to have kids, but proactively trying *not to*. Wear a condom. It will not only protect you against becoming a father at a young age, it will also protect you and your partner against a wide range of sexually transmitted diseases. If you don't have a condom then abstain from vaginal sex until you get one. It's that simple.

Maybe it's too late and you've either had kids or you're going to have kids before your time? If that's the case then you've got even more work to do than the rest of us. Not only be a great dad and to raise happy kids, but to also find time to educate yourself, develop your skills and grow as a man so that becoming a young parent isn't the only example you end up setting for your children.

Being a teen father doesn't mean that your responsibilities are any less than for the rest of us, so man up and read on... there's a lot of work to be done.

Nurturing Your Core Values

Our values-based approach to parenting revolves around the idea that our children learn more from *our* words and actions than from anyone or anything else.

Our children look up to us and they emulate us. We are their role models and our values become their values. Our beliefs become their beliefs. Our behaviours become their behaviours.

This is, of course, unless they eventually reject our values or behaviours, which is indicative of a flaw in those values and/or in the relationship between parent and child.

It is scary how young in life our children start observing and emulating our behaviour - from the moment they are born they are looking to us for reassurance and guidance. They read our emotions and they are in tune with our thoughts and feelings, even when they're too young to understand what any of it really means.

It is important, therefore, that we take time to identify and nurture our core values - the values that we hold most important and that we seek to live our lives by. These core values will form the foundations upon which the example that we set our children will be built. Without strong values these foundations will be built on sand, meaning we set an inconsistent, irresponsible or downright dangerous example for our kids to follow.

My mother had strong values around equality and human rights and I'm proud that I inherited these. She also had negative values around honesty and theft - she abhorred the idea of people stealing from each other but, to her, stealing from organisations was fine. In her mind stealing from organisations was a victimless crime and my brother and I witnessed many examples of casual theft as children. From her stealing items from work to lying about our ages to get us into the zoo for free, we grew up thinking it was fine to steal as long as it wasn't a fellow human being who we were ripping off.

Unfortunately these negative values also became my values and I too became an opportunistic, petty thief who wouldn't hesitate to steal from organisations, including an employer here or there, if given the chance.

But of course I was stealing from people. I rationalised it to myself that companies had insurance and that such petty theft was a mere annoyance to my victims if that - no company was going to go broke based on the scale of my offending.

I used to think that people didn't steal were naive, that they were too straight or too scared to help themselves when the opportunity arose. Now I realise who was naive and that it actually takes greater self-control and courage to display integrity than it does to take that which does not belong to you.

It troubles me that it took so long to come to this realisation and it troubles me greater to think of things that I have stolen over time. We're not talking a lifetime of crime here, far from it, but it was still ugly and I regret it.

I don't blame mum for my actions, as I chose to steal, but it is clear to me how strongly her core values around theft and dishonesty became my core values and how difficult it was for me to finally realise how flawed and downright wrong my values, and my behaviour, were.

And so it is for us with our children - their core values will mirror ours. More than we'll ever realise. They will learn what's right and wrong through us well before they have the ability to ask whether or not our example is a poor one.

There are lots of reasons why we should nurture our core values and live values-based lives. Our values give us direction and inform our decisions. They help us to continue to grow and develop over the entire course of our lifetimes. Most important, they help us to become better parents and to set better examples for our children.

I can't tell you what your core values should be any more than you can tell me mine, as our values are our own. Whether my values are compatible or not with yours is not important. What is important is that we nurture our core values, our most important values, and that we live by them.

It took me far too long to realise that stealing, any kind of stealing, was wrong and for me to make integrity one of my core values. Over time this value has become increasingly important, however, and now I am proud of the fact that now no temptation is too great - I can't remember the last thing I stole and I've never been happier about it. I used to think that people who didn't steal were fools for not taking advantage of pilfering opportunities that would arise from time to time. Now I see that I was the fool and that any idiot can rip someone else off. Most of all I can see how likely it is that my kids would have turned out to be common thieves if I hadn't starting *living* my core value of not stealing.

I can't tell you what your core values should be, but here are a few guidelines that we can all benefit from:

- Live your core values. Start now. Talk is cheap - in fact, those who talk the most about their values are often the least likely to demonstrate them in their actions. Live your core values and let your example talk louder than words.
- Prioritise happiness. What's the point of anything if it doesn't make you and your loved ones happy? It's fine to value hard work and a great education, I certainly do, but these things are meaningless if you and your family are not happy, so don't lose sight of the wood for the trees.
- Use the power of good. Values are not an excuse for hatred, violence or bigotry. Your core values are your own, but take some time to reflect on them carefully - are there any that you (or any well-meaning person) would not want to pass on to your children? If so then get rid of the bad and embrace the good and be proud of your values and actions.
  Don't rationalise or make excuses for bigotry. You can't justify bigotry against gays because of your religion, for example - it's still bigotry and bigotry has no place in our core values.
- Conduct regular health checks. Our values change and evolve over time. It pays to regularly reassess them and to

make adjustments as necessary.

One of my early parenting values, for example, was to have well behaved, respectful children who did what they were told, when they were told and without question. Obedience and conformity, when it came to children, were definitely a core value. Over time, however, I've come to realise the importance of letting them display their personalities, even if it means letting them misbehave ever so slightly sometimes.

Take time to regularly assess your core values and how they are working out. Think as objectively as possible about what's working well and what you need to change.

- It's never too late. It's never, ever, too late to start living a values-based life. It doesn't matter how old or how hopeless we think we are - our lives and the lives of our children will benefit from each and every one of us identifying, nurturing and living by our core values.

  Many of us are stuck in cycles of poverty, abuse or destructive behaviour. We certainly suffered from our share of sexual abuse, alcoholism and dishonesty in our family. Too often these are patterns that have weaved themselves through generations.

  Unfortunately these factors can darken our souls well before we are old enough to form values systems of our own, but none of us is beyond help and it's never too late to better ourselves.

Take a moment to write down your core values and what they mean to you. It may feel a bit trite, but it's worth the time and effort. Keep the list short enough that you can easily memorise your core values. It's easy enough to write pages and pages of *values* but each of us only has a handful of core values that we live our lives by.

Getting Your Relationships Right

Life is about relationships and it is meaningless without them. We are defined by the relationships that occur during our short time on this planet. Our relationships, not our material wealth, shape us and have a profound impact on our happiness and sense of fulfilment.

This is why, in study after study, scientists find no correlation between wealth and happiness. In fact, often they find a negative correlation between wealth and happiness. This means that, excluding the destitute, who are unlikely to be happy for obvious reasons, the wealthier we become the less happy we are with our lives. This is often because the wealthier we become the more we prioritise the acquisition of wealth over maintaining strong relationships. Being wealthy can also mean being preoccupied with work, being constantly stressed out and having little time for your families.

The strength and quality of our relationships, particularly the relationships with those closest to us, will also have a profound impact on our children.

If we don't have our relationships right then we can't be great dads. We can't expect our kids to develop meaningful and rewarding relationships themselves if they haven't learned to do so from us. If you find it hard form positive relationships with those around you, especially those closest to you, then you'll also find it harder to form positive relationships with your kids, making it harder for them to form positive relationships with their kids and so on.

Getting your relationships right has nothing to do with being popular and everything to do with loving and being loved. Happiness is not brought by the *quantity* of the relationships we have with others, but the *quality* of those relationships.

Start with those closest to you and work your way outward. Think about the health of each relationship in terms of how happy or otherwise having each loved one in your life makes you feel. Are you always happy to see each other? Do you fight or do either of you inflict harm on the other (emotional or otherwise)? Do you find yourself wishing for someone else?

It's Quantity Time, Not Quality Time

Your family needs your time and attention. It's not enough to just be there, you have to be there *with them*. There's no such thing as 'quality time vs. quantity time' - your family just needs *your time*.

For me and my wife this can mean going on date nights, but we're just as happy on the couch watching TV together, often too tired to talk after a stressful day of work and family demands.

My kids love special activities with me and my wife, but nothing is more special to them than the one on one time that we have with them or dad lying with them in bed for 20 minutes at bedtime to talk about their day.

If you don't have enough time for your family then you have a problem that this book won't help you solve. You have to make time for your family. If this means making difficult life choices then make them, as you only get one chance to do this right.

You also have to make time for your friends. I don't see my friends nearly as often as I would like, but we do organise a number of annual get-togethers that allow us to remain close, even if we haven't seen each other for long periods in-between.

Say I Love You

Everyone in your family should hear you tell them you love them at least once per day.

There are no more powerful words in the English language. In any language for that matter.

You should tell your kids that you love them even before they're old enough to know what the words mean and keep telling them. They need to hear it.

I read about a recent study from the UK that showed a quarter of adults felt too awkward to tell their fathers that they loved them. One in four. This is a sad and ridiculous statistic.

Now if you're reading this and thinking 'that's not what we do in our family', 'we know that we love each other without having to say it' or that kind of thing then you're fooling yourself. It's bullshit.

Of course your family knows that you love them, but they also *need to hear it*. When they're old enough they need to be able to say it too, so make it normal. Make it expected.

Show your partner, your kids, your parents and all of those closest to you that your love is unconditional. If you've fought with your partner and you're still frosty with each other then still tell each other you love each other if one of you is going out or off to bed.

If you're one of those who feel too awkward to say I love you to one or both of your parents then for fucks sake grow up and pick up the phone and tell them right now. Sure there will be a history between you and things that are unsaid, but fuck all that. One of you might be hit by a bus tomorrow and by then it might be too late.

This isn't just about you and the adults closest to you. It's also about your kids. They need be reassured that the people they love the most also *love each other*.

So pick up the phone and tell your parents that you love them. Don't blurt it out at the end of the conversation and then slam the phone down - make it clear and deliberate. Let it hang there. If you get an 'I love you too' then great, but be prepared for the fact that your mum or dad might be taken by surprise and they may duff their chance to reciprocate.

That's ok. Our love is not a prize that must be won or a payment that must be earned. We don't withhold saying 'I love you' because we're afraid that we might not hear it back.

Someone once told me that by saying 'I love you' too much you run the risk of making it meaningless, but this is far from the truth. Love is oxygen for the soul. Without it we wither inside.

So tell your kids that you love them. Tell them often and tell them always. Never follow it up with 'but' - we just love them and they deserve to hear it.

Fun

What's the point of life without fun? The daily grind can sap us of our energy, leaving us tired, grumpy and short tempered. Often our sense of humour is first to go, which is counter-productive, as nothing makes the grind more bearable than having fun.

Relationships are important, but they should never be too serious. You should be able to crack jokes with your loved ones that you'd never dare crack in public and in situations that don't always call for humour. There's no better end to an argument than when someone cracks a joke or lets a fart rip and cuts the tension with the sharp knife of wit. Ok, hot make-up sex is an even better end to an argument, but let's be realistic. Anyway, not all arguments are going to be with your partner.

Fun and spontaneity go hand in hand, but sometimes spontaneity needs a bit of help, so think about injecting fun into your relationships, particularly those at home. Sing. Be goofy. Don't be afraid to ham it up and make a dick of yourself. Book a trip away as a surprise to the family. Take everyone out for a cheap meal to celebrate Tuesday. Yay, it's Tuesday!

If it's a nice night then pile them into the car for a trip to the local park, for a walk on the beach or anything that involves time together. Even if it's just for half an hour, something is better than nothing.

Being fun can be easy, but all too often we forget to stop worrying and stop rushing and just have a laugh.

Your kids, like mine, are *hanging out* to have fun with their dad. Give them a hint that they're about to get a tickle or a tussle and they'll light up. My kids won't remember how great dinner was or how clean the house was tonight. In thirty years from now, however, they will remember that every night I'd sing to them, tickle them, tuck them in and, every now and then, lie next to them, give them a cuddle and ask them about their day.

They'll remember the trips to the movies where dad was acting like a dick while it was still fun for dad to make a dick of himself in public. In no time they'll be horrified to be seen in public with me, let alone when I'm being an idiot, so I'm cherishing this time, too.

I can't express how important having fun is to building strong relationships with your kids and to making them feel good about themselves. When you have the confidence to horse around and play the fool that gives them the confidence to do the same. When you sing and play fight with your kids you're expressing love, intimacy and tenderness that is like oxygen for their souls.

I never felt like I could initiate horseplay with either of my parents and, looking back, this makes me profoundly sad. I can't put my finger on why this is the case, but whatever the reason it shouldn't have been that way.

Having fun with your partner is just as important. Having fun is an expression of your love for each other. It makes you both happier and more comfortable in each other's company. If the kids are around then it helps them understand what a healthy, respectful and, yes, fun relationship looks like.

So take fun seriously and make an effort to have a laugh. Even on those nights when you get home late, you're tired and grumpy and the house is a mess... sounds like rumble time to me. Grab the kids and have a play fight. The mess can wait.

Your Partner

Every relationship is different - some of us are married, some of us have same-sex partners and some of us are bringing up kids on our own. I'm married and I refer to my wife often throughout this book, but also use the word 'partner' interchangeably if talking about our significant others in the general sense. I trust that you can relate the messages to your personal situation.

The relationship between you and your partner is of fundamental importance to the emotional development of your children. Let your kids run riot and be totally misbehaved and they'll still have a fighting chance of becoming well-adjusted adults. Be deadbeat parents who don't love and respect each other and you're very likely to fuck them up for life, often condemning them to repeat many of the same mistakes and mess up many of the same vital relationships as you did.

If this sounds over the top it's not.

It doesn't matter what you say or do to your child - nothing will influence how they relate to others more than the example that you set them within the home.

So you have to set the right example.

If your relationship is healthy and vibrant then your children will learn from this and they will have significantly improved prospects for healthy and vibrant relationships of their own. If your relationship is hollow, unfulfilling or unloving then, well, you get the point.

This shit is important dad, so take notice.

All of our relationships are different, but one thing that every healthy spousal relationship has in common is mutual commitment.

You'll know that your partner is the love of your life, your great love, if you're fully invested and fully committed to that love. If she's the one who you can't wait to get home to and the only one that you could ever see yourself waking up next to then she's *the one*. And if she's the one then there's no better mother for your kids.

Let commitment be your yardstick. You will know, deep down, how committed you are to your partner and how committed she is to you.

If you're half-arsed about it and always looking for something, or someone, better then it's never going to work. It might be that you love each other, but you're not fully *in love* with each other.

There's nothing wrong with a relationship to which either or both parties aren't fully committed - we've all had flings or girlfriends who were fun, but weren't 'the one'. If she's not the one, however, or if either of you aren't fully committed then don't bring children into the relationship - at least not until the both of you have figured out that maybe you are right for each other after all.

Just remember that there's a lid for every pot. If you're not with the love of your life then she's out there somewhere, you just have to find her.

Keep the Fire Burning

Many of us find that the romance rapidly fades once kids are on the scene. There are things that all of us can do to keep the fire burning bright. For example:

- Treat her like a queen. A real man is not afraid to put his partner first and to put her on a pedestal. Respect her, look after her, listen to what she has to say and support her.
- Learn how to argue without fighting. Arguments are a fact of life and we shouldn't try and pretend to our kids that mum and dad don't disagree (and maybe piss each other off) sometimes. Never let an argument escalate into a fight (i.e. a situation where you're trying to hurt each other), however:
    - Stick to the issue at hand. Forget what she did or said last week or the week before. If you have to argue then stick to the issue that you disagree on. You'll end the argument quicker.
    - Actually listen. When we're angry we can display a tendency to just talk. Loudly. Our ability to listen and to empathise with the other party diminishes and we raise our voices to try and get our point across. Try listening. Hear what your loved one has to say and think about it. Pause before saying your piece and try not to interrupt her. If she interrupts you then ask her not to but don't start shouting over the top of each other - it's unproductive.
    - Never use 'never'. Accusations like 'you always', 'you

never', etc. have no place in an argument. Stick to the facts and avoid useless generalisations.
- Keep it clean. Calling each other names or swearing, getting physical, trying to intimidate each other - it's all fighting and there's no place for it. Don't do it, even in retaliation. Don't put up with abuse either - walk away. If it's serious then stay away and call the police.
- Get over it. Many couples fall into the trap of freezing each other out after a fight (i.e. not talking to each other, storming around the house, etc.) It's childish and it's pointless. If you need some time to cool off then say so. Chill out, get over it and then...
- Make up. An argument shouldn't last a second longer than absolutely necessary, but don't try and make up too soon or another argument is likely to break out. Be prepared to agree to disagree - if you're not able to see eye to eye then you'll have to find a compromise. If you play your cards right you might even be able to wangle a bit of make-up sex. The kids don't need to know about that bit of you do.
Just remember that compromise is a two-way street and you'll both need to be ready to meet in the middle.

- Do your bit, plus a bit more. Whether it's the housework, your finances, or any other aspect of the relationship that involves work.
It's human nature to overestimate our contribution to the relationship and to underestimate the contribution made by our partners. If you both do your bit, plus a bit more, then there's more chance of you meeting in the middle and not leaving each other with an unfair share of the work. Don't keep score of who does what - the ledger will never balance, as both of you will feel like you're doing more than the other.

- Keep the romance. Love and romance go hand in hand. Buy her flowers. Take her on a date at least once a month, even if it's only for an hour or two. Take her shopping and buy her something nice for no reason other than to make her feel special. Don't keep score. We're not romantic because we expect to be repaid in kind - we do it because it makes our partner happy.
- Sex it up. Every couple grapples with declining sexual desire, especially after they have kids. Women often lose their libido a lot more quickly than men do and that can be hard to take when you're the one trying to initiate sex and having to deal with being rebuffed.

  A healthy sex life is an important part of a healthy relationship, so don't take it personally if you get the brush off and don't get resentful. Have a frank and open dialogue with your partner about sex and how to maintain your sex life, but keep your expectations realistic. Hoping for a blowjob in the morning and sex every night is probably just going to end in disappointment.

If you're reading this and thinking that it all sounds a bit soft, then you're right. It is soft. Your partner needs to see your tender side more than you might realise.

This does not make *you* soft, nor does it make you a pushover. Being compassionate and loving is a sign of strength, not a sign of weakness.

What if We're Separated/Divorced?

Being separated or divorced from the mother of your child does not excuse you from treating her with compassion and respect. This can be difficult, as there can be unresolved resentment and raw emotions between the two of you, but you'll just need to get over it.

Your job as a parent is to demonstrate to your children how people should be treated, no matter how angry or betrayed you feel. Remember that hate is not the opposite of love - indifference is. When relationships break up we can end up hating each other, if only for a little while, because we still have strong feelings for one another. Rather than letting hate and anger consume you, set the example that you'd want to see your kids follow one day, even if you feel betrayed or otherwise aggrieved.

If you and your 'ex' continue to fight and abuse each other, even if it's out of view of the children, then it's your kids that will suffer the most. They will feel the tension in the relationship and they will become fundamentally conflicted by it. This will not only make the break-up much more stressful for your children, it will leave them with emotional scars that they will carry with them long after.

If you and your ex are adult enough to treat each other with compassion and respect during (and after) a break-up then all of you (children and adults alike) will be happier. The break-up will be less traumatic and you will all recover faster.

Work

Work, and our work ethic, is one of our biggest defining factors. It's scary to think that many of us will spend more time at work than we will in the company of our children over our lifetimes, so it's important that we enjoy what we do. Through working we provide a great example for our children, as well as bringing home the bacon.

Get a Job

If you're a father and you don't work then you've got a real problem dad, as your kids are watching and the longer you stay out of work the more likely it is that they're going to see this as normal and follow suit.

No one should be out of work. No one.

Do you lack the skills and experience required for the job you want? Then get your arse back to school or go and get a job flipping burgers.

Anything is better than nothing. There is no excuse to be idle.

If paid work is not available and study is not an option then find a company who you can *volunteer* for. Working for free beats not working at all. At least if you're working for free you are moving. You will be picking up skills and experience and you'll be making yourself more employable by the hour.

When we're not working (and not studying) we're wallowing. Our motivation seeps out of our bodies and our self-belief fades. We start making excuses for our lack of productivity and the more we repeat those excuses the more we begin to believe them, which damages our long-term prospects even further.

I know how demeaning minimum-wage work can be. I spent many years stacking supermarket shelves and flipping burgers myself, but I always knew it was simply a means to an end. I knew that I'd better myself and that, one day, I'd work my way up into a job, and a profession, that I could be proud of.

Even finding minimum wage work can be difficult at times. When I was at university I remember being one of two dozen applicants for the graveyard shift at a supermarket stocking shelves. I got that job and I hated every minute of it, but I stacked the shit out of those shelves. The job was totally forgettable, but it was instrumental in helping me develop strategies for finding and excelling at work. Strategies that served me well in the decades that followed and that have helped others who I've coached over the years.

These strategies helped me work my way up from a minimum wage job to a six figure salary working with IBM within five years, despite being a university drop-out. I have since gone on to found a successful business using the skills that I picked up over two decades in the IT industry.

These strategies work every time - I guarantee it. I've included them below - try them and they'll work for you, but they do require courage.

Getting the Job

I sat in the office at the supermarket and told myself I was going to get that job. I *needed* that job. Our rent was overdue and we were running low on food. My girlfriend (now wife) had exams coming up and financial worries were getting in the way of her studies.

I was going to get the job. I had to get the job.

They told me they'd had dozens of applications, many of them from university graduates, and that they'd be interviewing from a shortlist of three. I returned three times and filled out three different application forms. When they told me I hadn't made the shortlist I turned up for an interview anyway, but arrived 30 minutes before the first interview was due to start and blagged my way into the manager's office. He asked me why he should choose me over his short-list of university graduates. I told him that no one spends three years getting a degree just so they could stack shelves for a living.

I started the job that night.

I also learned a valuable lesson that day. I learned that, when you're up against your peers, a university degree isn't enough to get you a job stacking shelves at a supermarket if you can't differentiate yourself from the others. If you don't stand out, especially if there are lots of applicants, then it's a lottery and your chances of getting an interview are down to just that - chance. There's only a chance that your application is going to be viewed and an even smaller chance that you are going to get in for an interview.

I learned that people don't hire qualifications, they hire personalities. People hire with their hearts, not their heads and hiring decisions are rarely rational.

This helped me work my way up and now I am in a position where I regularly advertise jobs and hire people.

Now that I am the manager and I'm doing the hiring I see the same thing happen again and again. I advertise a job and I get a flood of applications - often too many to review them all. I look at them in some order (often the order in which they were received) and create a shortlist from the first five or so who take my fancy. The rest don't even get looked at - I have no choice but to send them a form email saying that we've already found our shortlist and that their applications will not be reviewed.

I advertised a job recently for which I received over 300 applications. I had my shortlist after reviewing 30 or of them, meaning that roughly 90 percent of the applicants weren't even looked at.

If you need a job then this isn't how to go about it. You could have the best CV on the planet, but if the employer doesn't see it then it's not going to help you. What makes matters worse is that employers and recruitment agents don't have time to properly read all of the CV's that they do read - each of those carefully written CV's will typically get a cursory glance at best. The reader will typically decide within the first 20 seconds whether they're interested in the candidate or not.

So how do you find a job against such odds? If applying for jobs is such a lottery, then how do you improve your chances of getting a ticket, let alone winning?

The answer is - don't play the same game.

Jobs are everywhere around us. Even during the deepest recessions and the most drastic downturns there are jobs to be had. You just have to be ready to work and you have to have the courage to get out there and *find* that job.

Be Ready to Work

Being ready to work means being prepared to take the job you can get, even if it's not the job you want. I'm not saying you shouldn't aim high - as we'll see below, getting ahead in your career involves a continuous process of working your way into roles that you're not completely qualified for. If you can't get the job you want, however, then there's no point in deluding yourself. It's also impossible to work your way from unemployment into the job that you want - you have to work your way up from a position of employment.

You might even have to give your time away for free to get the foothold that you need to start working toward the career of your dreams. This is certainly the case for my industry, the IT industry, where there is a shortage of highly-skilled workers, but a glut of under-experienced, newly minted graduates.

You'd be amazed at how many of these graduates bristle at the thought of working for free, despite having spent the last three years paying someone for the privilege of sitting in their lecture halls.

Be prepared to work for free - but not for long. Anything more than a month or three and the employer is just exploiting you - demand that they give you paid work or move on to something else.

Take Courage. Get the Job

Finding that job takes courage because it requires you to get out from behind your keyboard, to get out there and sell yourself. It requires you to make cold calls (including phone calls and in-person visits) to potential employers. It requires that you swallow your pride and pound the pavement and be ready to hear 'no' again and again until you finally hear a 'yes'.

In my experience this approach works 100% of the time, as sooner or later you're going to find someone who will give you a chance, but only if you don't give up first.

Every 'no' is a learning experience - you have to ask the employer why they're not interested and what three pieces of advice they'd give you about trying to get work with their company.

The secret to this approach is persistence. Return to employers who have said 'no' and show them that you've addressed the issues that they raised (within reason - if they require you to have a certain type of qualification then it may be difficult to simply pop out and get one). Cold-call and door-knock employers you haven't spoken to. Keep going and going, refining your pitch as you go. Find out who the decision maker is and figure out how to talk to that person. There may be gatekeepers to get through - receptionists, assistants, etc. whose job it is to stop you from distracting the decision maker. If so, you'll need to figure out how to get around them.

Be prepared to come face to face with the decision maker or to get her on the phone. You don't want to waste all of that hard work getting an encounter only to clam up and stutter your way through it.

Develop your pitch and *practice it*. Be prepared to tell the prospective employer why they should hire you. Make it smart, but not desperate. Your pitch should be polished before you need it. If you're too lazy or too shy to practice it on family members or friends before you get to the decision maker then you've wasted your time and theirs. Be ready.

Don't just talk. Ask the employer questions about what they do and the issues that they face. Use that information to inform your pitch. Figure out what they need. Maybe they need staff who can work a night shift, or who can be on call during the weekends. Whatever it is, find out what it is that they need and be prepared to offer it.

More than anything else employers want employees who are going to work hard and make their lives easier. They want someone who will show initiative and who will learn quickly. We all want to feel good about the hiring decisions that we make, so we will tend to give preference to the plucky fighters.

Don't settle for a lottery ticket. Be the fighter. Make the call. Talk to the decision maker. Get the job.

And don't tell me that this approach isn't working. If it hasn't worked yet then you simply haven't been trying hard enough, for long enough, yet. In my experience this approach has a 100% success rate, even when the candidate has been long term unemployed.

So keep going. Don't cop out and hide behind email in the hope that someone will notice you.

Make Work Meaningful

We spend too much of our lives working to do work that we don't enjoy and find satisfying.

We need to be careful to not measure our success or fulfilment using financial metrics alone, but there is also no excuse for being stuck in a minimum wage, go-nowhere job for the rest of your life either.

Low-income work is unfulfilling and meaningless and is bad for the soul. Further, those in low-paid jobs have less transferable skills (have less chance of finding work elsewhere) and have the lowest job security.

This is not to say that we're all born with the same chances in life. We're not. Getting ahead can be more difficult for some of us than for others, but we all have an obligation to ourselves to at least try.

It's important that we invest ourselves fully into whatever work we're doing. Whether it's stacking supermarket shelves, flipping burgers, working behind a bar or cleaning toilets. I've done all of these jobs and they all sucked, but I worked my ass off at each and every one of them. This didn't always make me popular with my minimum wage colleagues, some of whom thought I was trying to show them up, but I didn't care.

From the beginning I knew that if I couldn't do really well at unskilled work then it would be silly to expect that I would be able to work my way up into a meaningful career.

I have no patience for those who consider themselves 'too good' for the job they're currently doing.

None of us are too good for our current job. If we were then we wouldn't be there.

We all deserve the jobs that we have right now.

Those who think they're too good for their current job usually do a poor job of it, which causes them to slip backward rather than moving forward.

They usually find excuses to justify their poor performance and lack of commitment, but it's too easy to blame a clueless employer or poor working conditions for our own shortcomings.

Amazingly, it's not just in low-paid workplaces where you see these attitudes. In large corporations, where salaries are higher and resources more plentiful, you'll still find that a significant number of your colleagues do just enough to get by. Sometimes just enough to avoid being fired.

Wherever you work and whatever you do, ensure that you always do *more* than is required.

Take the initiative. Do the work that no one else wants. Don't compete or compare yourself with those around you, as petty rivalries will only distract you and slow you down.

Make your work meaningful. Make it meaningful *to you*. If you're flipping burgers then make the best burgers, faster than anyone else. If you're cleaning toilets then clean them until they sparkle.

Your work may not be saving the world, but it still has importance. People need to eat and they need to crap. We all love good burgers and we all appreciate a clean toilet.

Most important, your hard work is propelling you forward. Every burger, every toilet, every shelf stacked, takes you one step closer to what you *really* want to do with your life.

Make no mistake, working hard at a minimum wage job is unlikely in itself to be enough to propel you into the career of your dreams, but learning to work harder and smarter than those around you is an important skill. Learning to recognise the meaning in your work is critical - both to your success and, as we will see later, to your ongoing happiness.

Better Yourself

All of us have to continue moving forward or we slip backward.

The human mind will not let us sit still. It is always seeking new and exciting things. It needs to be challenged. *We* need to be challenged.

This is why such a large proportion of retirees find that their mental and physical health deteriorates rapidly after they retire. We all need purpose. We all need meaning. If you have nothing to replace the purpose and meaning that your job gave you then what point is there in continuing?

I'm not saying that we should all work until we drop dead. Nor am I saying that you can only better yourself at work.

There is a multitude of ways we can better ourselves. On the sports field. By picking up a new interest or hobby. By learning and mastering a new skill.

The important thing is that we continue to better ourselves until our last breath.

This is exercise for the mind. It gives us purpose and it makes us feel good about ourselves.

Most important, it sets an example for our children to emulate. By observing us as we strive to continually better ourselves they learn the importance of doing so. They are inspired by our actions.

As you better yourself you're also making yourself more employable.

It helps if you're focusing on areas that are related to your work, but it's the process of striving, of constantly wanting and trying to be better, that will make you better at work.

The Manual

When I was younger I used to read software manuals. Partly because I was generally interested in them, but mainly because I wanted to break into the IT industry. I lacked the money for formal training and I didn't have any experience (beyond tinkering with my own computer) so I read those things from cover to cover. Software manuals used to rival phone books in thickness in those days - you don't see either publication anymore.

My wife jokes about how we'd go to the beach and everyone would be building sandcastles or sunbathing and I'd be sitting there hunched over a manual for Novell NetWare.

But it worked.

Not only did this help me learn about every little feature of these products (most I'd never even used) but the very process of reading those manuals gave me skills that I still rely on today, more than a quarter century later.

My reading and comprehension skills are better. My attention span is longer. My work ethic is stronger.

What you're striving toward doesn't even have to be work related for it to make you more employable. The very process of striving, of bettering yourself, makes you more determined, better rounded and more motivated to take on new challenges.

Now that I'm an employer I will always hire someone who displays an active interest in bettering themselves over someone who is happy to coast.

Move Up

Never be satisfied with your progress in the workplace. Like it or not, you have to keep moving up to avoid slipping backward.

Once we become complacent, and we stop developing ourselves, our value to our employer starts diminishing. Slowly at first, but becoming more rapid over time as our skills become increasingly obsolescent and as others emerge to shine as brightly as we once did.

This decline soon becomes a downward spiral. We become resentful that we don't command the same respect that we used to (despite being party to our own demise) which saps our motivation and causes us to fall even further behind.

Most of us have seen this happen - if not to ourselves then to others. The 'golden child' rests too long on their laurels and before long they start being viewed as a liability rather than an asset.

All too often we see it happen to those above us in the pecking order when middle managers, or even executives, are promoted into positions above their level of competence. They do a mediocre job but, due to the Dunning Kruger effect, they often overestimate their own competence and fail to recognise the competence of those around them.

Working for incompetents is difficult, as they're no longer upwardly mobile, so you're often stuck with them as your manager, or as your manager's' manager. They often fail to recognise your skill and hard work or, worse, they're threatened by your competence and they treat you like a liability rather than an asset.

If you find yourself working for such a person then you have to work that much harder and smarter to find a way to keep moving up in spite of them.

Avoid politics or vendettas - they'll only harm you in the long run. Realise that you may need to change employer, or even to become your own employer, to escape their clutches and to keep yourself moving upward and forward.

But never stop moving up. Never stop moving forward.

Money

Parenting, in short, is expensive. You're going to need money.

You don't need to be rich to give your kids a happy childhood, but believe me, being poor can make happiness a lot more difficult to sustain.

Life is unfair and without mercy. Get used to it.

The less money you have the less power you have. The less money you have the less choices you have.

Is this really important? Lots of us grew up poor and happy - should we really care?

Yes, we should.

Yes it is possible to grow up poor and happy and it's true what your grandmother used to say - money can't buy you happiness. Study after study shows that there is no correlation between wealth and happiness. In fact, happiness appears to *decrease* as people become both very poor and as they become very wealthy.

If you are poor, however, then your kids are much more likely to become a statistic of the unwanted kind. They are much less likely to gain formal qualifications and much more likely to be a victim of sexual or other types of abuse before they're adults. They're much less likely to pull themselves out of poverty and much more likely to be single parents and to have kids in their teens.

In short, the statistics, when you are poor, are stacked against your kids, so being poor shouldn't be an option.

But don't panic - none of us has to be poor if we choose not to be. We can't all be rich, no matter what they say in the self-help books (the only person those books often make rich are their authors).

But none of us has to be poor.

So why are some people poor? The reasons for this are complex and varied and there's no room in shaming or blaming the poor for being poor. No one chooses to be poor and no one chooses to stay poor. But we can decide to change. We can decide that poverty isn't for us or for our kids.

If you've yet to have kids then remember that pulling yourself out of poverty is a lot easier *before* they come along. Also bear in mind that kids are expensive, real expensive, so you're going to have a lot less disposable income once you're a dad.

I came from a deprived background but my wife and I worked hard to build a comfortable income and lifestyle for ourselves before we started a family. We were thus able to travel the world and make decisions about where and when we'd settle down before having the financial burden of kids and (as my wife was a stay at home mum) one less income.

If you're already a dad and you're struggling then don't worry - it's going to be harder to get ahead, but you can do it and you'll need to. You're going to find it a lot harder to be a good, attentive dad and to give your kids all of the opportunities that they deserve if you spend their childhoods struggling just to get by.

Even if you're not short of a bob or two, financial security is important and, although money won't buy us happiness, it's hard to have too much of it, so all of us can benefit from:

Getting Ahead at Work

See above. Never stop striving.

Reducing Debt

Most households have far too much debt and, more important, spend far too much money servicing that debt (i.e. paying interest and charges). Credit cards, overdrafts, hire purchases - it's all high interest borrowing for items of little resale value or for things, like vehicles, that rapidly depreciate.

We live in a time of easy credit and far too often we choose to borrow rather than save for the things we want.

The problem with buying stereos, clothes, travel, cars and other desirable items on credit is that the cost of those items can end up being significantly more than they're worth once you've finally paid them off. If you ever pay them off.

Lenders such as credit card and finance companies bank on us running up balances that sit there earning high rates of interest, year after year.

Consumer credit is different to productive forms of credit such as trade, real estate and other forms of credit that are designed to give the lender the opportunity to make, rather than lose, money.

Consumer credit is designed specifically to allow you buy the things that you can't afford. It is often advanced without collateral (i.e. without you having to offer up any assets as security), meaning it is, by definition, expensive. High interest rates, high fees, high penalties - consumer credit has it all.

The poorer you are (and the lower your credit rating) the more expensive consumer credit will be, as the lender will charge you a premium to compensate for the higher perceived risk of lending to you.

Servicing that debt means paying, at least, the minimum amount required to stop the lender from calling in the debt. As there's no security, 'calling in' the debt usually means repossessing the goods. As the goods are of little to no value once used, the lender is likely to come after you to recover the difference between what they can get for them and the amount you owe (including collection charges). Of course, they're going to slap all kinds of penalties and charges on you and your credit rating is going to take an absolute beating, making it difficult and expensive to obtain credit in future.

In my home country of New Zealand the majority of families have no significant assets. Most own cars, furniture and other personal effects, but these are rapidly depreciating assets that, while useful on a day to day basis, often have little resale value or, in many cases, are worth less than the owner owes for them.

As depressing as it is, a significant portion of parents have a *negative* net worth when they have their first child, meaning their liabilities (debts) are worth more than their assets.

The effects of this are disastrous, as many parents struggle to meet the minimum payments due on those debts and end up spending more on interest and fees than the items they purchased were worth in the first place. Worse, it means that they live hand to mouth, without the reserves needed to get us through those hard times.

Case in point - imagine you decided to treat yourself and racked up $2,000 worth of debt on your Visa to fund a holiday and then decided to pay the debt back at the minimum rate required by the credit card company. At current standard Visa lending rates it is likely to take you over 60 years to repay the debt and you'd repay a total of almost $11,000 over this time. Now you may be thinking 'yeah, but only a chump would take 60 years to pay off a debt like that' and you'd be right. The problem is that most of us are chumps - the majority of adults in the western would live with a significant balance *permanently* on their credit cards (or other high interest revolving credit facilities) and end up burning much, much more than this over their lifetimes.

So step 1 to reducing debt is: Stop borrowing and cut up those credit cards! If you can't afford it then don't buy it. Ignore those 'interest free' deals - they are often interest free for a while only, meaning you'll end up paying exorbitant interest rates once the interest free period is over. Besides, you'll be able to negotiate a much better purchase price if you forgo the interest free offer and pay in cash.

Don't wimp out and put the credit card in the freezer or other half-arsed measures - cut it up. Cut them all up. If you can't afford it then buying it on credit won't change that - it's just going to make your purchase even less affordable later. It doesn't matter how strapped you are - just stop borrowing.

Think about other forms of credit that cost you more than they should - mobile phones are a great example, as mobile operators often try and sting you with 'overage' charges (for exceeding your plan data, etc.)

that are often more than your monthly rental. Switch to a pre-pay account so you know you'll never spend more than you've budgeted for. Mobile operators make much less money on prepay customers for a reason - they typically get a better deal than 'post pay' customers.

While you're at it, think about other unnecessary costs that you can avoid. Speeding tickets (or other traffic-related fines), excessive power charges because you bought a cheap, inefficient heater and left it running for a week, the cost of replacing the stuff you had stolen when you left your bag unattended - it can all be avoided with a little care.

If you *must* have a credit card (e.g. because you need to buy stuff online, etc.) then make a rule that it must remain in credit. Reduce the credit limit to the absolute minimum you need and be disciplined enough to keep it in credit at all times. If your bank offers a 'debit card' option (i.e. you can buy with it like a credit card, but only if you have funds in your account) then use one instead of a credit card - remove the temptation to spend money you don't have!

Step 2 to decreasing debt: Increase your disposable and discretionary income. Your disposable income is essentially the income you have left after you've paid your taxes. Your discretionary income is the amount you have left after paying all of your necessary costs of living, such as rent, finance charges, food, transport costs, medical costs, etc.

You can only increase your *disposable* income by increasing the amount you earn. We've covered this in the work section already, so we won't cover it again, although I will say this - if you tell yourself that you can't increase what you earn then you're probably right. If you want to improve your job prospects and increase your earnings then you can.

There are *two* ways of increasing your *discretionary* income - increasing the amount you earn and decreasing the amount you spend. Many of us are reluctant to decrease the amount we spend, because doing so means making sacrifices. Essentially we need to lower our standard of living. We may need to move into cheaper accommodation (even moving in with the parents!), sell the car, give up smoking, reduce booze intake and make other sacrifices to increase the amount of money left over, our discretionary income, each month.

It is notoriously difficult to reduce the amount we spend, as old habits die hard, so make a budget. Write it down and be careful to include everything. Make a budget then *stick to it*. If you overspend in one area then underspend in another to compensate. If you can't make a budget, or if you're having trouble sticking to it, then get budgeting advice - you'll probably find non-profits that will give you good budgeting advice for free (or for a donation) if you need it.

Most important - be aggressive. The more you increase your disposable and discretionary incomes, the more you will have leftover to pay down debt. The more you have to pay down your debts the faster you will get rid of them and the sooner you'll be able ease back on some of the sacrifices.

Step 3: Reduce your actual debt. And fast! Making minimum payments won't cut it - you'll be chipping away at that debt forever. Literally. Remember that consumer debt is often designed to cost you much more than the original price of the product over time.

You've got to reduce that debt permanently. All of that high cost debt - the credit cards, HP's, overdrafts, etc. - they've all got to go!

List all of your debts (your liabilities) twice - firstly in the order of how large each one is (i.e. the total amount that you still owe) and then in order of how expensive each one is. For the latter, don't order them by how much you have to repay each month, but rather the effective rate of interest (including charges) you're paying - the higher the interest the faster we're going to want to pay it off, regardless of how big or small it is.

Now get strategic about how you pay off your debts.

Look at getting a debt consolidation loan, for example, but first check that the loan will help you pay your debts off faster and that it will cost you less. I am fairly financially astute, but there's no way I'd take out a debt consolidation loan without getting independent advice first, as many such facilities are simply traps designed to help you move from one pool of quicksand to another.

As well as looking at how long a debt consolidation loan will take to pay off and its overall cost, you also need to be careful that you don't have to put up collateral that you couldn't afford to lose if everything went wrong. I've seen people lose their homes because they used them as collateral against such loans - imagine that, losing your home because you bought a car that you couldn't really afford.

Also look for a debt consolidation loan that won't penalise you for paying it off early. Remember that our objective is to become debt free quickly - if we're not able to pay off our debts as fast as we can manage then that will simply give us an excuse to waste money.

Getting strategic about paying off your debts also means structuring payments to minimise their overall cost and the length of time required to get rid of them.

The following assumes that you don't take out a debt consolidation loan and that you decide to pay off your debts directly.

Structured Debt Repayments

Grab your second list of your debts (the one ordered by how expensive each debt is) and divert all of your available funds to paying off the most expensive debts first.

This means, for example, that you may keep paying the minimum monthly charge on all of your debts *except* the most expensive debt on your list. Use every last penny to pay this off as quickly as you can, then move on to the next one. Be as aggressive as you can and lance that thing like the festering boil that it is.

Using this approach you will significantly reduce the amount of time and money required to reduce your debts. But don't get complacent -

don't stop pushing yourself until all of those debts are gone.

As each debt is paid off move to the next most expensive debt. You'll have more and more money to spend on each successive debt. If you're disciplined you'll be amazed at how quickly you can pay down those debts and regain your financial freedom.

I've seen people go from 'drowning in debt' to 'debt free' in less than a year using this approach.

Saving

Having assets is important.

Expenses can arise, often unexpectedly.

Crises can occur, such as health problems, redundancy or worse.

Without resources you can be left unable to cope and/or forced into debt as a result.

You also need the financial freedom to make decisions from time to time. You might choose to buy a house or to move you and the family to another city (or country), particularly if you decide to move into a better school zone.

It's also not just important to build up assets for the short and medium term. We must, of course, start planning for our golden years early on. Our life expectancies continue to increase, meaning our retirements get longer and longer.

Even the richest countries are finding it harder and harder to support their ageing populations, resulting in shrinking pension entitlements in many of them.

So don't just think of saving as something you do to buy an item you want.

Building your asset base, or your net worth, is what's really important. So get yourself in a position where you can save some of your income (by reducing debt and increasing your earning power) and then investing that money wisely.

Protect that asset base by being careful about risk. Make sure you have adequate insurance and avoid being stupid. A moment of madness, such as a decision to drive drunk or to steal something that doesn't belong to you, can have catastrophic results that you, and others, may have to live with for years. Possibly forever.

Anything that adversely affects you will typically affect your kids too. Both directly and in terms of the example you set for them to follow. So be smart and don't do anything stupid.

Assess risk and take adequate steps to avoid it.

Put a savings plan together and invest wisely - get advice on how to do so without putting your savings at risk.

Fit Body, Fit Mind

Most of us have heard the expression 'dad bod' and it's perfectly normal for us to develop a few curves as we progress through parenthood, particularly as we approach middle age.

If you're blessed with the genetics or the motivation to stay trim and toned through adulthood then good for you, but as you become a parent your appearance becomes secondary to remaining fit and healthy and, most important, setting an example that you want your kids to follow.

If we are obese then our kids are significantly more likely to grow up obese. Same if we're sedentary.

Your kid's attitudes to diet and exercise will be formed primarily during their childhood. Where will they learn those attitudes? From observing you, of course.

Being a dad, while simultaneously being a great husband and striving to get ahead in life, is also arduous, continuous work. If you're not 'match fit' then you won't be up to the challenge.

If you're not fit and healthy then you will struggle with the constant demands for you time and attention that your kids place on you.

Tragically for them, most of the time that they will spend with you will be your 'rest' time (after work or in the weekends) when all you probably want to do is have a beer on front of the TV.

Don't do it. Don't put your rest ahead of their precious time with their dad.

Put those shoes back on and take them for a walk, or to the park. Build a tree house together. Do something. They will remember it for life.

They will look back at how dad would come home and help with dinner and the dishes then, instead of shutting them off and sinking into the couch, would give *them* his precious time. Not because they'd been good or they'd done something else to deserve it, but just because he wanted to.

The fitter you are the easier it will be to do it. You have to be ready to come home and leave your stresses and frustrations at the door. You have to be ready to do something physical with the kids - inviting them to watch TV with you doesn't count!

I struggle to balance time to keep fit and time with my family. I found that going to the gym, or going for a run, would eat into my precious time with them.

This was only a challenge until they became old enough to exercise with us. Now I help teach them Kung Fu before I do adult classes. We go on family walks or even runs through New Zealand's beautiful forests.

The kids are lighter and fitter than me and a good run can be painful, but I wouldn't give them up for anything. They are amazing bonding experiences and we all end up tired, but happy. Later the kids will regale us with tales of their forest adventures as if we weren't there to witness them in person.

I don't know what happiness is, but the feeling after these excursions is about as close as I think I could get to being truly happy.

It won't last forever. Before long they'll struggle to fit me into their busy social lives, so I cherish every opportunity to do something outdoors with them. Having a modicum of fitness makes this possible.

Kids also give us a reason to live to an old age.

The most effective way to extend your life is, of course, to remain fit and healthy. This also happens to be one of the best ways of keeping your *mind* healthy too - exercising and eating well is a great way of helping you maintain a positive outlook, a great state of mind and motivation to get out of bed each morning.

The health of our bodies and minds are inextricably linked - this section could just as easily be called fit mind, fit body, as it's difficult to motivate yourself to stay fit and healthy if you're depressed, in a rut or otherwise don't have your head together.

Yes, it can be a struggle. I have struggled with obesity my entire life, but it's a struggle we can win. And it's worth winning.

The best advice that I can give you, from my own experience, is:

1. Don't exercise for the sake of it. Find an activity that is strenuous and that you actually enjoy. If you can do it with the kids then all the better.
2. Use the kids as your motivation. Whenever I feel the temptation to skip exercise I think about my kids and the example that I want to set for them. I think about how I want to be around for a while and to not drop dead of a heart attack while they're young. That's usually all the motivation I need.

Fathering as a Single Parent

Don't Rush In

As careful as we are about choosing our life partners, it's a sad fact that most of our children will grow up in broken homes, or homes that do not include both of the child's birth parents.

Kids from broken homes have to deal with a range of issues that other kids don't have to deal with. Losing a parent creates an open wound for the child that never fully heals.

Being a solo parent means you have to be mum and dad. Breadwinner and homemaker. Nurturer and disciplinarian. Even if you find someone else (giving your kids a step mum or step dad) things are not the same, as then the 'solo' parent has to manage the relationship between child and spouse, while still having to wear both parenting hats, although possibly to a lesser degree.

This is why it's so important to take your time and to choose a life partner that you're likely to be with for life.

You should, of course, only stay in a relationship that is loving and supportive. But choose relationships that are healthy to begin with.

Don't rush into having kids. Of course it seems like a great idea to bring kids into a relationship when you're in the honeymoon period, but the honeymoon period only lasts so long.

Often those who find they've rushed in, either intentionally or accidentally, are soon disillusioned. They haven't given themselves time to truly get to know each other, or to build the reservoir of trust and goodwill that you're going to need to get you through the trials and tribulations of having young kids.

If You Can, Give Them Two Parents

You can be a great single parent, there's no doubt about it. It's a fact, however, that kids from broken homes do have a greater incidence of psychological problems, are more likely to display antisocial behaviour and are more likely to grow up in poverty than kids from two parent families.

So give them two parents if you can.

Double down on the relationship with their mother and do whatever you can to maintain the love, affection and romance that brought you together in the first place.

This isn't always easy, particularly as you'll have less time for romancing each other once kids have come along, but the potential rewards are worth it. Not only will you increase the chances of your kids growing up with two parents, but you're likely to find that your investment in your relationship pays dividends, for you and your partner, as you're both likely to feel happier and more fulfilled as a result.

If, despite your best efforts, you are unable to save your relationship and you still decide to break up then it's still vitally important that you give your children two parents, even if it is parents who live apart from each other.

It may be exciting to be single again, or even to enter into new relationships, but remember that you are a dad first and foremost. Everything else is secondary.

Your kids will be left feeling sad and confused about the breakup of the parental relationship and it's not uncommon for them to blame themselves, if only subconsciously.

They do not also need to feel that they have been discarded and forgotten by one (or both) of their parents.

They'll need your love and reassurance more than ever, so make sure they always know they have two parents, even if you do live apart.

Being a Single Parent: It's Tough

Being a single parent brings with it a host of additional challenges, particularly as 'single parent' can mean 'single breadwinner', 'single disciplinarian', 'single taxi driver' and just about anything else that you'd otherwise share with your partner.

You also have the added stresses of custody arrangements and a relationship (with your former spouse) that can become strained at times.

Worst of all, being a single parent can make you feel like you're doing it on your own.

Yes, being a single parent is tough. But you can tough it out.

As a single parent you have to work even harder and smarter to make sure your kids have the childhood they deserve. But don't make it harder, on you or the kids, than it needs to be.

For a start, don't make war with your 'ex'. Having an acrimonious relationship with the mother of your children helps no one. It helps your children least of all. They will only suffer from being torn between the two of you.

It's too easy to justify acrimony against your ex based on her behaviour, or on your desire to do what's right for the children. But post-relationship battles are very rarely 'for' the children. They are manifestations of the anger, hurt and resentment we all feel when a relationship breaks up

No matter how much it sticks in your craw to do so, swallow hard and maintain a respectful and courteous relationship with your ex - and her partner if she has one.

Don't just do this for the kids' sake, although clearly they will benefit.

By working with your ex (instead of against her) you maximise opportunities to be able to work together to share the workload.

If you both act like adults, and make an effort to let bygones be bygones, then you'll be surprised how quickly the feelings of anger and resentment subside. As surprising as it may sound, it is entirely possible to be friends with your ex and it's important that you at least try to do so. This will not only lessen the trauma on your children from the collapse of your relationship, but will also set an excellent example for them in their most formative years.

Tips for Single Parents

These tips easily apply to any parenting situation. When you're a single parent, however, you have less time and resources at your disposal, so they do take on an increased importance:

- Make time for the kids. This can be even harder for single parents, who often have to work all day, return home to cook and clean and put the kids to bed. As a single parent it can feel impossible to make time for yourself, let alone for the children. You must make for them, however - for your sake as well as theirs. They need time with you when they can have your undivided attention.
  Most important, give them constant love and reassurance. They need to hear that you love them as well as seeing it. They need to know that everything is going to be alright, even if you're struggling.
- Plan for emergencies. Put money aside for rainy days and keep holiday pay in reserve for unexpected 'holidays' spent at home looking after sick kids, going on school camps, etc. Ask friends and family in advance if they'd be able to help when you need it - they'll often be happy to help regardless, but it can help to know in advance who to turn to in an emergency.
- Build your network and share the load. Make an effort to get to know other parents at school, at sports practice and anywhere else you need to ferry your kids to and from. Seek arrangements where you can take turns at caring for each other's kids and for taking them to and from events. This not only helps reduce your workload, but is also a great way to get to know other parents.
- Make time for yourself. You still need to have a life outside of being a parent. Get creative to give yourself 'adult only' time without disadvantaging the kids. You can, for example, take turns with other parents at hosting sleepovers, which can be simultaneously fun for the kids while letting you take turns at

being kid-free for the night.
- Be mum and dad. Be the disciplinarian, but find time to be nurturing also. Never be afraid to show your kids your vulnerabilities - it's a sign of strength, not weakness, to let them know that you're vulnerable too, just like them.
- Seek out role models. You have to be mum and dad, but no matter how good you are at filling both roles, your kids are still going to need the company and guidance of women in their lives (or men if you are female). A new partner could help fill this role (see below), so too could a family friend or one or both of the kids' grandmothers.

  Seek out positive role models of the opposite sex and arrange for your kids to spend quality time with them.

Choose new partners carefully. Whenever you start a romantic relationship with someone else you will be bringing them into the relationship with your kids. Choose carefully and remember that the needs of your kids always come first.

Chapter 3: Getting Pregnant

Right, let's get down to business. Literally. Getting pregnant involves sex and sex is fun, so getting pregnant should be fun too, right?

Hopefully. Although, like most things related to having kids, it's not always so simple.

From watching TV or the movies you'd be excused for thinking that all you had to do was decide you wanted kids, have sex and, hey presto, out pops a child 9 months later.

Although this is the case for some couples, for many of us the process can be a lot more difficult.

For a start, women's fertility levels start to decline around their mid-20, declining most quickly from about the age of 35.

Men's fertility starts declining as we age also, but less dramatically, meaning our age has less impact on the overall probability of conception.

You also have to time sexual intercourse correctly (i.e. from a few days before, until just after ovulation) to have any chance of success.

This can be great fun during the first couple of months, as you've got the heady excitement of having sex combined with the possibility that you could be making a baby.

If, like most of us, you don't manage to conceive during the first couple of months then things can quickly turn for the worse.

Roughly 20% of couples will conceive in the first month of trying. 85%

will conceive within a year and 95% will conceive within two years.

It's perfectly normal, due to the merciless effect of probabilities, for healthy, fertile couples to take two years, or more, to conceive.

If you thought it was impossible to ever see sex as a chore, spare a thought for those of us (I've been there) who have to have sex twice a day for several days straight (according to a strict schedule outside of your control) for 24 months solid. Add in the stress and emotional trauma that goes with struggling to conceive (trauma that only increases with each unsuccessful month) and you've got the recipe for a total passion killer.

Dealing with Infertility

Infertility (which is defined as either being unable to conceive after 12 or 24 months of consistent trying, depending on which definition you use) is actually no joking matter. The anxiety and pain of not being able to conceive are very real. This pain is usually felt most acutely by the hopeful mother, so be prepared.

To make matters worse, infertile couples often have to deal with false alarms, miscarriages and watching others around them become pregnant (and even have babies) while they try desperately to become pregnant themselves.

If you find yourself in this position then don't bury your head in the sand. Be prepared for the fact that your partner may be struggling. Possibly more than she lets on.

Avoid the temptation to minimise the issue or to tell her that everything will be ok. You don't know that everything will be ok and neither does she.

Avoid the temptation to play it down by saying that 'no one's dying', 'you'll still have each other' or anything equally true, but unhelpful. Struggling with infertility can be just as traumatic to a woman as being diagnosed with cancer, so playing the situation down is unlikely to help. If anything it's only likely to make her feel more isolated and desolate than she already does.

If you find yourself in this situation then the best you can do is to be as loving and supportive as possible. Remind her, and yourself, that it's normal and expectable to become emotionally fraught about infertility.

There are support networks for infertile couples in most cities, so consider seeking them out. No one understands how difficult infertility is except those who have been through it, or who are going through it, so these support networks can be invaluable.

Remember that most infertile couples end up conceiving in the end, so don't give up hope. There may come a time, however, when you need to start considering medical intervention. There are a range of procedures available to help infertile couples, the ultimate of which is IVF.

Start doing research early. Talk to medical professionals about your options. Depending on your situation you may or may not qualify for state funding for some or all of the procedures available to you.

Fertility treatments are improving all the time, but they are expensive if you're picking up the bill. Be prepared for this. Not only might you need to raise the funds, but there's no guarantee that any fertility treatment will be successful, so steel yourselves for the fact that you may spend a lot of money and not have anything to show for it in the end.

My wife and I had to fund our own fertility treatment. We had two unsuccessful rounds of artificial insemination (IUI) followed by a successful round of In Vitro Fertilisation (IVF). The financial cost was significant, but it was well worth it in the end.

If you do decide that it's time to get help with trying to have a baby then for goodness sakes don't waste your time, money or hope with any of the myriad sham companies, diets or other schemes that promise to help.

There is an appallingly large industry of charlatans and snake oil merchants who thrive on the desperation of the infertile.

Don't be fooled by them. Seek medical advice from *qualified* medical professionals. Any good fertility specialist will be able to give you factual, scientifically proven information about what treatments work (and their success rates) and which don't.

Finally, be prepared for hopelessly misguided, but well meaning, comments from friends and family. I lost count of how many friends told me that we 'just needed to relax'. It had, of course, worked for them, so surely it would work for us.

Preparation for Pregnancy

At time of writing it's still not possible for men to become pregnant, so here's not a whole lot you can do to prepare for pregnancy. There are men's vitamins and a range of other products that claim to benefit men somehow or another during the conception process, but they're all bogus.

As long as you're reasonably fit and healthy then you're ready to go. Oh, you should abstain from masturbating and oral sex (if you should be so lucky) for a week or two before, and until a couple of days after, your partner ovulates each month.

There are a few things that you should think about before getting started.

Once you start having unprotected sex you have made the decision to become a father. With this decision comes great responsibility, so make sure that:

1. You're ready to be a dad. You're old enough and mature enough and that you have the required resources.
2. You're confident that you and your partner will, together, make great parents and that you've got a good chance of staying together.
3. You and your partner are free from STD's, drug or alcohol dependencies or other conditions that may harm either of you or a baby.

Your partner will need to do a little more preparation than you. For a start she'll need to start taking folic acid to prevent neural tube defects such as spina bifida, which are rare, but can be devastating. There are a range of over-the-counter supplements for mums-to-be that include folic acid - these are typically taken prior to and for a period after conception.

She may also want to begin tracking her menstrual cycle and maintaining an ovulation calendar. There are several methods for tracking ovulation - from tracking body temperature to using over-the-counter ovulation tests (similar to pregnancy tests). Advice on this is outside of the scope of this book, but it's definitely worthwhile doing your research, as there's only a short period during each month when intercourse is likely to result in conception.

Doing the Deed

To maximise the chances of conception, you should have sex twice per day (morning and night) from 5 days before ovulation until the day after ovulation.

If this sounds like fun to you and your partner then enjoy it while you can - it's doubtful that you'll ever see this much sex again.

If you and your partner struggle to keep up this kind of regime, however, then don't pressure yourselves. Sex once per day is likely to be adequate and you can even throw in a rest day here and there if you need to. Try and maintain a sense of fun and adventure and to enjoy the act for what it is, as you may have to repeat this process for a while.

Your partner will be most fertile during the period from two days before ovulation until the day of ovulation itself, so if you can muster it, try and have sex on each of these days, or at least on the day of ovulation.

Is She Pregnant?

If you're trying for a baby then the wait between ovulation and finding out if your partner is pregnant can be excruciating.

Try to take both of your minds off of it. Don't track the days or talk about it incessantly. Go about your lives as normal and you'll find that the time passes a lot more quickly (or at least less painfully).

The most obvious sign of pregnancy is, of course, a missed period, which is going to be roughly two weeks from the date of conception. Do remember that this isn't an exact science - periods can be late and women can display symptoms of having a period (including vaginal bleeding that's very much like menstrual bleeding) when pregnant.

The trick is to be calm and patient. Always remember that this is your partner's' body that we're talking about, so she gets to make the decisions. She should be able to do so without feeling harassed or pressured.

Pregnancy tests, when used correctly, are effective from the day of a missed period (roughly two weeks from conception), although some newer tests can be accurate even earlier in the cycle. Pregnancy tests are expensive, however. If you are going to use them then consider buying cheaper multi-packs and waiting for two or three days past the expected date of her period, when they are likely to be more accurate.

There are a range of other symptoms of early pregnancy, so you need not buy pregnancy tests if you don't want to. Remember that every woman, and every pregnancy, is different, so she may experience some or all of these symptoms, or none of them at all - it's best to be aware of these, but let her tell you about them in her own sweet time.

Spotting or Cramping

After conception the fertilised egg attaches itself to the wall of the uterus. This can cause one of the earliest signs of pregnancy, as it can result in spotting (light implantation bleeding) and cramping.

These symptoms can be similar to the early symptoms of menstruation, which can be really confusing.

Tender, Swollen Breasts

The breasts can be a barometer of her surging hormones, making them tender and sore. This usually subsides as her body adjusts to the changing hormone levels.

Nausea

'Morning sickness' doesn't always strike in the morning and it may or may not be accompanied with vomiting. Some women avoid morning sickness altogether, while some report distinct changes in tastes and aromas (wine can suddenly taste as if it's gone off, etc.)

Increased Urination

The amount of blood in her body increases rapidly when she becomes pregnant. This makes her kidneys work harder, which results in more urine to her bladder.

Fatigue

Those surging hormones may not only make her feel nauseous - they can also make her feel fatigued and sleepy. Remember to be supportive - it's easy to forget that she may be pregnant and to become irritable at any sudden onset of fatigue. She may in fact just be tired, but give her the benefit of the doubt and insist that she puts her feet up.

Other Common Symptoms

Other early symptoms can include bloating, cramping, moodiness (look out!), constipation and food aversions.

She's Pregnant! What do We Do?

Yay, she's pregnant! Congratulations! How exciting and nerve wracking at the same time!

Now what do you do?

Apart from your partner having to watch her diet (see next chapter), you might want to do absolutely nothing at all.

Your partner is now in her first trimester (i.e. the first three months of a nine month pregnancy). The first trimester is the most tenuous, as roughly 15% of pregnancies end in a miscarriage during this period (i.e. the period between three weeks and twelve weeks from conception).

A miscarriage is defined as a pregnancy coming to an end without explanation within the first 20 weeks. A loss of the baby after this period is known as a stillbirth.

Miscarriages and stillbirths can be deeply traumatic and upsetting to the both of you, although your partner is likely to suffer most intensely from such a loss. Most miscarriages remain unexplained and some couples will suffer from multiple miscarriages while starting a family, even after successful live births.

For some of us this is just bad luck - the laws of probabilities mean that some couples will never experience miscarriage, while others will have to endure multiple miscarriages simply due to the luck of the draw.

For others there are a range of medical and/or environmental factors that result in a higher than normal incidence of miscarriage. The exploration of these is outside of the scope of this book, but it is worth reading up on these prior to trying to get pregnant and cutting down on risk factors (such as smoking) early.

Always remember that miscarriage is a tragic but normal part of life and more couples suffer through it than you realise. You have every right to react to a miscarriage however you deem fit and so does your partner. If you're not overly bothered by it then there's nothing wrong with that. If either of you is devastated, emotional and feeling the need to grieve then *grieve*.

If your partner grieves more than you, possibly more than you think is reasonable, then grieve with her. Be supportive. She doesn't need to justify her pain. Help her through it. If she struggles to get through it then consider reaching out for help - there are support networks and counsellors in most places who specialise in helping couples recovering from miscarriages or stillbirths.

Thankfully we're relatively safe once she's past the first trimester, as the chances of miscarriage or stillbirth reduce significantly after this period, but it can make the first trimester pretty nerve wracking.

So think carefully about when you want to let family and friends know about the pregnancy.

Remember that the pregnancy is going to be a keen topic of conversation from the time you let the cat out of the bag, which can make for some awkward and painful situations if she miscarries.

Unfortunately even our most loved ones can say things that are foolish and misinformed when faced with tragedy that they don't understand. They can make clumsy comments like 'oh well, at least you didn't lose a real baby' that are insensitive and that trivialise the pain that the suffering couple is going through.

You might want to consider only letting your closest, most trusted friends and family know about the pregnancy during the first trimester, or maybe no-one at all. It is your choice. This pregnancy belongs to you and your partner alone.

Chapter 4: Pregnancy

Your role during the pregnancy will vary greatly depending on whether this will be your first child, or whether you already have kids.

Either way, the 9 months of pregnancy are full of joy and wonderment, as well as a fair amount of struggle. Mainly by your partner, of course.

There is a baby, your baby, growing inside of her. Every day over the course of the pregnancy your son or daughter develops at an astonishing rate. Truly pregnancy is a miracle.

There are a number of great, free services that provide regular updates over the course of the pregnancy, keeping you informed of progress as baby grows and develops. We signed up to a weekly email service which was excellent - it was always exciting to receive each instalment and to imagine baby's' development at each stage along the way.

Keeping Her and Baby Safe

There are a number of precautions that you and your partner will need to take to keep her and baby safe during pregnancy. We discuss some of the key risks here, but this is by no means an exhaustive list. It is a good idea for you and her to research these together, seeking professional where appropriate.

Some of these risk factors, such as smoking or drinking while pregnant, are significant and serious, while others, such as avoiding shellfish and sushi can seem obscure and almost pointless. So should we bother with them?

My advice is to avoid risk where you can. Pregnant women are advised to avoid shellfish, sushi and other possible sources of listeria because others have suffered miscarriages as a result of contracting listeria from these foods. Is this likely to happen to your partner? Probably not. But why run the risk in the first place?

What she chooses to do with her body, and what she chooses to put into it, are up to her. You are in a position to support her, however, and you should.

If you both smoke, for example, then you both must give up together. If she struggles to avoid some foods she knows she shouldn't be eating then banish them from the house. If she loves sushi then learn how to make sushi (fresh, home-made sushi is safe) - with a bit of practice you'd be surprised at how delicious it can be.

Things to Avoid

Both of you should avoid smoking and smokers. If either of you smoke then it's time to stop. Not only is smoking dangerous during pregnancy, it's dangerous around babies and children full stop. No excuses. No smoking outside. Just stop.

Your partner also needs to be careful of:

- Drugs of any kind. She shouldn't take any illicit drugs whatsoever. Anything else should be carefully checked with your doctor or a specialist pregnancy information service. Avoid alternative medicine too unless cleared by her doctor. Alternative medicines are rarely tested adequately, particularly with pregnant mothers.
- Alcohol. Any amount of drinking can cause foetal alcohol syndrome, which the child will live with for life. Some studies suggest that small amounts of alcohol are safe during the second and third trimesters, but I don't see why anyone would risk it.
- Foods that can harbour listeria or other such nasties. Soft cheeses are out, so too are rare steaks, pre-prepared salads, shellfish, sushi, almost all small goods and a range of other foods she won't think she'd miss until she can't have them.

It's important that you both research what foods and substances are, and are not, safe during pregnancy and that you agree together what your partner's approach will be. Remember that your job isn't that of policeman, but you may need to be supportive, particularly if she's having moments of weakness.

Antenatal Classes

Antenatal classes are offered in most towns and cities and you may find that classes are subsidised (either partially or fully) by the state and/or by non-profit entities in your area.

These classes are a must for any first-time parents. They generally run one or two nights per week for a month or two and cover a range of topics from pregnancy to birth and looking after a new-born.

A good antenatal class will be taught by an experienced professional, such as a midwife, and will be full of useful, practical tips and advice. They also provide an excellent forum for asking questions and discussing any concerns you or your partner might have.

Antenatal classes are also excellent places to meet other expectant couples, which is really valuable.

Pregnancy and childbirth can be isolating, particularly for mum and especially if none of her friends are pregnant or having kids.

At an antenatal class you are likely to meet other couples from similar socioeconomic backgrounds (as often the class will comprise people from a common geographic area) and, most important, who will become first-time parents about the same time as you.

Most antenatal classes will help attendees to organise 'coffee groups' or other regular get-togethers. If they don't then suggest it to the group yourself.

Some antenatal coffee groups peter out only after a couple of meetings, but many of them go on for many months or years. Long-term friendships can be formed - my wife still regularly sees friends from her antenatal coffee group from over a decade ago, and she's not unique in this respect.

There is also a wide range of other types of classes available to expectant mums and couples. From massage classes for pregnant couples to aromatherapy for labour pains - you'll find just about everything you can think of if you look hard enough. It's all completely unnecessary, but mostly harmless. One hospital midwife once told me that 'You can often tell the first-time parents when they come into the delivery suite - they have their oil burners, whale music and massage oils. They don't often bother bringing those things the next time.'

Around Home

Remember that your partner is going to be feeling the effects of being pregnant from the very early stages of the pregnancy right through to the birth and beyond.

She's likely to be a lot more tired and restless, hungry and nauseous - often all at the same time! She may experience mood swings, which can leave her irritable some of the time and in tears at others. Or irritable and in tears at the same time.

You get the picture.

Be prepared. Be calm and don't be swept up in her mood swings. This will be good practice for when you're a parent.

Be calm and be supportive. Be ready to shoulder more of the domestic burden, particularly if you have kids already.

Presents from Family and Friends

If you're lucky you'll get presents for baby from family and friends. This might be during a baby shower for your partner, or simply presents that people spontaneously give you before or after the birth.

Be prepared for the fact that most people receive more presents for the arrival of their first child than subsequent children. This doesn't mean that people care less about the subsequent arrivals, but it is the case that the novelty does wear off. Your loved ones also might consider that you have more of the things you need after baby number one (meaning their help is less important) and they may have had to shell out for numerous other presents (for other couples) since your first baby.

If you do anticipate receiving presents, and assuming you're comfortable doing so, then don't be afraid to try and coordinate the choice of presents a little.

You only need so many outfits for baby between the ages of 0 - 6 months, for example, but if you're not proactive you may find that's all that people buy you. If you have a large and/or fast growing baby then you may find that she only gets to wear those cute outfits once or twice before she's too big for them. I have known couples with exceptionally large babies who didn't get to put their babies in their gifted new-born clothes at all.

Many of your friends and family will welcome advice about what to buy, so don't be shy to make requests.

Preparing for Baby's Arrival

On average it will take about 40 weeks for your baby to make an entrance, but it pays to be prepared well ahead of time, just in case he or she decides to arrive early.

If you have kids around the house already then it's important to involve them in the preparations so they feel like they are welcoming baby into the family, rather than being replaced by the new addition.

Early Sleeping Arrangements

The best place for baby to sleep as a new-born is in the same room as you and mum, but in a separate sleeping space.

As appealing as the idea is of sleeping snuggled up with your new-born, it's not safe for you to share a bed in her early days. This can be difficult for some parents to accept, particularly if there's a cultural element involved, but you should always put baby's safety first.

She's going to need a bassinet, preferably one that can stand near your bed so that you and your partner can remain close to her at night.

If you absolutely must have baby in the bed with you then you'll need a bassinet that provides her with her own mattress, bedclothes and walls to keep her safe from errant adult bedclothes or rolling parents. Even this isn't as safe as giving her own standalone bassinet.

Regardless of where she sleeps, there are lots of precautions that you need to take to make a safe sleep space for your new-born. These include:

- Ensuring that her bassinet is safe, fit for purpose and properly constructed. Avoid bassinets with unnecessary bits and pieces - they may look good, but they can pose a hazard.
- Providing her with a new mattress. To minimise the chances of Sudden Infant Death Syndrome (SIDS), mattresses should be replaced for each new baby. Look at buying a mattress wrapper designed specifically for new-borns.
- Having appropriate, clean bedding. Avoid using bedding that

is too big for the bassinet - you don't want baby to wiggle her way under a heap of bedclothes that she can't breathe through.
- Keeping the bassinet away from objects that may fall on or into it. Even the drawstring from blinds can pose a hazard, so make sure nothing is close enough to fall in.
- Figuring out how to keep the cat out. Cats can be attracted to small, enclosed, warm spaces such as bassinets with babies in them. This may sound cute, but babies have died from asphyxiation from cats sleeping on their faces - figure out how to keep the cat well away.

It's also a great idea to have a second, portable bassinet that you can carry baby around in. We had one that clipped onto a pram (stroller), which was really useful.

The Nursery

Babies are beautiful, but they're also noisy. Even when they're not crying they can make a good old racket with all of their sniffling, cooing and snoring.

Babies can also be light sleepers and you'll need to give them their own room (if possible) when they're about a month old.

The nursery should be an oasis of calm. As much as *you'd* love to hang a mobile above her crib or to paint a mural on her wall, you should focus on soft colours and removing visual stimulation. Babies, particularly new-borns, can easily become over-stimulated, which can prevent, rather than help them sleep.

Essential items in the nursery are:

- A crib. Look for a crib that baby will be able to stay in until she is 2 - 3 years old. It should have sides (to stop her from rolling out, or climbing out in future), suitable mattress and bed wear.
- A feeding/cuddling chair. Somewhere where baby can be breast or bottle fed, cuddled and winded (burped) between sleeping sessions. Make it a comfortable chair with cushioned arms - a recliner is ideal.

- A change table. Look for one that is safe and stable and in which baby will lie at a comfortable working height. The change table should also have lots of storage space for nappies, wipes and other essentials that you will need to be able to reach while you have one hand on baby.
- Your nappy system. Whether you decide to use disposable or cloth nappies, you are going to need A LOT of them. You need a good stock of nappies, plus a system for processing dirty ones, etc. You can't leave the room to dispose of nappies while baby is on the change table, so make sure everything is within your reach.

You may also want to consider a baby monitor, although these are not strictly necessary. I had an elevated (albeit irrational) fear of one of my kids dying of SIDS, having lost a relative to it when I was a child. So we had a baby monitor that included motion sensitive pads under the baby's mattress - an alarm would sound if the baby stopped breathing. This was admittedly a little neurotic, but it let us rest a little easier, so it was worth it.

Food and Feeding Utensils

If your partner is planning on breastfeeding then you're not going to need much in the way of food or utensils for baby's first weeks. As we'll discuss in the next chapter, however, first time mums should always have a backup plan in place in case, like many women, they have trouble breastfeeding and they need to revert to a bottle, even if only temporarily.

If you're going to bottle feed baby then you're going to need formula (make sure it's for new-borns!), bottles, sterilising solution/equipment and something suitable for carrying bottles around in.

While you're waiting for baby to arrive it's also a great time to start making and freezing meals for baby (once she's old enough for solids) and for yourselves.

When my wife was pregnant with baby number one we bought a chest freezer and filled it to the brim with home cooked meals (lasagnes, shepherd's pies and others that froze well) as well as tons of cooked and pureed fruit, vegetables and meat for baby.

This required a bit of planning and effort, but the results were more than worthwhile.

During the haze of exhaustion and sleeplessness in her earliest days we had a steady supply of nutritious meals that we just had to thaw and put in the oven.

More important, we had an excellent supply of 'solid' food (as you'll see, this is a misnomer, as baby's first foods are anything but solid) that allowed us to avoid having to buy expensive processed baby foods.

To prepare your own baby food, simply boil fruits, vegetables and meats (choose meat that's high in iron, such as kidney and liver) on their own (don't mix the ingredients yet) until they're really, really well done. You want to cook them until they're really soft - a lot more than you'd normally cook them for yourself.

Then just puree each ingredient, adding water that it was boiled in to achieve a good consistency. Spoon the puree into ice trays and freeze until solid.

You can then transfer the frozen cubes of food to separate containers (we used zip lock bags) and repeat the process until the freezer is full.

The beauty of keeping the ingredients separate is that you can mix and match them how you like before you feed them to baby.

Just pop out a few cubes (of whatever ingredients you've chosen), zap them in the microwave, mix them up (you can add some baby rice cereal powder or similar to make it more substantial) and let it cool before feeding it to baby.

You probably won't feed her solids until baby is 6 months old or so, but you may have a lot less time for preparing these solids after she's born. We did this with all four of our children and it worked an absolute treat.

Ben Gannon

Midwife or Obstetrician?

One of the bigger decisions you'll need to make in the first days of your pregnancy is whether you'll opt for an obstetrician or a midwife to be your lead carer during the pregnancy.

Your options may be different in your country, but in New Zealand the state funds birth care with a midwife as your lead carer, but you can choose to use an obstetrician if you want to pay for one.

An obstetrician has superior medical training and capabilities than a midwife, but that doesn't always make them the best choice for every couple. Some would argue that obstetricians can be too quick to use medical interventions, while midwives are happier to support natural childbirth.

We chose to use an obstetrician for the birth of all four of our children because we liked the additional diagnostic capabilities our obstetrician he had at his disposal (he had his own ultrasound machine, for example). We also liked the idea that he could intervene directly if anything went wrong during delivery.

Every couple is different and no two medical professionals are the same. There is no right or wrong answer about whether you should use an obstetrician or a midwife, but you should do your research. Whoever you choose to be your lead carer you should talk to others who have used them and make sure you're comfortable with their philosophy and methods.

Good obstetricians and midwives can be booked up well in advance, so it can pay to make up your mind and choosing your professional before your partner becomes pregnant. This may sound ridiculous, but it's better to at least know what your options are before the pregnancy begins.

It can be difficult and awkward to change your lead carer after pregnancy has begun and some couples end up scrambling to find someone if they leave it too late.

Ben Gannon

The First Trimester

For us as fathers (or fathers to be) the first trimester can be the least satisfying, as there are no bumps to talk to, scans to fawn over or baby kicks to marvel at.

Baby is developing fast, however, and your partner's body will be undergoing an enormous about of change, so she may be a lot more aware of her condition than you are.

This trimester runs from conception until week 13. During this time her uterus will change so it can support the attachment and growth of the placenta. Hormone levels change rapidly, and will remain elevated for the duration of the pregnancy, and her blood supply will increase significantly. Her heart rate will also increase and remain elevated throughout.

Some women are susceptible to elevated blood pressure, gestational diabetes and other unpleasant pregnancy suite effects, so be prepared to help her keep an eye on her health.

We used a Doppler baby heartbeat monitor so we could listen to baby's heartbeat from the latter stages of the first trimester. Many health professionals recommend against them, as they can be hard to use - it can be difficult to find baby's heartbeat. This can cause distress for expectant parents (who often think the worst if they can't find the foetal heartbeat) but we used to love hearing his or her tiny heart beating away.

The Second Trimester

The second trimester (weeks 13-27) can lure you both into a false sense of security. Your partner will develop a pleasing bump and she will probably start feeling somewhat normal again, meaning more restful nights and more energy during the day.

The arrival of the second trimester also coincides with a sharp decline in the likelihood of miscarriage, so many couples choose now to tell their loved ones the good news (many time the announcement after the foetus has been screened for Down's syndrome, as below).

Your partner is likely to suffer from indigestion, heartburn, leg cramps and/or other fun side effects that come from a baby displacing a bunch of her vital organs.

Remember that many over the counter medicines and remedies are not safe (or at least are not proven to be safe) for pregnant women, so be careful that your desire to make her feel better doesn't result in her taking something she shouldn't.

Many pregnant women decide not to take any drugs at all when pregnant unless it's an emergency. In any case your doctor or obstetrician are best to advise on what's safe and what's not.

There will be a number of scans and other diagnostic procedures during the second and third trimesters. You shouldn't skip these, as they are important. If your partner is busy then see what support you can provide so she can find the time for them.

One important test is the nuchal scan (sometimes called the 'nuchal fold' scan), which occurs around the 13 week mark and is a screening test for Down's syndrome.

If the foetus is assessed as having a high likelihood of having Down's then you can opt for more invasive procedures to confirm one way or another.

If the foetus has Down's then you and your partner will need to decide whether you want to terminate or to continue with the pregnancy. This choice is yours and hers alone - no one can make it for you and you should never feel guilty or ashamed for whatever choice you make.

If you choose to continue with the pregnancy then you will have a lot of additional planning to do for having a baby with Down's - the sooner you get on to this the better!

My favourite thing about the second trimester is that, if you're lucky, you should start to feel some of baby's movements.

Whether or not you do is subject to a wide range of factors (such as baby's position, orientation, activity levels, etc.) so don't freak out if it takes longer than you'd expect to feel baby moving around.

Regardless of whether or not you feel her moving, you should talk to her regularly. She will be able to hear the sound of your voice more and more and this is your opportunity to start building your relationship with her.

At the end of the second trimester the foetus starts becoming viable, meaning its chances of surviving a premature birth start to increase.

This is a good time to prepare your hospital bag (see below) and to make arrangements for various labour scenarios. Who will look after your existing kids if your partner goes into labour in the middle of the night? What numbers will you ring in an emergency? Get a plan together and make sure everyone knows what to do.

The Third Trimester

If you thought the second trimester sounded uncomfortable for your partner, you wait until you see what the third trimester has in store for her!

The final trimester is, of course, the most visible to others, as her bump will generally be big enough for all to see and she may develop a bit of a waddle as she has to work harder to carry it around.

Your partner will be in full bloom and will look as beautiful as you will ever see her. This is partly a result of all those hormones (making her hair, skin and eyes look amazing), but mostly because you'll have feelings of love and protectiveness that are stronger than you may have ever felt. This is evolution's way of ensuring that we care for the pregnant mothers in our 'clan' (despite their hunting abilities being temporarily impaired), but there is also more to it than that.

Enjoy this time and be careful that you don't both wish it away. Although she will feel uncomfortable and you'll be dying to meet your new baby this time is so precious and so fleeting. Blink and you really will miss it.

On the down side, your partner will probably suffer from a range of ailments over this trimester - most of these will miraculously disappear after the birth, but that won't make them any less uncomfortable in the meantime. Common third trimester afflictions include:

- High blood pressure and associated symptoms
- Gestational diabetes and associated symptoms
- Weight gain. Every woman, and every pregnancy, is different. Remember that she may feel self-conscious about her changing shape and weight. Reassure her and support her - remind her that she looks beautiful each chance you get.
- Backache, varicose/spider veins, swollen ankles, haemorrhoids, frequent urination and vaginal discharge. Some things make you feel lucky to be a man. These symptoms are common and they can make her uncomfortable

and embarrassed. Remind her that they're normal (if not often discussed) and remember that a good foot rub can work wonders.

If you travel regularly for business then it may pay to put a stop to it during this trimester - both to minimise the chances of being out of town when baby comes and because you're not going to want to miss these special last months of pregnancy.

During these precious months baby may respond to light and sound and even to your touch. Such a special time.

Your Birthing Plan

Your lead carer should advise you nice and early on the creation of your birthing plan.

The birthing plan should set out where and how the baby will be born.

For example, will you have a home birth or will it be at the hospital? Will it be in bed or a water birth? Will she use pain relief or tough it out without it?

It's important that you both think these things through and decide on them ahead of time. You don't want to be stressing your partner out during labour expecting her to make decisions that she could have made weeks earlier.

Where and how your baby is delivered are deeply personal decisions that are completely up to the two of you. When choosing where, however, please bear in mind that nowhere is safer than the hospital for your partner to have her baby. The idea of a home birth may appeal and most home births go without a hitch.

But sometimes things do go wrong. Sometimes they go wrong quickly, meaning that urgent intervention is required.

It's a fact that home births are a lot riskier than giving birth at the hospital.

If you're thinking about a home birth then do your homework and, most important, listen to the advice of your lead carer.

In particular, seek advice on pain relief, even if your partner wants to go without. Some mothers will change their mind on pain relief once labour is underway, so it's important that you understand what the options are ahead of time. In the movies pain relief comes via a syringe and is instantaneous. In reality some forms of pain relief involve complex procedures that may only be available from certain medical specialists.

In New Zealand, for example, an epidural is a delicate procedure that can only be performed by an anaesthetist. An anaesthetist has to be available to perform the procedure and the epidural takes time to take effect. Epidurals are not always effective the first time, too, which further complicates things.

It's important for you and your partner to understand her options are likely to be at the time of the birth. She will need to understand how early in the labour she will need to ask for certain forms of pain relief for those options to be available.

There may be cost implications for certain forms of pain relief also. If so then be prepared - she should be able to make her own choices regarding pain relief, irrespective of the cost.

When it comes to the birthing plan, remember that it's your partner's body. She's the one who's going to be pushing a bowling ball out her vagina, so at the end of the day it's her call whether she wants to be sitting in a bath or on a bed, or whether or not she's going to have pain relief.

Chapter 5: The First Year

Hold on dad... your life is about to change forever. Baby's arrival is going to bring some big changes!

So much will change over the course of the first year. A year that starts with a helpless, tiny bundle of joy and ends with an inquisitive, crawling, babbling wonder on all fours.

Before we look at what to expect over the first year it's important that you and your partner prepare yourselves for what's ahead.

In truth it doesn't matter how many books you read, how much advice you receive or how ready you think you are - you're never *truly* ready to become a parent for the first time. Knowing you're not ready is the secret.

Often first time expectant parents, who are organised and successful in other areas of their lives, approach parenthood as they do everything else. They research, reading books and talking to others, they plan and they prepare.

This is all normal and important.

The mistake that many of us make, however, (I was certainly guilty of this) is that we convince ourselves that we're *more ready* than those who came before us.

We have read more and prepared more than they did, so it follows that we're going to find the birth, and the first year, easier than our friends and family did with their kids.

Don't kid yourself!

For a start, you often won't hear about the bad stuff until it happens to you.

Many parents, unfortunately, feel the need to present an overly-positive picture of how parenting is going, particularly in the first few years. It's as if they are afraid that others will think less of them if, like all of us, they struggle with aspects of parenting.

Parents also won't want to be overly negative when discussing their experiences with parents to be. Yes there were nights when we were so tired we were physically sick and yes I have had my baby's poo on just about every part of my body, including in my mouth, but do I really want to terrorise expectant parents with these anecdotes? No, I don't. Instead I talk about the fun stuff and smile knowingly at the other parents in the room. 'They have no fucking idea what's about to happen to them!' we're silently saying to each other.

Also, all of our experiences are different. Every child is different. Some babies will be a dream during the first few months. Others will make your life *miserable*.

This can leave you shocked and confused. You'll ask yourself 'I've read all the books and I'm doing it all right, so why is this baby STILL CRYING?!?'

Remember that baby hasn't read your books. He cares nothing for the techniques that you've learned that are supposedly going to make him sleep like a, will, baby.

No matter how much you have read, no matter your preparations, you are going to be faced with a huge learning curve. Get used to this idea.

You won't have all of the answers and, at times, you may feel exhausted and at your wits end.

This doesn't make you bad parents. It makes you normal.

Embrace it. If it was easy bringing children into the world it would be boring.

Your baby will cry. Sometimes he will cry inexplicably and it will seem like nothing you can do will soothe him.

Your baby will sometimes refuse to sleep. He will refuse to sleep and he will cry at the same time.

You will care - his crying and lack of sleep will drive you and your partner around the bend.

And this is a good thing. If you didn't care, and you were able to ignore your sleepless, crying baby, then there really *would* be a problem.

Be ready for the fact that you're not ever going to be completely ready for what's about to happen. Be prepared for the fact that your partner, who's probably used to overcoming whatever challenges that come her way, is going to be affected by the trials and tribulations of baby's first days most acutely. Be understanding and be supportive. Remember that you might not have the answer, so try not to rush in and try to fix every problem.

Mum will find her way - your job is to reassure and support her as she does so.

The good news is that it does get easier and normality does return.

As baby gets older his patterns will be easier to read. You'll become more comfortable as a parent and you'll be better at anticipating and understanding his outbursts.

If you later have more children then they will offer up their own unique challenges, but you'll be surprised at how much easier these are to overcome with each subsequent child. By the time we had our fourth child it was a breeze!

Labour and Birth

The big day has arrived! How exciting! Baby is on his way!

Don't panic! Most women will labour for hours before they need to go to the delivery suite. Hopefully your lead carer will have advised you on what to do and when.

In a very small number of cases labour may be very quick and baby may start arriving unexpectedly. If this happens to you then don't be shy - ring an ambulance straight away.

No matter what happens, stay calm! Your partner needs your help. She does not need to have to look after you as well as dealing with labour pains, etc.

Be attentive. Be prepared for her to experience some discomfort. Even be prepared for her to act a little strange - the combination of pain and hormones affects every woman differently.

Our obstetrician told us of a patient he had who squatted in the corner and clucked like a chicken. They managed to coax her back onto the delivery table, but apparently she continued clucking right through the delivery.

This kind of thing is rare and is very unlikely to happen to your partner. Unlike on TV, however, where labour only ever takes a few minutes, your partner is likely to labour for hours before baby arrives. It's common for women to labour for 8 hours or more, so be prepared to wait. And wait. And wait.

This is why your lead carer won't want you to head into the hospital straight away when your partner goes into labour - you'd just end up hogging one of their beds while your partner waits for nature to take its course.

Your carer should advise you on when you should bring your partner into the birthing suite and this will usually be based on the frequency and strength of contractions. Make yourself useful and record the time between those contractions so you can get an idea of when you should be heading in.

There are procedures that your carer can perform to try and speed things along, although unless mum or baby are distressed then it's usually better to just wait it out. That baby will usually make an appearance when it's good and ready.

Once your partner's cervix is fully dilated (i.e. the cervical opening has increased to 10cm) then she will normally have an hour or two of pushing before baby is born.

This can be traumatic, painful and exhausting for her, particularly if she's opted not to have pain relief.

Ready yourself for this. It can be upsetting for you to see your partner in such distress, but now is not the time to freak out. You have to remain calm and supportive. Reassure her and encourage her.

Have faith in the health professionals around you. They will know if there's a problem that requires intervention, otherwise your partner is just going to have to tough it out.

If things do start to go wrong and the professionals decide to intervene then they are likely to do so swiftly. Intervention can involve anything from a forceps delivery (where they help baby out with the aid of forceps) to a ventouse delivery (where they attach a vacuum cap to baby and pull him out by his head) to a caesarean section. No matter what happens you must stay calm and stay out of the way. Reassure your partner - it's very likely that she and baby will be fine. Hang in there!

There are a number of things that you're not often warned about prior to entering the delivery suite. Don't say I didn't warn you:

- Unwelcome deliveries. As your partner is pushing hard to get baby out she can make deliveries of an unwanted kind. If poo comes out then don't make a big deal about it. Your carer will usually clean it up without your partner even noticing.
- Tearing or incisions to the vagina during birth. Tearing can occur due to the pressure of baby's head on the vagina. Your

lead carer may try and relieve this pressure by making an incision first. Either way, the result can be gruesome. If you don't want to see it then stay away from that end.
- Meconium on, and/or in baby. Meconium is baby's first stool. It's thick, black, sticky and generally unpleasant. Sometimes it comes out of baby before or during labour. If it's on baby it can be harmless, if baby aspirates it (breathes it in) it can be more serious.
- Screaming (by your partner). If this comes as a surprise it shouldn't. The pain of childbirth can be intense to the point of becoming overwhelming. Don't freak out - help reassure her that it will be over soon.

When baby finally arrives it is the most overwhelmingly emotional experience you are ever likely to have. Two of you walked into the delivery suite and now there are three of you.

Suddenly there is another tiny human in the room and he relies totally on you.

Your life will never be the same again.

If all has gone well during the birth your carer will put baby on mum's chest, allowing her to have that important first hug. You will be a bit of a third wheel for a while, so be patient - you will have plenty of time to hold baby soon enough.

Your carer will usually ask if you want to cut the umbilical cord if this isn't already in your birthing plan. If not then don't be afraid to ask. It is a magic experience severing that sacred connection between baby and mother. That cord has sustained baby through his entire life to date, but he doesn't need it anymore.

If there have been complications during birth, or if baby is just a little cold, then he may be whisked away for checks and possibly to spend some time in a foetal incubator to help warm him up.

Almost always baby will be fine, so don't worry. Take care of your partner and reassure her - she has just been through an experience that is almost as traumatic as it is magical. She may be worried about baby, however, and she may be exhibiting signs of shock, so take care of her.

Breastfeeding

Before we look at what to expect during baby's first week, let's spend a moment discussing what can be a ridiculous situation surrounding breastfeeding.

The act of breastfeeding is wondrous and beautiful. In fact, feeding your new-born is a beautiful experience regardless. I'm pretty sure that if we had breasts it would be even more special.

So breastfeeding is great. What's the problem?

The problem is that, in many communities (mine included) everyone seems to have an opinion about others' breastfeeding decisions (i.e. whether women should breastfeed, when and where they should be able to breastfeed, etc.) despite it being absolutely none of their business.

Whether your partner breastfeeds or not is her business and her business alone.

You're the dad, so you get to share your opinion, but it's still her choice at the end of the day.

Unfortunately as a society we've forgotten this and it's mum's who suffer as a result.

In many Western countries there is a vocal and powerful pro-breastfeeding movement that doesn't just promote breastfeeding - they vilify bottle feeding as well.

This is a problem because all parents deserve the right to receive fair and balanced information on the feeding alternatives available to them at each stage of their child's life. Parents (namely the mother) should then be free to choose how to nourish their child, free from judgement and interference from others.

Unfortunately this is not how things usually turn out and mother's end up suffering as a result.

This may sound a little strong, but let me share some of my

experiences and observations from my home country (New Zealand):

- During antenatal classes, our instructor was *only permitted* to talk about breastfeeding and even then only in positive terms. She was forbidden (by the government agency that she worked for) from talking about, or even answering questions about, bottle feeding in class.
- At most postnatal care facilities in New Zealand (which are state funded) they are not allowed to supply you with formula or baby bottles, even if mother is unable to breastfeed for any reason. Instead you're forced to bring in your own formula as if it's some type of illicit substance.
- There are restrictions on advertising baby formula. Even unrelated ads that have shown babies being bottle fed have been pulled for fear of causing some form of bottle feeding epidemic.

Mothers are bombarded with messages that breastfeeding is safe and easy and is 'what's best for your baby'. They are made to feel inadequate or even that they're bad mothers if they have trouble breastfeeding, or if they simply choose not to.

Many mums are so self-conscious about bottle feeding their infants that they won't do it in public. This comes as no surprise to me, as I've seen complete strangers chastise mothers in public for bottle feeding their babies.

Can you imagine how upsetting and humiliating it would be for a complete stranger to criticise you in public for how you choose to feed your baby?

This all creates a situation where mums can feel pressured to breastfeed and, worse, as if they're failures if they don't (or can't).

There are two key facts that get lost in all the noise:

1. Breastfeeding isn't always easy. In fact, for many first time mums it's downright difficult. For a small minority it's impossible. It's hard to find reliable statistics on this topic, but my (unscientific) experience is that most women have at least

some difficulty breastfeeding (see below).
2. Formula-fed babies are, on average, just as healthy as breastfed babies (assuming the correct, high quality formula is used). In fact, I once asked one of New Zealand's leading paediatricians whether he could tell the difference between breastfed and bottle-fed babies. After thinking about it for a while the only difference he could think of was that bottle-fed babies are 'bonnier' (plump and healthy looking).

My advice is to ignore all of the noise and to let your partner decide what's best for *her*.

Yes, breastfeeding is magical, but it's no one's choice whether she should do it other than her own.

If she decides to breastfeed then be prepared, however. I doubt there is anything in this world more stressful than watching your partner unsuccessfully try to latch a hungry, screaming baby onto her breast for several hours at a time. Believe me - I've been there, and it was excruciating for the both of them and awful to watch.

Thankfully, after several days of my wife struggling to feed our daughter, someone put us in touch with a lactation consultant (I didn't know such an occupation existed before then) and she worked wonders.

Lactation consultants are not cheap but, of your partner decides to breastfeed, I cannot recommend engaging with one strongly enough.

Our consultant helped my wife with her technique and helped her understand all of the complexities of milk supply that no one had explained to her earlier.

You see, it's perfectly normal, and expected, for it to take a while (i.e. 2 - 5 days) before mum's milk 'comes in'. Before this the breast is either dispensing colostrum or *nothing at all*. Also, breastfed babies will normally lose 7 - 10% of their weight during their first 5 - 7 days from birth.

The lactation consultant helped us to understand these facts and she helped my wife with her breastfeeding technique. We didn't hesitate to call her again when my wife had baby number two - we didn't need her for babies three and four.

Help your partner to prepare for breastfeeding in advance. Talk to her about what she wants to do and be supportive of her decisions.

If she is likely to try breastfeeding then make sure she talks to other mothers about their experiences. Remember that breastfeeding is a deeply personal experience and some mothers may feel self-conscious talking about any challenges that they may have had. Your partner should seek out friends and family who are likely to share all of the gory details, good and bad, with her.

It's also a good idea for her to find a lactation consultant in your area and to check with him or her that they are likely to be available around the time that baby is due. This can be a sensitive subject, as you don't want to cause her to feel anxious or inadequate about breastfeeding, so approach the subject with caution!

The First Week

A friend of mine, whose wife was at the time expectant with their first child, did once assure me that 'having this baby isn't going to change us'. They weren't going to change their schedule to suit the baby - the baby was going have to work around them.

I tried not to laugh when I saw him a week after his son was born - he was so tired that he was almost asleep on his feet. The baby had obviously missed the memo about whose schedule he was supposed to be operating to and he had been keeping mum and dad awake almost constantly since birth.

Nothing can prepare you for this first week of wondrous torture.

It is a week of firsts - baby's first poo (meconium - don't worry, this vile substance doesn't come out of them for long), first smile, first sleep, first bath. Don't wish this week away. Stop every now and then and take in what's happening - it may feel like torture at the time, but this beautiful, chaotic moment will never be repeated.

Forget any thoughts of parenting techniques or philosophies this week. Forget any thoughts of going into work or working on the house.

All you need to focus on this week is making sure your bundle of joy is fed and that both mother and baby get plenty of rest.

Crying

It may come as no surprise that your baby is going to cry. What may be a surprise is *how much* he cries and, sometimes, how little you can do to stop it.

Now not all new-borns cry a lot, so if yours is contented then don't worry that he should be crying more - be happy for your good fortune.

If he's like most new-borns and he cries a lot then you're going to have to find ways of dealing with it.

Your baby doesn't need much - he needs food, comfort (from you), a clean nappy and lots of sleep.

If he's fed and still crying then burp him and try to feed him again.

If he's full and if his nappy is clean and he's still crying then he probably needs sleep. Unfortunately he can get overtired, in which case he's probably going to need to torment you with his crying for a while until he gets off to sleep.

Sometimes you won't know why he's crying and maybe he won't know either. Babies cry. Deal with it.

You do need to remember that mothers often *feel* baby's crying much more deeply than you will. There's evidence to suggest that there are evolutionary reasons for this - if prehistoric mum could easily ignore baby's cry then baby probably wouldn't live very long.

Find opportunities to take baby off your partner's hands and to give her a break whenever possible.

You may also find that baby cries if mum picks him up, but seemingly not when you do. He may also cry unexpectedly if you hand baby to her. This can be upsetting to your partner, who can find this behaviour confusing. Reassure her - baby isn't crying because he doesn't like her. He's crying because he knows that mum has boobs and he wants to be fed. The only way he knows how to ask is to cry. Loudly.

Feeding and Changing

New-borns should be fed on demand, which is likely to be roughly every 3 - 4 hours. Feeding can be relentless at first - baby has no concept yet of day or night. He will cry whenever he's hungry. Sometimes you'll get a few hours of respite. Sometimes you'll get a few minutes.

It's common for both of you to feel exhausted as a result. It can be like you're walking in a daze. I remember wondering out loud how something so small could have such a big impact on our actions and on our state of mind. Everything revolved around feeding her and changing her and putting her back down for sleep.

Baby is not going to be overly sociable during the f[irst...] he's not feeding or crying then he'll likely be asleep [... get as] much sleep as he needs, even if it means not bein[g held] as much as you or your family would like.

Resist the urge to get him out of his bassinet when [someone] comes around to visit. If he's already awake then there will probably be time for a quick cuddle, but otherwise your guests will have to wait.

If your partner is breastfeeding then you can help by ferrying baby between mother and bassinet, by changing him and burping him before putting him to bed.

Baby needs to be burped after every feed. Drape a towel over your shoulder (or your lap, if you prefer) and drape baby over the top of it, tummy down. Now either rub your hand up his back or firmly tap his back until he produces a satisfying burp. He should only need one belch before going back down, but if he's restless look for discolouration around the lips and/or him bringing his knees up toward his chest - these are signs that he's got trapped wind.

Remember to check his nappy often and to change dirty nappies straight away. Even if he's only wet his nappy it needs to be changed ASAP to prevent skin irritation.

Bear in mind that baby's stools come out primarily in liquid form and they tend to squirt out with a fair amount of velocity. I always make sure I slip a new nappy in quickly when I'm changing new-borns in case they decide to squirt all over the change table.

With boys it's also worth covering their penis with a clean nappy or a cloth when removing their soiled nappy, as the sensation of cold air on their willy can cause them to spontaneously pee. You'd be amazed at how far it can go, too!

Bottle Care

Until your baby is about a year old he's going to be particularly susceptible to harmful germs, so you will need to be careful to not only clean, but also sanitise bottles and pacifiers (if used) regularly. Use a

...able sanitising agent and follow the instructions carefully.

Sleep

New-borns sleep. A lot. It can be a little disappointing for new dads to find out quite how much they sleep, as between all of the feeding, changing and sleeping you might get less time holding him than you expected. Don't worry - this doesn't last forever and you will get plenty of time to hold him as he gets older.

At night you should change baby and put him down to sleep straight after each feed. You and your partner should get back to sleep as quickly as possible, as there's no telling how long you're going to get before he's awake again.

During the day you can keep him up for a while but look out for signs of tiredness - you don't want him to get overtired, which will make it more difficult for him to get off to sleep. Watch for him pulling at his ears, closing his fists, yawning, frowning or making jerky movements. His eyes might start rolling around and he can have trouble focusing on things. He may also start sucking on his fingers in an attempt to settle himself.

Resist the temptation to let baby sleep on you too often. Every now and then is fine, but any more than this and baby will soon start relying on you (i.e. on being on you) for sleep. He will also tend to cry when he opens his eyes (babies do this often while they're sleeping - like they're checking that everything is still in order) and finds that you're gone. Your baby needs to be put down to sleep when he's tired but still awake.

DO NOT get into the habit of holding or otherwise being with your baby when he goes off to sleep. It's lovely to experience them drifting off from time to time, but at no point in his development should he *rely* on your presence to get off to sleep. Not as a baby, toddler or child. Such a practice is not good for him or for you.

Infants should be swaddled in bed, as swaddling them makes them feel safe and secure and prevents them from jerking themselves awake. You should swaddle your baby in a blanket that's made for swaddling (a 'swaddling blanket' or 'swaddle') - you'll find these in most department stores. Buy lots of them (we used ones made of a muslin-type cloth), as you don't want to run out of swaddles if baby has been particularly generous with his secretions (i.e. if they're all dirty).

Start by laying the swaddle in a diamond shape on the bed with one corner pointing toward you. Foid the opposite (top) corner down and lie baby on the swaddle so the fold is behind his neck. Now wrap the left corner over the front of him and tuck it under his left side - now both of his arms should be snugly tucked at his side. Wrap the right corner over the front of him and the bottom corner up behind him. Voila - one swaddled baby who's ready for bed.

When putting him into his crib make sure he only has bedclothes that he can breathe through if they end up over his face. I like to use just one knitted blanket (no top sheet), which I tucked in snugly all around him. This makes him feel secure, stops the bed clothes from rolling up over him and helps keep the swaddle intact.

Always lie baby down on his back when putting him to bed - never on his side or on his tummy, as these sleeping positions can be dangerous. If you find he tends to roll over on his own then it might be worth looking at buying a bed cushion to prevent him from doing so.

Remember that baby can't tell you if he's too hot or cold, so take care to keep an eye on his temperature.

Resist the temptation to use props to try and get your baby off to sleep. He doesn't need a mobile above his bassinet or other distractions - if anything these will cause him to become over-stimulated and he'll struggle to nod off.

If your baby has trouble sleeping then you may need to let him cry a little. This can be agonising for you, but remind yourself that he's safe and warm and well fed. His crying might feel like it's hurting you, but it's not hurting him. He's a baby. It's what he does.

During his first week you should let him cry for 5 minutes or so at a time before you go in - time yourself to make sure you don't cheat and go in sooner. You can try gently patting his chest and singing to him softly to get him off to sleep.

Once he's down remember not to rush in when you hear him cry. He might wake himself up and cry out for company before calming himself down and going back to sleep. He might even babble for a while, which is adorable, but wait for him to really start wailing before you come into his view and/or get him up out of the bassinet - the trick is to let him sleep as much as possible.

Bath Time

If there's anything more beautiful than bathing a baby, I don't know what it is. It really is a special time and it can be a good opportunity for you to bond with your new baby while mum grabs a few moments to herself.

All you need to bathe your baby is a suitable baby bath, some warm water and a couple of facecloths. It's not a good idea to chuck him in the family bath - this is too big and too slippery for it to be fun for either of you.

Don't use soap with your new-born - water is fine. If you really want to use something make sure it is designed specifically for bathing new-borns - normal soaps will dry out his skin. He also doesn't need a bath every day - a few times per week is fine. You can bathe him more than this, but watch out for his skin becoming dried out if he's bathed too often.

Get yourself set up before you put baby in the bath - everything needs to be within easy reach, including towels, nappies and a change of clothes. You should never, ever, leave your baby alone in or around water even for a second.

The room needs to be warm enough that baby won't get too cold before or after the bath, but be careful not to put him directly in front of the heater - his skin is much more sensitive than yours.

Be very careful with the water temperature - put cold water into the bath first then add hot water. The water should be a degree or two above body temperature, or about 38 degrees Celsius (about 100 degrees Fahrenheit). Use a thermometer if you have one or use your elbow to check the temperature if not. Remember that your skin becomes less sensitive each time you dip it into hot water, so be careful not to convince yourself that the temperature is fine simply because your elbow has become less sensitive to it.

Baby might cry a bit as you take his clothes off and as he first feels the water against his skin, this is normal. Lie him in the water with your hand under him. I just support his neck so his face is out of the water but the rest of his body is floating. Now the important bit - dunk one of the face clothes in the water and spread it over baby's chest and tummy so the bottom of the cloth is covering his penis (to prevent unexpected fountains). This will make him feel warmer and more secure and this is usually when he'll stop crying and will start chilling. Take a moment to stare into his eyes as he enjoys floating around.

Now use the other facecloth to give him a good clean. Be gentle but thorough. Remember that babies often shed skin during their first week, so don't freak out if you see what looks like rashes under his arms, between his legs, etc. Start by washing his face and end by cleaning his bum and genitals. Don't leave him in the bath for too long, as the water will be getting cooler and you don't want him to be too tired as you get him dressed.

His umbilical cord stump will take a week or two to shrivel and fall off - gently clean around it, but don't try and pull it off prematurely. Doing so is likely to cause discomfort and bleeding and could open the door to infection. When it falls off you can simply throw the shrivelled stump away.

When he's all clean lift him out and hold him over the bath for a few seconds to let the excess water run-off. Lie him on a towel and quickly wrap him up to keep him warm and make him feel safe. I use baby towels with a pocket in one of the corners to put over his head - this makes it easier to keep his head warm while I'm drying him, not to mention making him look really adorable.

Make sure you dry him thoroughly - including all of his crevices, before getting him dressed. You don't need baby powder or other such products - in fact some of these can be damaging to baby's health. He just needs his nappy, his clothes and a cuddle.

The First Six Months

Congratulations - you've made it through the first week! Hopefully with your sanity intact.

I'm not sure if things get any less crazy during the rest of the first six months, but if you can survive the first week you can survive anything.

The great thing about this period in your baby's development is that you start to see his personality emerge.

You should see him lifting his head, smiling, making noises and maybe even laughing by the three month mark.

He will discover (and keep rediscovering) his hands and he'll start to use them, albeit very clumsily at first. He'll reach out for and grab things and will try and mouth just about everything.

Crying, feeding, changing and bathing are pretty much the same as they were during the first week, although you should be seeing more of a pattern to his behaviour as the days go by. Your partner's milk should have come in by the end of the first week (if breastfeeding) and baby is likely to be eating more and more by the day.

Sleep

Baby should sleep for longer and longer over time and should manage to stay awake for longer periods too. It's not realistic to expect baby to sleep through the night at this stage, although you may get lucky from time to time.

This is, of course, until baby approaches the magical 5kg mark (about 11lbs). Until baby reaches 5kg he should continue to be fed on demand. Once he reaches 5kg it's time to move him into the nursery and to start building toward him sleeping all night.

Note that not all babies reach 5kg during the first six months - some can take a little longer. When he does reach 5kg, however, it's time for him to start learning how to self-settle and eventually how to sleep through the night.

This is our first section on building and maintaining effective sleeping habits, so pay attention. If you're disciplined you're going to have a child who sleeps soundly through the night. If not then sleep, or lack thereof, is going to become a total nightmare for you and your partner.

If sleep does become a challenge then remember that your child doesn't develop poor sleeping habits - you do.

Notwithstanding a tiny minority of children that have bona fide medical conditions that affect their sleep, if your child struggles to get to sleep and/or to stay asleep on a regular basis then it's because *you've* developed poor sleeping habits for him.

Parents with poor sleeping habits struggle with children who do not sleep. When *he* doesn't sleep *you* don't sleep. And guess what? It's less of a problem for them, as they don't have to work during the day.

If you instead choose to develop and maintain positive sleeping habits with your children then you will remain blissfully unaware of the torment that parents of 'bad sleepers' live through.

Let me stress this for emphasis: if your child doesn't sleep it's your fault. But don't despair - you can fix it and it won't take long.

The problem with poor sleeping habits is that they creep in without you realising until one day you find yourselves at your wits end.

As parents we also tend to undermine ourselves. Our parenting instincts work against us. Instead of allowing our baby to cry for a reasonable amount of time (before he goes off to sleep) our instincts compel us to rush in and sooth him until he nods off. In doing so we inadvertently make him dependant on us to get to sleep.

When he's older and he comes into our room in the middle of the night our instincts compel us to let him into our bed rather than taking him back to his bed and getting him back to sleep.

In doing so we inadvertently create and then enforce a pattern of behaviour, encouraging him to wake us whenever he wakes in the middle of the night.

The Manual

Be the lighthouse, not the sea.

Don't give in to your parenting instincts - they won't help you in this situation.

Be methodical and don't cop out. There is no such thing as a 'bad sleeper'.

Once baby reaches 5kg of bodyweight he's got sufficient metabolic resources to last through the night, or between 6 - 8 hours at a stretch. Here's how to help him get there:

1. Put baby in his own room to reduce the likelihood of you or your partner waking him up as you move around.
2. Put baby to bed at 10pm every night, no matter what. Even if he's recently had a nap, or is already asleep, give him a dream feed (see below) and put him down.
3. Before baby goes down at 10pm give him a 'dream feed'. This is the top up that's going to sustain him through the night. No matter how recently he's been fed or how much he takes do this religiously at the same time each night.
4. As soon as he's fed, burped and changed, swaddle him and put him down for the night. Give him a kiss and walk out of the room while he's still awake.
5. When putting baby down for the night, let him cry for at least 10 minutes before calling out to him or going in to him. Time yourself if you have to and don't give in early. This should be uninterrupted crying. If he stops crying for 10 seconds or more then start the clock again. Also don't leave him crying for much more than 10 minutes, as by this stage he's probably going to need a bit of comforting.
6. Once baby has been down for 10 minutes without crying you can consider him down for the night. You can go to him if he cries, but only if he cries consistently for a minimum period of time (the 'crying interval'). If he stops crying for 10 seconds or more then reset the clock. The crying interval will start at 2 minutes and increase by 30 seconds each night. Again, don't cheat - time yourself to make sure. The crying interval carries

over from night to night, getting 30 seconds longer each time you go to him.
7. If you do go to him, don't turn on the light or talk to him. Just pat him on the chest gently to let him know you're there. Only get him up if you think he's soiled himself or if he's winded. Be strong - getting him up now just for a cuddle would be for your benefit, not his.
8. Do not get him out of bed until 4am at the earliest. After this time only get him up if he's clearly hungry (i.e. crying and won't go back to sleep). Stretch this time out further and further each night. Within a couple of months you should be getting him up after 6am. Try and stretch him past 6am, but be realistic - during the first six months anything past 6am is a bonus.

And that's it. If you follow this regime religiously you will have a baby that sleeps through the night in no time at all. Our four children were sleeping through the night after just a few nights.

It will only work if you don't undermine yourselves, so you need to both be on board before you start.

The hardest part will be to let your poor, defenceless child cry in the darkness, but let him cry you must.

Being able to self-settle is a skill he must learn and he won't learn it if you swoop in to save him each time he cries.

Rely on the clock to keep you honest.

Remind yourself that his crying is natural and that he is fine. He, and you, will be happier as a result of both of you developing good sleeping habits. He is not suffering and his crying will not result in long term emotional damage - it won't result in damage at all.

Continue to put baby down during the day when he's tired as normal. He's now developing day and night sleeping patterns that will last a lifetime.

Play and Exercise

As baby gets older his awake time will get longer and longer and he'll become increasingly interactive with you. He'll discover that life exists beyond his fingers and will reach out for and play with objects more readily (usually by mouthing them).

You should give him practice lifting his head by regularly laying him on his front, arms out in front of him. He might do very little at first, but over time he'll lift his head more and more and will eventually learn to get up on his elbows. Never leave baby unattended while he's on his front - he'll start to get distressed after a while and will need to be rolled back over.

The rest of the time baby will be on his back. You can give him a mobile or similar to play with (i.e. a toy that suspends above his face when he's on his back), but remember these aren't for sleeping with.

You can also use a bouncenette, which will give him a better view of proceedings (allowing him to look around instead of just up).

Getting Out of the House

It's important that you and mum get out of the house regularly, this may be particularly important for mum if she's staying at home to look after the baby while you're getting adult companionship at work.

Coffee groups are a great idea for trips out by the primary caregiver, as these can give you the opportunity to share experiences with other new parents, ask for and share advice and to generally be around people who understand what you're going through. It's great to see childless friends too, but until you've been through it you can't really appreciate what being the parent of a new-born is like.

If you're not the primary caregiver then your job is to make sure that your partner gets time to herself from time to time. Ask her what she would like to do. Does she want to go out and meet her friends? Maybe she'd just like to have a shower and read for an hour in her favourite chair without having to worry about the baby for a while.

If you're heading out it's important that you're prepared. No, seriously - be prepared! There's nothing like having a baby that's hungry and inexplicably covered in shit (how did it get all over him?!?) to make you regret leaving home adequate preparation. The days of being able to leave the house with nothing but your car keys and wallet are over.

Get a nappy bag that's big enough to carry everything and agree to always keep it in the same place when it's at home, as this will save you having to run around trying to find it when you're trying to get out the door. I like to use an over-the-shoulder bag with a big flap that lets you get in there and fish around for things with one hand. You'll see how handy this is when you're trying to deal with shit-zilla with one hand while reaching for wipes with another.

Always check your nappy bag inventory before you go out and make sure you have more of *everything* than you think you'll need. Your nappy bag should include:

- Nappies
- Plastic nappy disposal/storage bags (put soiled nappies in these and tie them at the top to seal them up - you do NOT want shitty nappies to be floating around in your nappy bag)
- Baby wipes
- At least one full change of clothes - I carry two for particularly productive days
- A change mat. Once you get to change your baby on the floor of a public toilet you'll see how important one of these is.
- If baby is bottle-fed, bottles. You can either make up formula before you head out or carry sanitised bottles and formula powder so you can make up bottles on the run. Carry clean water if you live in a country where tap water can be suspect.
- A sipper cup of water.
- Something to protect him from the elements. Something waterproof you can put over his capsule/pram if it's raining and something to keep him out of the sun if it's sunny.
- Toys to keep him occupied while he's being changed. Also useful for distracting him while you're trying to have a

conversation.
- When baby is a bit older, food. Lots of food. Choose non-perishable foods that aren't going to easily leak through the bag. I like to carry baby food (homemade, of course), baby rice and rusks.

Baby Blues

Perhaps unsurprisingly, given the raging hormones and the physical ordeal involved in giving birth, many new mums experience the baby blues for a week or two after the birth. This can cause mood swings, crying spells, bouts of anxiety and insomnia.

This is unfortunate, but all too normal.

If your partner suffers from the baby blues she may or may not even realise. If she does realise then she may not feel like saying anything about it, as some mums can feel embarrassed or inadequate as a result. 'What kind of mum am I that I'm crying when my baby needs me'? That kind of thing.

Be on the lookout for symptoms of the baby blues. Ask her how she's feeling. Dig below the surface.

In our society it's perfectly acceptable to talk about physical injuries. We are quick to sympathise with those who have broken their leg or suffered some other form of injury or disease. Unfortunately this is not always the case when those injuries are mental rather than physical.

If a new mum has a caesarean section she's likely to get flowers and will wishers and sympathy while she recovers.

If she suffers from the baby blues, however, she's unlikely to experience much sympathy at all.

She's much more likely have others downplay the seriousness of her condition or, worse, tell her that it's 'all in her head' and that she just needs to pull herself together. A friend of mine 'Sarah' once told me that her mother, upon hearing that she had full-blown postpartum depression, told Sarah 'You've just had a child for chrissakes! What more do you want?' Unsurprisingly, this did not help Sarah's state of mind.

Don't be this person. Mental illness, even if temporary, can be just as debilitating as physical injury or even more so.

If she is suffering from the blues then it's unlikely to last long. Reassure her of this. Remind her that she's doing a wonderful job and that you and the baby are lucky to have her. Don't brush her feelings under the carpet - they're real, even if they're the chemically induced. Remind her that her condition isn't a sign of weakness or a character flaw - it can, and does, happen to anyone.

The more supportive you and your family are the easier it will be for her to get through the baby blues unscathed.

For a small minority of mums the baby blues don't go away, however. In fact they get worse.

This is called postpartum depression (also called postnatal depression) and it's much more serious and requires prompt medical attention.

With the right treatment and support postpartum depression can be managed, but it should never be ignored.

If you're worried that your partner may be exhibiting signs of depression then help her to get help as soon as possible, starting with your GP. There is no shame in suffering from postpartum depression and the earlier she gets help the easier it will be to manage.

Months 6 - 12

You'll be amazed at how much baby develops over his second six months. During this period he's likely to start crawling, then walking, eating solids and maybe even talk a little. It truly is a wonderful time in their development.

Before we go any further it's important to note that no two babies ever develop at the same rate, so don't worry if your baby takes a while longer to develop in one or more areas.

It's also a good idea not to assume your baby is gifted of he starts talking or walking or even growing teeth earlier than his peers. My children were all very early to develop teeth and, sadly, none of them are gifted with superhuman strength or intelligence.

As an aside, I believe that a third of parents of toddlers worry about one or more aspects of their child's development, one third don't think much about their child's development and a third are convinced that their kids are baby Einstein's. This is obviously very unscientific, but guess what... the first third end up relieved (when their kids end up the same as everyone else), the second third are don't think too much about it and the last third end up disappointed. This is because, development wise, almost all of our kids end up the same in the end.

My kids had teeth first, but this didn't make them unique in the long run. All of their peers ended up with the same number of teeth in the end.

The trick is to marvel at their development while not worrying too much about it.

Feeding

Somewhere between the ages of 6 - 12 months baby is going to start showing an interest in solid food. Don't rush this - he'll let you know when he's good and ready. Until then he's fine on the breast or bottle.

Baby should also be able to sit up in a high chair before he starts on solids. You should never feed a baby solids while he's lying down.

We used to prop our kids up in their high chairs with a cushion when they first started on solids, as they could sit on their own, but this made them more stable in a high chair that was too big for them.

Never be tempted to feed baby food that he can't swallow without chewing. He doesn't yet have teeth, doesn't know how to chew and will even struggle to swallow, so don't make if any harder for him than it needs to be. Baby food should be simple, natural and mashed/pureed.

He won't thank you for rich or challenging foods, or big spoons for that matter. Try mashing up some carrot or banana and offering it to him from time to time on a baby-sized spoon (soft rubbery ones are best).

If he takes an interest then start him on solids slowly. Choose baby food that is age appropriate, or use food you've prepared yourself. You can mix it with a little rice cereal and water to give it a bit of substance and a pleasant texture.

Always, always test the temperature of food before it goes anywhere near baby. Unlike you and me, he doesn't know how to spit out food that is too hot, so it will just sit in there burning him. Don't ever let this happen.

Always feed him solids after he's had milk - solid food will supplement milk for a while rather than replacing it, so always go breast or bottle first. You can then feed him solids until he's full (i.e. he stops showing interest and/or he starts spitting food out). Remember that sometimes they force food out with their tongue by accident when they intended to swallow it - you'll soon be able to tell the difference.

Keep baby's food as varied as possible to get him used to lots of different flavours. Think different fruit, vegetables and meats rather than prepared foods.

This variety of foods is both good for him and it will make him less fussy and finicky about food as he grows older.

Sleep

By the time baby is six months old he should be sleeping all night (at least six hours per night, preferably 8 or more) in his own bed without interruption.

If you're not there yet then go back to the last section and think about what's going wrong. Don't kid yourself that your baby is different or unique to justify any bad habits. He's not different - he still needs to sleep.

This is particularly important as baby will learn to stand and may even try and climb out of his crib during this period. He's going to have a much bigger bag of tricks at his disposal to try and convince you to give him attention when he should be sleeping. And he'll use them.

Watch for bad habits developing and nip them in the bud before they have a chance to take root.

You should not have to go in to him after you've put him down to try and settle him. His job is to settle himself.

You do not have to live with a nightly routine of having to go in and settle him if he wakes in the middle of the night.

The sleeping patterns that he's learning now are going to be reflected and amplified for years to come, so do yourself a favour and get it right.

Around the six month mark it's also a great idea to start reading to him each night before bed.

Get into a routine that he'll recognise, such as feed, burp, story, swaddle and down to sleep.

Choose books that are age suitable. At 6 months a story should only last a minute or two. Anything more than that and you risk over stimulating him and that touching moment together is likely to become a bit less fun.

Reading to your kids on a daily basis is so unbelievably important. Not only does it help them wind down and get some cuddle time before they go off to sleep, reading to them regularly - daily - is absolutely critical to their ongoing development.

Exercise

It's during this period that baby will start crawling, pulling himself up and walking.

This can be both exhilarating and exhausting.

It's amazing to watch your little human crawl for the first time, take his first step, kick his first ball.

It can also be exhausting, as his motor skills develop a lot more quickly than his common sense. Babies of this age have no fear. They haven't yet learnt the consequences of stupid, so there's no limit to the madcap things they'll do. If he finds a poo in the kitty litter it will quickly become a toy to be played with and put in his mouth.

You will need to make your home toddler friendly before they get moving (see below).

There's lots you can do to encourage baby to roll over, crawl and walk, but remember that play time should be about play. Be careful not to become a drill sergeant - there's no great rush to reach each developmental stage.

Before he's moving on his own give baby plenty of tummy time. As he develops strength try sitting him up for longer and longer periods, but be very careful to not let him fall backward (or forward for that matter), as he can hit his head hard on the way down.

When he's sitting but not moving try putting a basket of toys next to him and let him pull them out one by one and examine them. When he's pulled them all out you can just collect them up again and put the basket on his other side. What's this? A new basket of toys for me to explore!

If he's about to crawl you can place toys strategically beyond his reach to encourage him to move across the floor to them. If he learns instead to bum shuffle then don't despair - bum shuffling is a perfectly respectable method of getting around and has the added advantage of providing hours of entertainment. My youngest bum-shuffled until she walked. She never crawled. It was hilarious.

Before baby walks he'll start pulling himself up, both so he can see what's going on and to strengthen his legs. Make sure he has lots of safe places to do so. It's a good idea to put mats and other forms of cushioning in places where he may fall. It's also time to secure objects (like TV's, speakers, vases, etc.) that he may pull down on himself. Glass top coffee tables have to go also, as baby will like nothing more than to smash at that glass with the heaviest thing he can find.

You can encourage him into his feet by lifting him gently while holding his hands. You can even walk him along a bit when he is confident and strong enough to do so. Always offer lots of encouragement and praise in a soft, high pitched voice. He'll get a buzz from the sense of achievement and from your obvious approval.

From the time he starts moving, and until he's almost an adult, this kid is going to fall over. A lot. Most of the time it's not going to hurt him at all. Sometimes there will be scratches and scrapes. As he gets older he may even injure himself more seriously, ending up with cuts or broken bones that require medical attention.

Whenever he hurts himself it's important that you're the lighthouse and not the sea. You need to be compassionate, but not overly soft. If you molly coddle him every time he falls over he's likely to learn to over dramatise it every little time. He's going to expect, no, need you to run over and fuss over him, even if he's not hurt at all. This would not be good for you and it most certainly would not be good for him.

We want our kids to grow up feeling loved while being robust. We don't them to fall apart and cry for their mum and dad each time they run into trouble.

This is where that attitude starts.

When your child falls over don't make a big fuss about. If it was minor then ignore it. There will be hundreds more where that came from.

If it was a bit harder and he's upset then give him some attention, but let him calm himself down. I like to name the event to distract baby from it. Names like 'oopsie' and 'boof' are great, saying things like 'poor baby' not so much, as they invite too much sympathy. Before long baby is saying 'boof' each time he falls over, dusting himself off and getting on with his business.

I'm not saying for a second that you shouldn't comfort your baby if he's distressed or genuinely hurt. Of course you should.

If he's not hurt, however, then don't make a fuss. Ignore it altogether if you can. As you will see, this is the first step toward building strong, robust adults who know how to bounce back from setbacks.

Out and About

Take the pram everywhere you go, even if he's walking already, as he will tire quickly. Trust me when I tell you that you don't want to be stuck miles from home (or from your car) with a baby you have to carry in your arms. I'm a big guy, but for me even small babies become a lot of work to carry after 10 minutes or so.

Alternatively you could invest in one of those packs that let you strap baby onto yourself and carry him on your front or back. I love these things - they are hot to wear in the summer, but they hold baby close to you and they seem to like them a lot.

Discipline

Baby's personality really starts to shine through during this period and you start to get a feel for what he's going to be like as he gets older.

As his personality develops, so do his needs and desires.

So how's he going to get what he wants?

Is he going to walk over and take it?

No, he can't even walk yet, let alone carry things around with him.

Is he going to ask for it?

No, he can't do more than babble, maybe sounding out a word or two with a vocabulary in single digits.

How's he going to get what he wants?

He's going to cry, of course. Oh, and as soon as he's old enough to figure out how, he's going to start throwing tantrums.

But hang on a second... am I really saying that a baby is going to be able to control grown adults with nothing more than a wail?

This is exactly what I'm saying and if you don't believe me on this then just watch how quickly adults, all adults, scramble when there's a crying baby in the room. The baby might be crying because he's hungry, but clearly he's not starving to death. Notwithstanding this, all of the adults in the room (or the house) will scramble to help get that baby fed (and hopefully quiet) as soon as he starts wailing.

The other kids in the room know the ruse and they're not buying it. You won't see kids climbing the walls to stop a baby from crying. Most of the time they won't care... they might admire another child's ability to control every adult in sight, but they know that the crying baby ain't dying.

Here's a great example of the power that these little bundles of joy can exert over us if we let them.

I visited a friend once and found their family of four sitting in the dark in their lounge. I knew the power hadn't gone out, as other lights were on, so I asked them why they were sitting in the dark.

They told me it was because Matilda didn't want the lights on.

Matilda wasn't even two years old, but here she was controlling not one, but two adults and her 10 year old brother. If one of them *dared* to turn the light on she'd fly into a raging tantrum and they'd quickly turn the lights off again.

Amazing.

Of course, we are not going to get ourselves into this position.

We are going to let our children wield influence over us, but only when and where it is appropriate. We will never neglect our kids, so we will keep responding to their cries for food, sleep, etc. but otherwise they are going to have to use their manners.

In this section we are going to start utilising techniques that we'll continue to use throughout his childhood and into adolescence. These techniques are nothing more than common sense - there's nothing ground-breaking here.

The trick is to apply them consistently.

Your child isn't going to learn good manners if you're firm with him some of the time and not others. He'll just learn that bad behaviour will be rewarded if he's persistent.

He also isn't going to learn good manners if you and your partner both accept different standards of behaviour. You're only going to confuse baby and leave him feeling frustrated. You and your partner both need to agree on exactly what your expectations are early on and you need to agree that you adhere these standards consistently, whether or not each other is in the room.

But hang on a second, my baby can't even talk yet? How's he going to use his manners?

For a start, he's not going to cry for what he wants. If he does he's going to find himself not getting it.

As soon as he's old enough to start reaching out for things start saying 'ta' each time you either give him something or take something off of him. He'll soon learn he's that he needs to ask if he wants something - at first by reaching out for it and waiting patiently and later by asking for it ('ta').

Of course you need to remember your manners too. When you want something from him you should also get his attention, stretch out your hand, look him in the eye and say 'ta'. Only snatch things from him if there's a reason (e.g. he's picked up something he shouldn't have) - babies still have a sense of justice and they'll usually know if something is being taken off them for a reason or not.

If you've said 'ta' and he ignores you then get his attention and say it again with your hand still outstretched, but say it slightly firmer than you did before.

If he still refuses to cooperate then you should gently take the item from him.

Don't cop out at this stage - you've used your manners, but now it's time to remind baby who is in charge (it's you, in case you weren't following). Hey may protest, but don't give the item back to him under any circumstances, as this would demonstrate that he just needs to lose his shit to get what he wants.

If you see your child snatch something off of another child then you should intervene to show that such behaviour is not acceptable. The other child may be crying at this stage, but they're within their rights to do so - they've just suffered a great injustice and only the return of the treasured item will put this right.

Move to where your child can see you and get his attention. Tell him that what he did is wrong (e.g. 'no, Lisa had that, please give it back') - even if he can't understand you, he'll get the gist of it. If he doesn't give it back then say 'ta' twice as above before taking the item off of him yourself and returning it to the rightful owner. If he does hand it over then try and engineer it so that he hands it back to the other child himself.

Remember that discipline is not just about reacting to bad behaviour. It is just as important to reinforce positive behaviour too.

If uses his manners then congratulate him on it, particularly if he does so without you prompting. Make a big deal about it. Use a high pitched voice and say something like 'Good, Sammy, ta!' (assuming he's just asked for something or given something to you - you get the drift). He will feel well chuffed with himself and this will reinforce the positive behaviour he's demonstrated.

Make congratulating good behaviour a habit.

All too often we comment only on negative behaviour while ignoring good behaviour. Children crave attention and if they learn that the best way of getting attention (of getting **any** attention) is to misbehave then guess what they will do?

Look for opportunities to congratulate them at least a few times per day, even while they're too young to understand your words.

Conversely, when your child is misbehaving you should ignore him every chance you get, particularly if he's throwing a tantrum (see below). If he's in danger or if he's hurting someone else then clearly ignoring him is not the way to go, but if he's just acting grotty and getting on your nerves then **ignore the bad and praise the good** - encourage him to give you less of the former and more of the latter.

This is also very important if you have more than one child, as it's often the ones who are behaving who are ignored when someone else is misbehaving.

If one of your kids is misbehaving then heap ample praise on those who are being good. Reward them with your time. You can say something like 'You are being so calm and polite - should we play together?' You'll be surprised at how quickly the misbehaving child will want to join in - but only let him if he starts behaving himself.

Remember that, before the age of 3, there's absolutely no point in punishing your child for bad behaviour. He's too young to learn from it, so don't bother.

If he does something wrong and you catch him in the act then tell him not to in a stern voice. Use his name and tell him what he's doing wrong by relating it to how the family behave. Saying 'We don't try and ride the cat in our family' is a lot more powerful than simply saying 'don't do that!'

Remember to always criticise the behaviour, not the child. For example 'Sam, no! We don't pull the dog's tail' is criticising the behaviour, 'Sam, naughty boy! Don't do that!' is criticising the boy.

This may sound like politically correct nonsense, but it's not. Kids are much more aware of labels than adults are - if you label a child 'naughty' (or stupid, disruptive, etc.) then this is how they will start seeing themselves.

If you call a boy naughty then don't be surprised if that's how he starts acting. Worse, don't be surprised if that's how he starts thinking of himself.

Tantrums

Kids cry to control others and to get what they want. When crying isn't enough, however, they'll go for the nuclear option and throw a tantrum.

We all know a tantrum when we see one. The child kicks and screams. His body stiffens with rage. He might stomp his feet, pound the ground with his hands and flail about like someone set him on fire.

Let him.

Once a tantrum has started there's nothing you can do except wait for it to burn itself out.

Starve it of oxygen. Don't talk to the child. Don't even look at the child. Try as hard as you can to have a conversation with someone else - show Mr Tantrum that you're not interested in his carry on.

If you're in public then this may be a bit embarrassing, but get over it. Other parents will understand (they'll be thanking their lucky stars it's you and not them). Non-parents may not understand but what do you care?

My eldest child had the mother of all tantrums once at a department store when she was about two years old. I'm usually not bothered by such behaviour, but she was screaming so loud that I eventually pushed her outside (she was sitting in a shopping trolley) and stood next to her until she had screamed herself out.

When we went through the checkout of the same store 15 minutes later, the cashier commented on what a wonderfully well behaved girl my daughter was. She then said to me under her breath 'you should have heard the little monster that was in here before.... she almost screamed the place down!'

When it comes to tantrums the most important thing is to never, ever give into the child's demands, no matter how long the tantrum goes on for.

If you cave then expect more tantrums. If you wait before caving then expect longer tantrums, as your child will learn that he'll win if he just screams for long enough.

Don't cave and don't undermine your partner by encouraging her to cave if she's dealing with a tantrum.

If you demonstrate to your child that tantrums will get him nowhere then he will stop subjecting you to them.

I have four children and none of them would have had more than 4 - 5 tantrums in their lives. I know of families who experience more than five tantrums *per week.*

If your child regularly throws tantrums then it is because you are rewarding them for doing so. It's that simple. Stop rewarding them (i.e. don't cave and don't give them attention) and the behaviour will stop.

As always, be prepared to celebrate positive behaviour. If your child throws a tantrum then ignore him until he gets bored of it and moves onto something else. As soon as he does so, praise him for something. Reinforce the fact that only positive behaviour will attract your attention.

Teething

If there's anything as cute as a child with his first one or two teeth poking out hopefully from his bottom gum I don't know what it is. There's something almost cartoonish about their appearance and with every tooth he looks less and less like a baby and more and more like a little boy.

Unfortunately teething can bring a lot of pain and suffering too - for you and for him.

Some kids hardly notice the arrival of teeth, while for others it can be a miserable experience. Baby's teeth will normally break through around the 6 month mark, although this can vary widely.

Usually you'll see the lower middle teeth appear first, then the top two, then the others from front to back. Again, no two children are the same, so don't worry if your child doesn't follow this pattern exactly.

The teeth that are most likely to give your child trouble are the molars, which normally appear when he's about two years old.

There are several signs to look out for as an indication that your baby might be teething, these include:

- Irritability or fussiness
- Excessive drooling (which can cause a facial rash)
- Swollen, sensitive gums
- Gnawing or chewing behaviour
- Refusing to eat
- Trouble sleeping

Before baby starts teething buy a few teething rings (these are filled with water) and pop them in the fridge. Baby will bite on these. The pressure and the temperature will provide temporary relief from the pain.

You can also rub baby's gums lightly - you may find that he bites down in your finger or even that he grabs your finger and sticks it in his mouth so he can squash it against his burning gums.

If baby is eating solids then try cold foods such as yogurt or pureed fruit, which can also provide temporary relief. Rusks are also great, as they give him something to chew on while promoting swallowing, which results in less drool.

If he's really suffering then you can also try topical creams such as Bonjela, which numb the gums slightly. Use any such products sparingly and only if strictly necessary.

If baby is in extreme pain then take him to the doctor. Don't use *any* kind of painkiller without checking with your doctor first. Under no circumstances should you try homoeopathic or herbal remedies - very few such products have been clinically tested to demonstrate efficacy and safety when used with young children.

Most important, be on the lookout for the signs of teething and be patient when they present themselves. Baby isn't grizzling because he wants to be difficult - give him lots of hugs and reassurance.

First Birthday Party

There's nothing quite like your child's first birthday party. What a milestone! Not only are you celebrating his first anniversary, you're also celebrating the fact that you and your partner made it this far, maybe a little jaded, but all in one piece!

Have a great party. Celebrate. Enjoy yourself.

Although, as you're organising the party, bear in mind he won't remember it and neither will his friends.

He will enjoy it, of course, but make sure you do too.

Many parents go all-out on the first birthday party, spending a fortune and exhausting themselves in the process. And what's the point?

Birthday parties should be about you and the kids enjoying yourselves, not about trying to outdo other families in a quest to have the most extravagant party.

Ironically, the most extravagant parties are a spectacle, but they're often the most awkward and the least fun.

My wife always bakes the kids a themed cake for their birthdays. At first this was an arduous and stressful affair, but (now that she's created over 30 of them) it's a lot easier. This is her tradition and one that our family loves.

Otherwise our kid's birthdays are about maximising fun for the kids while minimising stress and expense for us.

This is a good lesson to learn early on. Make your child's first birthday party fun, but don't celebrate this amazing milestone by exhausting yourself (or your bank account).

Chapter 6: Ages 1 – 5

You made it through the craziness that is the first year. If you're anything like me you'll be relieved that you made it through in one piece, while being anxious that your 'baby' is growing up so fast.

You ain't seen nothing yet.

Your child starts this period as a toddler. She ends it a little girl.

There will be so many more firsts you'll be excused for losing count. If this is your first child then siblings may arrive during this period also.

Just remember that your child's development is unique and will run to its own schedule. Don't stress out about the timing of her developmental stages.

The Importance of the Early Years

Your child's early years (i.e. until they're about 5) have a profoundly important impact upon their development. We are only just starting to understand how important this phase of their life is and the evolutionary reasons for this, but research shows that one thing is certain - their experiences over this period will shape their personalities, drive and happiness **for the rest of their lives**.

Children who suffer a lack of love, support and learning interactions during this phase of their lives are likely to be negatively impacted in a variety of areas. The bonds they form with their parents and with others will be weaker. Their future physical, cognitive, emotional and social development will be stunted and they will suffer from lower levels of self-esteem and happiness.

Can children who have been neglected or maltreated during this period go on to have successful, happy lives? Yes, of course, but they are far, far less likely than their peers to do so.

It can be difficult to give your kids the amount of time, love and attention that they deserve during this period, as we can have a large number of conflicting priorities during this stage of our lives. For many of us our careers can be taking off, we have mortgages to pay, neglected social lives and a range of other distractions.

None of this shit matters. Your child doesn't care how well you are doing at work or if you're going to get that promotion.

All she cares about is *whether you are there*. So be there. This period of their lives is so profoundly important and there are no second chances.

It's Not Quality Time, It's Quantity Time

For most dads this stage of your child's development will coincide with the busiest time of your professional life. Your career is probably more important to you than it ever has been. Goodness knows the financial pressure of a young family will have you concentrating on getting ahead at work.

Don't lose sight of what's important.

Tend to your career. Support your partner if she wants to tend to hers, but always remember that your child doesn't care how quickly you're climbing the ladder at work.

She needs you. She needs your time and attention.

This period of her life goes by so fast that you'll hardly believe it.

During this time her world is incredibly small. You and her mother are central to just about everything she does and everything she thinks about.

Enjoy this while it lasts, because before long you'll be sharing her with others and wishing for more time with her.

Remember that it's quantity time, not quality time, that counts. If your career has to take a back seat then don't worry - you'll be able to focus on it again before long.

Besides, no one ever lays in their deathbed, surrounded by those they love, thinking how glad they are that they put in those extra hours in the office.

Favourite Toy or Comfort Blanket

Most kids identify a favourite toy or blanket that they start to rely upon for comfort, particularly at bedtime. This is not usually a problem. In fact, blankey (or whatever it's called by your baby) can be instrumental in helping to settle your child or to get her off to sleep.

They will outgrow this attachment before too long, so there's no harm in the attachment itself.

Where you can run into problems is if you only have one of said item. Then it can become ratty (it will spend a lot of time in her mouth) and it can get lost, which can seem like a disaster.

You can't avoid her becoming attached to an object and I'm not sure if you'd really want to. What you can try and do is encourage her to become attached to a *type* of object, rather than an individual thing.

My wife is an avid knitter and she knitted blankets for each of our children. The kids somehow named these 'boogies' and all but one of them carried their boogie everywhere they went. Third child instead chose the muslin sheets that we used to swaddle her with when she was a baby.

These comfort blankets (including the muslin ones) were ideal, as they could be readily interchanged. It took my wife a while to knit all of those blankets, but each child had two of them, and we had stacks of muslins.

If one was dirty or left at a friend's house we could swap it out with one of the spares while it was being cleaned or retrieved.

You can influence what she becomes attached to, but you have to act early. If you notice her becoming attached to an object that you don't want her to become attached to (such as a toy that you only have one of) then consider removing that toy from view for a while and replacing it with something you *do* want her to attach to.

If she does become attached to a toy then you might want to consider buying a few of them. It's likely that the attachment will last for several years - you're likely to want to wash it and possibly replace it more than once. If you have more than one of them then just make sure you rotate them regularly so they all age evenly - if you present a brand new version of the item after the others have faded then you might find it being rejected by a child who recognises your deception.

Sleep

By now your child should be sleeping through the night every night. She may wake on the odd occasion if she has a nightmare or something, but in no way should this be a regular event.

Somewhere between 18 months and three years of age you're going to want to move her from her cot to a bed. If she hasn't learned how to climb out of her cot already it will mean that she can get out of bed at will. Unless you want nights to be miserable, you're going to need to implement positive sleeping habits from the absolute beginning.

In this section we build on the skills and techniques that we learned in the previous chapter. The techniques below supplement, rather replace what we learned earlier.

If followed systematically your child will go down easily at bedtime and sleep through the night. If she doesn't then either you're not implementing these techniques properly or you're using them inconsistently.

If so then don't give up. Assess what's going wrong and address the problem.

At the age of 1 your child will probably need several naps during the day and should then sleep for at least 10 hours at night. By the age of 5 she probably won't be napping during the day anymore, but she should be getting 10 - 12 hours of sleep per night.

This sleep is critical. To you and to her.

Don't fool yourself into thinking your child doesn't need much sleep or that she simply likes to go to bed late. This is a cop out - your child needs just as much sleep as everyone else. Without it she will be irritable and will have trouble concentrating during the day. Her behaviour will suffer also, as she will be less able to control her actions or her emotions.

This causes misery at night and during the day for parents who don't have their kids sleep under control.

Misery at night because you'll spend an extraordinary amount of time trying to get your child to sleep, getting up to comfort her at night and generally missing out on your sleep and/or adult time.

Misery during the day because you'll have an emotional, irritable child who doesn't behave herself.

Don't be one of those parents. It's unnecessary. Worse, it's unfair on your child, who relies on you to teach her good sleeping habits. Without adequate sleep she's going to feel grotty and she won't enjoy being in trouble all of the time as a result.

Bedtime Routine

The bedtime routine should be as consistent as possible every night.

Don't surprise your kids by simply declaring it's time for bed. You should give them a couple of warnings, say 30 minutes and then 5 minutes before bed. This will help avoid outrage at the injustice of being sent to bed without adequate time to get dolly, pat the dog or whatever important tasks she still had to do.

Make sure they're well fed so they don't wake up prematurely to answer hunger pangs. Our kids are allowed to eat as much fruit as they like between dinner and bedtime. They eat a lot of fruit. This is a good thing.

You need to follow up the warnings with action. Once 5 minutes have passed since the 5 minute warning it's bedtime. No negotiation, no 'I just need to...' or 'I'm hungry'. Bedtime.

Your kids need to know that, once you've said 'bedtime' it's bedtime and there's nothing they can do to wriggle out of it.

Always follow the same routine at this stage. In our house the kids all have to brush their teeth next. Until they're 6 you should help them (you brush first, then they do). Until they're in their early teens you should watch them brush to make sure they're doing it properly. Before this age kids simply don't have the maturity or the attention span to consistently brush properly on their own.

Then it's toilet time, they kiss mum goodnight and then we meet in someone's room for a story.

We read in a different room each night and the kids take turns to choose a book. During story time there's no talking or playing. The kids get opportunities to read and to turn the page, but otherwise they're expected to sit quietly and listen to the story. By now playtime is over.

Because my four kids are similar in age (there's only 63 months between all four of them) they all go to bed at the same time, but the older kids can read for longer.

Don't hurry through the story - it can be tempting to skip a page here and there so you can get back to the couch, but resist the temptation. This is their special moment to snuggle up to you, wrapped in the security and warmth of your voice. Don't short change them.

Conversely you don't want to read to them for so long that they get bored. If you notice them becoming fidgety and distracted then ask if they want to stop and pick it up again the next day. If they're getting really scratchy then just wrap it up - you don't want it to descend into tears.

Now it's time to get them into bed. As soon as they're old enough they should get themselves into bed.

Once they're under their covers visit each one, youngest to oldest, and ask them how their day was, or some other open-ended question. Give them a chance to talk to you one on one. Just for a minute or two.

The next step is optional, but I think it's so beautiful. Before you kiss her goodnight, look your child in the eyes and sing her a lullaby. It doesn't matter if you can't sing. Goodness knows I can't. She won't mind. I never feel closer to my kids than when I'm singing to them.

Finally kiss your child, tell her you love her, wish her goodnight and tell her you expect her to stay in bed.

I say something like 'Ok, off to sleep, you're not allowed up until morning, unless you need to go to the toilet, ok?'

Easy.

Now leave the room and turn off the light (or return later to turn off the light if she's old enough to read for a while). And that's it.

Your routine, like mine, should be simple and effective.

She will rattle the fence from time to time to test your defences and to see if she can't squeeze that last little bit of attention out of you. In the next section we'll look at strategies for neutralising these tactics.

She Won't Be Quiet/Won't Stay In Bed!

Your child will try everything in her power to get you back in her bedroom or to get just a few more minutes of uptime.

Now we don't want to become tyrants when it comes to her sleep time, but it is imperative that *we* remain in control, not her. This is so easy that those of us who are in control struggle to understand the frustration and lack of sleep experienced by those who don't.

It's not rocket science. Every response that we make should be simple, measured and consistent.

If your child won't be quiet or won't stay in bed then don't despair - it only takes a few nights to correct bad sleeping habits that may have been years in the making.

But remember they're *your* bad habits, not hers, so you will need to use your brain.

Always remember that you command much greater amounts of patience than she does. You can, and will, wait her out when needed. You won't give in and choose the 'easy' option. You will stand firm and teach her that playing up will get her nowhere.

Here are some of the common issues that you're likely to face when putting your child down to sleep (or trying to keep her there) and strategies for how to respond:

Distractions and Stalling Techniques

Teach her early on that nothing except the bedtime routine is acceptable once you've called bedtime. Make exceptions for genuine emergencies (she hasn't kissed mum or her comfort blanket is in the lounge), but don't let these become a stalling technique - tell her you'll retrieve important items once she's in bed.

Tantrums at Bedtime

These can be difficult, as dealing effectively with a tantrum involves waiting it out, which delays bedtime and can be used as a stalling tactic.

If the child is still small enough, quietly carry her into her room, place her on her bed and tell her you will kiss her goodnight once she's quiet. Then leave the room and wait outside for the tantrum to stop. Don't engage with her until the tantrum is over. Wait until she's quiet for a few seconds (look for the opportunity as early as possible, you don't need to time the quiet period or anything), run in, congratulate her on being quiet and kiss her goodnight. If she agrees to be calm then read her a story, but tell her you will leave at the first sign of trouble (which you should do).

If your child is a bit older then don't carry her to bed while she's having a tantrum, as this can result in a physical contest and/or one of you might get hurt as a result of her flailing about.

Consider waiting her out to avoid escalating the situation. You may be tired and irritable after a long day, but don't lose your temper. It won't help. Turn off the TV and don't talk to her - show her that her tantrum will not get her anywhere. You are the adult, you can out-last her, so don't cave.

If she's having a tantrum in the lounge then you could even turn off the lights and leave the room - this should put an end to her tantrum pretty quickly.

Alternatively, if you don't want to wait her out, tell her that you're going to count to three and then there will be no story. Count loudly and slowly and give her time if she starts moving, but don't give her additional time if she's not moving. No 'two and a half, two and the quarters, etc.' - when you get to three she's earned the punishment.

Once she's missed out on a story you need to think of another punishment. Be cool and calculated - avoid the punishment escalating to ridiculous proportions. It's not the punishment that will get her to bed, but the anxiety she feels as the punishments mount up. I'd suggest saying something like 'each time I get to three you're going to bed 5 minutes earlier tomorrow' and start counting. Slowly and loudly - give her time to comply, but remember not to stop counting for stalling.

As with all of the strategies that she uses to avoid bedtime, you have to show her that tantrums are a waste of time and energy - that they won't get her anywhere.

Getting out of Bed

Nothing is more frustrating than trying to relax after a hard day, only to have a child who keeps getting out of bed. Thankfully this behaviour is also very easy to remedy.

When your child gets up the first time, simply say 'back to bed' and carry or walk her back to her room. Kiss her goodnight, tuck her in and walk away. Don't engage with her further. Don't answer questions or respond to her requests ('I need dolly, etc.) - three words are all you should utter before you turn and leave.

Every time she gets up from then on you should say nothing at all. Simply carry or walk her back to bed, kiss her and walk away.

Don't lose your patience and don't waver from the plan. If she gets up a dozen times then quietly put her back to bed 13 times.

In practice you should find that 2- 3 times will do it. She will soon see that getting out of bed is futile and she'll give up.

It's important that you get up and put her back to bed straight away, as you don't want to reward her with up time for even a few minutes beforehand. Don't call out to her to go to bed, as this is rewarding her with attention.

This also applies if your child wakes you and/or gets into bed with you. It's lovely to snuggle up together and you may feel too tired to get up straight away, but you must. As mercenary as it sounds, you can't reward her with time in mum and dad's bed, as this is like crack cocaine to a child. Before you know it she will be waking during the night and sneaking into your bed on a regular basis.

Won't Go to Sleep

In our house the rule is - if your head is on your pillow then you can read for as long as you like. We find this to be really effective, as it's useless to try and get them to sleep before they're ready. If we try then they invariably get bored and act out, which not only annoys us but it can prevent their siblings from sleeping as well.

We leave a hall light on which is bright enough to read by, but not so bright that they have trouble sleeping with it on.

We find that, when they're reading, their bodies will tell them how much sleep they need. If they're tired the reading won't last long.

Remember this - you can't force a child to go to sleep. Trying will just frustrate you and will probably make your child agitated, which will make it harder for her to go to sleep.

You can force your children to be quiet at bedtime, however. This is particularly important if they are sharing a room, or if they have a friend staying over - they're much more likely to play up after bedtime if there's someone in the room for them to entertain and feed off of.

Kids can quickly become over-tired, which means they become tired, cranky and in need of sleep, but also hyperactive, disruptive and unlikely to fall asleep.

If kids are sharing a room then give them a period of quiet talk. Unless it's really late, it's not really fair to expect kids to share a room and not be able to say boo to each other at bedtime. I tell my kids that they can talk for 10 minutes, but the quieter they talk the longer they get. If they start being silly that 10 minutes quickly becomes 5 minutes (or less). If they whisper to each other and don't do anything silly then they could find that they're rewarded - that 10 minutes can become 20 minutes or more.

Once they're told to stop talking, however, that's it. They need to stop talking.

Policing this is difficult, as kids will be kids and if you're not in the room with them it can be hard for them to comply with your wishes. It's just too tempting to hit their friend or sibling with a pillow!

In this scenario, try introducing a punishment if they don't comply. You can try something like 'I'm going to give you three strikes - on the third strike you're going to bed ten minutes early tomorrow'. If this strategy is ineffective, however, then don't keep at it past the first three strikes - you're only likely to frustrate yourself as they keep giggling and making noise.

At this stage try going into the room and standing there for a while to encourage them to go to sleep without talking. In my experience this is always effective - it's just a matter of how long you have to spend in the room before they finally go to sleep.

In my experience, once you're in there with them, you can get them to roll over and stop talking and they usually go off to sleep after 5 - 10 minutes. Don't engage in conversation with them and don't allow them to talk to each other. I take my phone in with me so I can check my Facebook or read the news so I don't get bored This also gives them a visual cue (i.e. the light from my phone) that I'm still there and they can't talk.

You always have the option of splitting them up, assuming there's somewhere else for the ejected child to sleep. I will resort to this fairly quickly if it's siblings sharing a room. If it's friends, however, then I'll usually only use this as a last resort, as it can be disappointing for the kids if they're not able to sleep in the same room if they have a friend over. Besides, you don't want a guest (i.e. your daughter's' friend) to get scared on her own and to want to go home in the middle of the night.

Potty and Toilet Training

The secret to potty training is to wait until your child is ready. It's as simple as that. If you find yourself struggling with potty training, having to deal with countless accidents, then just put her back in a nappy and try again later.

You should persevere for a while, sure, but you're only going to antagonise yourself (and your child) if she's not ready to ditch the nappy.

Well before you're ready to start with the potty training you'll need a potty.

Ask your child where she wants to put it. You might want to help guide her to find a suitable place that's central and easy for her to reach, but somewhere it's not going to easily be tripped over.

Congratulate her on finding a great position for her potty. Tell her that when she's a big girl she'll be able to do 'poos' on the potty.

This will pique her curiosity and she may ask if she can use the potty straight away. If so then let her try for as long as she wants to, but don't be disappointed if she doesn't do her business - the sensation of using a potty is completely different to the sensation of using a nappy. It can take practice.

Congratulate her every time she tries to use the potty, even if she doesn't manage to squeeze anything out. It's important that feels encouraged to keep trying.

If she does manage to do her business on the potty then make a big deal about it. Clap your hands, congratulate her in a high pitched voice and make her feel special. If you're lucky she'll learn to use the potty all on her own.

Until then try and find opportunities for her to observe others (such as friends or family members) using the potty. Not only will this let her observe how to use the potty, it will create peer pressure for her to do. Never underestimate the effectiveness of peer pressure to influence her behaviour, even at such a tender age.

You should also talk to her regularly about using her potty, particularly when changing her nappy. Keep it in her mind.

If she doesn't take to using the potty herself then take to putting her on it from time to time for a couple of minutes at a time.

Rapid Potty Training

If you become sick of waiting for your child to potty train herself (with your coaching, of course) then it may be time for a little rapid potty training. If your child is ready and able to toilet herself then this approach will work in 2 - 3 days, but (as with so many parenting techniques) consistency is key. If you blink first and put your child in a nappy (e.g. for convenience or because she's crying for one) then you may be giving up on all your progress and reverting back to day one.

Rapid potty training involves putting your child in underwear during the day. No nappies!

When she goes to the toilet without using the potty she will no longer have a nappy to draw moisture away and to keep her mess contained. Instead she will have wet, uncomfortable knickers and unpleasant fluids running down her legs. Yuck!

She won't like this at all. Neither will you, of course, but you won't need to do this for long.

The unpleasant sensation of soiling and wetting herself will rapidly teach her how to recognise the signs that she needs to go and will encourage her to do something about it.

In the meantime ask her to sit on the potty every two hours for about 5 minutes at a time. Remember - don't make it a prison. Forcing her to stay on it for long periods of time won't teach her to use it - it will only teach her to dislike being on the potty.

If she does go in her knickers then don't get cross with her. She's not doing it on purpose. Instead put her on the potty and encourage her to squeeze out a bit more. It's unlikely she will, but you want to encourage her to associate the sensation of doing her business with sitting on the potty.

Obviously you'll need to be prepared for cleaning up lots of accidents, so this type of rapid toilet training is best performed when you've got time off work and not planning on going anywhere. It's also a good idea to keep your child off of soft furnishings, etc. as much as possible for obvious reasons.

If you want to hurry the process along even further, you can add tangible rewards, such as lollies, for each successful effort. Don't offer rewards where there hasn't been a deposit - you're rewarding the act of using the potty, not of sitting on it.

Night-time Toilet Training

Sometime after your child has been potty trained she'll be ready to start working toward being able to sleep without a nappy and without wetting her bed. This means that she needs to learn how to hold on in her sleep and how to get up and use the toilet when needed.

Don't rush this. First she needs to be toilet trained during the day and she has to *want* to take this next step in her development.

Our third child, for example, steadfastly refused to allow herself to be toilet trained at night even though she had been using the potty for more than two years. It was only when her three year old sister started going the whole night without wetting her bed that she decided to finally make an effort. She was five and a half and decided she couldn't abide her younger sister doing something that she couldn't.

Until your child is 7 or 8, and hasn't wet her bed in over a year, you should keep a mattress protector on her bed. This should be suitable for keeping urine from seeping through to her mattress. This makes cleaning up after accidents much easier.

If urine does get on the mattress (e.g. if there was no mattress protector) then just strip off all of the bedclothes, take the mattress off the bed and stand it in a well-ventilated area until it's completely dry. You don't need to try and clean it or to dilute the urine with water -

doing so will just make the mattress wetter and harder to dry out. If it's wet for too long it will start to smell musty, so just get it dry and aired out as quickly as possible.

Always remember that it is not your child's fault if she wets the bed. There is never an excuse for being angry at her for doing so.

It is the case that she may urinate in her nappy because she finds it easier than going to the toilet, but even if you suspect that she's doing so there's no room for anger or acrimony. As with potty training, you need to make this a *positive* experience, free from feelings of embarrassment or shame.

When you think she's ready for night-time toilet training, buy her some 'pull up' nappies that she can take off on put on again herself. Ask her to put the pull-ups on *before* she goes to the toilet before bed. This gives her practice at pulling them down and up again.

Put her to bed as normal, but before she goes to sleep remind her that she has to get up and use the toilet if she needs to urinate. Ask her to try hard and congratulate her on her efforts to date, even if they haven't been completely successful.

If she does go the whole night without urinating in bed then make a big deal about it the next morning. Congratulate her and march her around the house so she can tell everyone else how clever she is.

If she doesn't manage it then remember to be encouraging - remind her that she can try again tonight and give it another go.

For most kids this will work and, apart from the odd accident here or there, they should be getting through the night with a dry nappy after a week or two.

You can offer a reward, particularly if your child has motivation problems when it comes to bed wetting. If you do offer up a reward make it something that she will *only* get once she's met the prescribed target. Make the target something definitive but achievable, such as three dry nights in a row.

If your child keeps urinating in her pull-up, however, then it's time to take things to the next level. The problem with pull-ups is that they are basically disposable nappies - they draw the urine away from the body on contact, providing a relatively comfortable and dry environment for the child. In short, the experience of urinating into a pull-up (or a nappy) is not sufficiently unpleasant to discourage her from doing it.

In this case it's time to pull out the 'big girl' knickers and to get rid of the pull-ups and nappies altogether. The idea behind this is that she's not going to have a nappy to contain her urine or to draw it away from her skin. Urinating at night is going to be wet, smelly and uncomfortable. It's going to be really unpleasant.

Yes, this also means that it's going to be uncomfortable for you, as you're going to have clothes and bedclothes soaked in urine, so you probably don't want to jump straight to this option. If nothing else works, however, then it's probably time to give this a go.

You should try going nappy-free for about 7 days. In my experience most children get the idea in a day or two and they soon learn to stop wetting the bed. If they've gone a full week without learning this then it may be too early for them to do so. It's probably a good idea to stop and to wait a few months before trying again.

Along Come Brothers and Sisters

As I have four kids it probably comes as no surprise that I'm a fan of larger families. Although having four kids with a 63 month age difference is manic, it's great that our kids always have someone to play with. They are never bored.

It has meant, however, that three of them have had to adjust to one or more new siblings coming along during their development. Three of them have had to adjust to no longer being the baby of the family.

When handled well this can be a magical experience for them and for you. If handled poorly your older children can be left feeling anxious, alienated and sometimes even resentful at the new arrival who's coming to steal valuable parental attention away from them.

It's important that your child is the first to know if she's going to have a sibling. Children can't be expected to keep secrets, so only tell her when you're ready for others to know also, but make her feel as if it's all of you who will be welcoming the baby, not just you and your partner.

Involve your child in the decision making. You can guide her decisions where necessary, but it's important that she starts developing a relationship with, and sense of responsibility for, the new baby as early as possible. You can ask her, for example, what she thinks the baby's name should be, whether you should tell others about baby yet, etc.

Even if your child is only one or two years old she won't be too young to start feeling and acting like an older sister.

It's also important that you keep her involved in baby's development in-utero. Tell her what's happening with baby. Let her feel baby kick. Encourage her to talk to baby through your partner's tummy. I challenge you not to tear up as she talks to her unborn sibling - I had happy tears running down my cheeks!

Your child will also be concerned about what baby's arrival will mean for her. Reassure her that you will continue to love her just as much. She needs to hear it. As an added bonus, she'll have a baby brother or sister who will love her too.

Tell her what will happen with the birth, when you and your partner will be away, who will look after her during the birth and all that kind of thing.

Give her a role in all of this. Ask her if she minds helping to look after baby and help her pick out a present that she can give to baby to welcome him or her to the family.

When baby arrives remember that her first meeting with baby is a very special moment for her, so treat it as such.

Ask her if she would like to say anything to baby and let her hold baby on her lap.

By putting your older children in a position where they welcome the new arrival into the family you will reduce the perceived threat that the baby represents while simultaneously giving them an active role in looking after the new arrival.

Don't forget to keep your older children involved in the care and feed of baby going forward too. This will promote feelings of empathy and a sense of responsibility for baby's welfare. This will reduce the likelihood of your older children feeling threatened, marginalised or alienated as a result of the new arrival.

It's easy to become preoccupied about the newest, youngest child in the house, so remember to make time for your older kids. Read to them when baby is asleep and make a point of taking them out for time without baby around.

Your older children are still having firsts all the time. Maybe they'll start school for the first time, notice boys for the first time, be invited to a birthday party or sleepover for the first time. These firsts are important - to you and to her, so don't let them pass unnoticed.

It doesn't matter how exhausted you are by having a new baby in the house - the physical and emotional development of your other children won't simply stop until things are less crazy, so make time for them.

The Manual

Pre-schooling

Every child should have a preschool experience. Even if one or both parents are at home with her during the day, your child needs the stimulation, socialisation and intellectual development that goes with preschool (also known as nursery school, pre-primary or kindergarten, depending where you're from).

Preschool and day-care are different in terms of intent, but similar in terms of delivery.

The primary purpose of day-care is to care for your children during the day. Generally the hours are longer, as preschool observes school hours, while day-care allows parents to drop off and pick up around office hours.

Whatever option you choose for your child, it pays to do your homework about where you'll send them.

Your child may end spending more of her waking hours with these strangers (at least they'll start out as strangers) than she will with you. This needs to be a positive, fun and educational experience for her.

Do your research on the options available in your area. Talk to other parents about their experiences and consider sitting in on a session or two before choosing a centre.

My wife chose a hands on option for our kids - she took all four of them through Playcentre, a New Zealand-based cooperative that focuses on parental-led learning through play. It may sound unconventional, but our children *thrived* at Playcentre. Mum found it challenging at times, particularly given the time commitment involved (she was required to undertake a significant amount of early childhood teaching training), but both of us are thankful that she made the commitment. Our kids benefited greatly as a result.

Regardless of which option you choose for your child, you should be involved.

If you don't regularly spend time at the facility then try and volunteer to help with outings or even to be parent teacher every now and then.

You want your child to gain self-confidence and independence, but it's also important for her to know you care and that you'll be around every now and then.

Although it can be hard to get time off work, etc., this can be really enjoyable and memorable for you too.

Diet

Ok, get ready to take this seriously. Your child is about to start learning the eating habits of a lifetime.

They're going to learn these from you.

Let's not waste any time with politically correct bullshit and face facts: if your (otherwise healthy) child is fat then it's your fault.

It's your responsibility to teach her healthy eating habits and you control her supply of food.

If your child is overweight then it's your responsibility to do something about it.

I'm not suggesting for a second that anyone should criticise other parents for having overweight children. That would be truly awful. I am saying that we are responsible for our children's weight at this age.

If your child is overweight then she is much more likely to be an overweight adult. The diet and exercise habits you teach her now are likely to be with her for life.

So let's get it right.

For a start, as soon as she's eating solid food she should be having more than five servings of fruit and vegetables every day. More than five. Ten is better. Get her eating raw fruit and vegetables early in her life and encourage her to eat them often.

Snacks should be fruit and vegetables, not crackers or processed foods.

Buy a book on children's nutrition. One based on nutritional science, no fad diets or kooky regimes. There's no such things as 'super foods' or 'cleansing diets' - if you own books with words like this in the title then whack yourself in the head with them before chuckling them in the bin.

Learn about the science of your child's nutrition and their neuronal needs. Understanding the practical details of why their nutrition is so important will make it much easier for you to enforce a healthy eating regime. Once you understand how damaging soft drinks and junk food can be to your children it will be a lot easier to limit their intake of these foods.

Then set some rules. Be serious and make sure that you and your partner are committed to them. These rules will not only dictate how healthy and active your kids are - they will also influence their attitudes to food and their eating habits into adulthood. Your rules will reflect your approach and priorities, but here's a selection of ours (i.e. from my own family) that you can use as a guide:

- Lollies (sweets) only once per week.
- Takeaways only once per week.
- Wholegrain bread only in our household.
- Healthy cereals only (e.g. wheat biscuits or rolled oats) although less healthy alternatives (sweetened cereals, etc.) are sometimes available once per week as a treat.
- Vegetables must be eaten at dinner time, no excuses.
- No treats or processed foods in school lunches. Only nutritious, healthy food.

Junk food, confectionary, soft drinks, etc. should remain treats and should not become part of their daily diet. It's not a good idea to deny them treats altogether - you want them to learn moderation, after all. It's important that they think of treats as exactly that - treats. Sooner or later they'll be making their own eating decisions.

Sometimes I think it's harder for dad to abide by healthy eating rules than it is for mum, as we're less likely to see what harm a chocolate bar here or a burger there will do. All parents like to treat their kids and it can be tough to say 'no' all the time (and kids do ask for treats *all* the time).

But we have to say no. We have to stand firm and think of their long-term health before their short-term satisfaction.

This is, after all, what healthy eating and looking after yourself is all about.

Of course there is room for exceptions, particularly when special occasions arise, but they have to remain exceptions.

You and your partner should talk regularly about the kid's diets and the treats that they've been having. Help each other to identify bad habits that may be creeping in (with you or with the kids) and agree how you'll handle these.

Also, avoid the temptation to force feed them. Kids are pretty good at listening to their bodies and knowing when they're full. When I was a kid it was customary for children to clear their plates - we would be sat at the table until we'd eaten everything that was put on front of us, regardless of how hungry we were that night.

You may choose to require them to eat their vegetables, particularly if they have already eaten more appetising components of the meal already.

If they don't eat their dinner then cover it and put it aside (in the fridge if appropriate). If they get hungry again before bed then they should be required to finish their dinner before they're allowed anything else.

If there's something on their plates that they don't like my kids will often try eating part of their meal and saying they're full, then asking for snacks a short time later. This used to be once they'd had a chance to throw their unwanted dinner in the bin. Now their unfinished dinners are kept until they go to bed, just in case.

When they Refuse Certain Foods

Your child should eat the food that you put on front of him. It's that simple. You choose what to feed him and you work hard to give him tasty, nutritious, healthy meals.

We start our children on a variety of foods from their earliest days of eating solids, in part to make them less fussy as they get older.

They will still develop preferences, of course, and there are foods that they will dislike and won't want to eat.

Allowing them choose what they won't eat is a slippery slope that I recommend you avoid.

Once you allow one child to pick the tomatoes off of his plate you'll have to allow all of your children to veto at least one food also.

In our house we use the saying 'you eat what you get and you don't get upset'. It's a quick and cheerful way of shutting down objections to whatever it is that they don't want to eat.

If your child digs his heels in and point blank refuses to eat a certain food then don't get into a standoff with him. A friend of mine told me that his son sat at the dinner table for five hours refusing to eat his mushrooms one night. Five hours. A little after 11PM my friend finally caved and sent his son to bed.

Although I was impressed at his son's stubbornness (that kid will go far!) it did strike me as a total lose/lose situation. My friend still ended up throwing out the uneaten mushrooms and his son, although victorious in the end, had an utterly boring and stressful night sitting at the dining room table doing nothing.

Instead of the standoff, if your child refuses to eat what's in front of him, simply let him clear his plate, but don't allow him to eat anything else until the meal is finished.

If he wants fruit to snack on before bed then let him... but only after he's eaten a sufficient amount of his dinner. Same with breakfast the next morning.

Do not cave and let him eat something else.

Once he is hungry enough he will eat his dinner and you will have sent him a strong message to him that he will remember the next time he thinks about turning his nose up at something.

If his pickiness becomes an ongoing issue then consider requiring him to eat his vegetables (or whatever item he dislikes so much) before the rest of his meal for a while.

Also, always remember to praise your children for eating what's put on front of them, particularly if another child isn't.

Ben Gannon

Exercise - Getting Out and About

Exercise is as important as nutrition when it comes to your child's long term health.

Again, the habits you teach them now will influence their habits of a lifetime. If you have sedentary children they are much less likely to enjoy exercise when they're older and they're much more likely to become sedentary adults.

Exercise is not only important for fitness and health. It's fun and an often social experience. It's also beneficial for mental health. Studies show that exercise can have a profoundly positive impact on depression, anxiety, ADHD and more.

Best of all, exercise wears them out, which can mean an early night for the kids and a peaceful night for mum and dad.

Just as with healthy eating, the best way to teach good exercise habits to your kids is to factor it into their daily lives from the very beginning.

Take them on excursions before they're even old enough to walk - show them how much fun and bonding can be achieved when you get away from the computer or TV and out into the wide open spaces.

In New Zealand we are very lucky to have an amazing array of outdoor options that provide excellent exercise opportunities all year round. We take all of our kids running through the bush (the younger kids get to do shorter walks), skiing, swimming in the sea and we enjoy a range of other activities. I can't wait for them to get a little older so I can also take them mountain biking, scuba diving and hunting.

We don't always have time to drive into the bush or off to the beach, however, so my wife and I make a concerted effort to keep them moving every day, including:

- Ensuring they walk to school at least twice per week. Their school has a walking school bus, where parents take turns to walk a 'bus load' of kids to school each day.

- Encouraging them to participate in school sports. This includes encouraging them to volunteer/try-out for various sports, providing logistical support (taking them to sports, providing food, drink, money, etc.) and helping them train for sports events. Yes, this all consumes valuable time and money, but it's worth it.
- Encouraging them to pursue extra-curricular activities that involve plenty of movement. All of our kids take dancing lessons, Kung Fu lessons, swimming lessons and perform a variety of other *active* extracurricular activities every week.
- Requiring them to do Saturday sports, at least during the colder months. Our kids are required to play soccer or rugby on Saturday mornings during autumn/winter months. We don't make this optional, but the kids really do love it - they sometimes put on a song and dance about having to get into their uniforms and out onto the pitch on cold Saturday mornings, but on balance they both enjoy and appreciate these sports.

I'm not telling you about all of the exercise that our kids do to be boastful or smug. I use my kids as an example because both my wife and I were sedentary children who were not taught the value of exercise. We exemplify how harmful a lack of exercise can be to child's development - both of us failed to meet our potential in sports and both of us struggled to incorporate exercise into our daily routines until we were approaching middle age. Both of us were worse off because of it.

Our kids, however, are paragons of how children benefit from being fit and active. They take amazing pride and enjoyment from their dance and sports.

They have boundless energy, are rarely sick and all have a positive outlook on life.

When I was a kid I thought I couldn't exercise because I was too fat and too uncoordinated to participate. Instead of encouraging me to give it a go, my mother facilitated my evasion of physical activity by providing me with notes asking my teachers to excuse me from physical education on medical grounds.

I grew up thinking that only some people were blessed with the skills and ability to excel at and enjoy sports.

Now when I see my children dancing, running and competing *for the fun of it* I can see how wrong I truly was.

They share my genes, so if I was genetically predisposed to a sedentary childhood then it would be reasonable to expect them to display some of the same traits.

They don't and this is great.

They are growing up with regular exercise as part of their daily lives and they will live longer, happier lives as a result.

You Should be Able to Take Your Kids Anywhere

Within reason, you should be able to take your kids anywhere.

I say 'within reason', as some places are simply not kid friendly. If the place is suitable for children, however, then you shouldn't be afraid to take your kids there.

Some parents avoid taking their kids shopping with them, as they are afraid of how they will act at the supermarket. What if they have a tantrum when they don't get what they want? It will be so embarrassing!

Avoiding such situations is exactly what we *shouldn't* do. By avoiding the situation you make the problem worse - if you don't learn how to 'control' your kids in public then you'll avoid taking them to more and more places and you'll find yourself in a vicious cycle.

I used to take all four of my kids to the supermarket with me when they were all younger than 6. I use to have two of them in the trolley and two on foot and I never had a problem with them. It was tiring, of course, and I had to be careful to keep them fed, occupied and not too tired, but I never had any trouble with their behaviour.

Just remember:

- For places you go to often, build a routine. When we went to the supermarket together we'd stop at the bakery for a bun beforehand (that they'd eat on the way around - helped with keeping them fed!) and they'd get a shoppers treat (if they behaved) at the end. They quickly learned the routine, what each visit would involve and, most important, that there was something in it for them if they behaved.
- Keep them fed and occupied. At the supermarket I'd employ the kids to help me find items on the shelves, collect items that they could bring back to me, hold the shopping list, etc. I also made sure they didn't become hungry, particularly as they were surrounded by food.
- Don't let them get too tired. You can't expect a child to behave once they become overly tired. If your child starts showing signs of fatigue then wrap up whatever you're doing as quickly as possible so you can get her to rest.
- Establish the rules before the excursion. Don't leave room for ambiguity - it will only give your child room for disappointment and outrage. Tell your kids how you expect them to behave and what will happen if they do (e.g. 'if you guys are really good then we might stay until closing time').
When we go to the supermarket, for example, my kids know that they only treat they'll be getting is the shoppers treat at the end and only then if they behave. This doesn't mean that you can't surprise them with things when you're out, but make it on your terms.
- Don't give in to demanding behaviour, particularly tantrums. Your child should know that this type of behaviour won't get her anywhere.
- Praise them for being good. Heap it on. Reinforce the positive. This is the most powerful tool that you have for promoting good behaviour while you're out.

Discipline

In the last chapter we learned how babies get what they want by crying. Crying is effective for babies. Evolution has made it this way.

Crying is not so effective once your baby grows into a child.

While a crying baby can have you and your partner literally climbing the walls, a crying four year old is probably going to annoy you rather than anything else.

So if crying becomes less and less effective as children get older, how will they continue to influence their parents and to get what they want?

They will have to deploy a much wider variety of techniques to influence their parents. These techniques are usually much more complex and subtle than out and out wailing, but they can be even more effective.

They are more effective, but often so subtle that you don't even notice that your darling child is busy twisting you around her little finger.

If she wants something and has a tantrum then this is easy to see and, I'd argue, easy to respond to.

What your child wants more than anything, however, more than toys or food or even fluffy animals, is *attention* and she will do everything in her power to get it.

Kids are bottomless pits for attention. They can never have too much and any attention is good attention, even when it's in response to them being 'bad'.

Understanding this is key to understanding how your child's mind ticks and, most important, how to prevent it from driving you all crazy, including your child herself.

You see, if left unchecked that sweet innocent child of yours is likely to become a tyrant who will rule your family with an iron fist.

This is not her fault, by the way. No child *wants* to become a dictator in their own home.

Without you, however, she has no control over the tools with which she would control you and demand your undivided attention.

Your job as her parent is to teach her how to control these tools. Your job is to teach her how to use her wily talents for good rather than evil.

Your job is to give her the love and attention that she wants and needs while teaching her the value of boundaries and mutual respect.

Your job is not to give in to her because you feel sorry for her or you want to stop her from crying.

Your job is most certainly not to become a tyrant yourself, so keep an eye on your behaviour too.

Remember that what you say to her becomes her inner voice. If you talk positively to her and fill her ears with praise then there's a greater chance of her inner voice being positive. Talk negatively to her and criticise her all the time and it's more likely that she will struggle with an overly negative inner voice.

In this section we will continue to develop our skills as a disciplinarian that will serve us into her teenage years and beyond.

As before, these skills are based on trust, mutual respect and forgiveness.

If you follow this discipline regime it will work. Your child will behave to the standard to which you expect, although this should *always* be suitable for their age. It is possible to have a four year old who is 'seen and not heard' but this would be awful for you and for him. Four year olds are supposed to be crazy - that's half the fun of it.

Aim for a balance where you allow your kids to be kids, albeit ones who act with courtesy and respect to those around them. Be tolerant and be ready to let them display their personalities. This does mean that sometimes they may overstep the bounds of what you're willing to accept as 'good behaviour', but it's better to have a vivacious child who tests the boundaries every now and then than one who's constantly afraid of punishment for stepping out of line.

Give them Food. Give them Sleep. Give them Attention.

I believe that hunger, a lack of sleep and a lack of attention are the three biggest contributors to bad behaviour in children.

Being hungry or tired it can make us adults grumpy, but we are mature enough to recognise the reasons for our irritability and to do something about it (i.e. eat something, take a nap, have a coffee, etc.)

Things are different for kids, who often feel lousy, but don't know why. Often they don't even realise they're feeling lousy at all, so they don't act on these feelings.

It may sound ridiculous, but even older children can lack the self-awareness to realise that they're hungry or tired and that they need to eat or rest.

Like us, kids also *need* attention. They've got to have it. If they don't get enough of it then they often start misbehaving to get more of it. Positive attention, negative attention - it doesn't matter. They just want attention.

Well, they'd prefer positive attention, of course, but they'll take what they can get.

So feed your child and feed them regularly (healthy food options, of course). Make sure they get plenty of sleep, including naps during the day if they need them. And give them plenty of attention.

Be proactive in preventing them from becoming hungry, tired and feeling neglected and you'll help avoid misbehaviour (and the need to dispense discipline) in the first place. This is better for you and for your children,

No Names or Labels

One amazing thing about humans is that, so much of the time, you can shape the entire arc of their lives with nothing more than a few words repeated on occasion during their formative years.

Tell a child that she is beautiful and friendly and smart and she will grow up to be beautiful and friendly and smart. She will do so because this is how she will see herself.

Tell a child that she is hardworking and industrious and she will see herself this way too.

Tell a child that she is lazy, useless or naughty and what do you think will happen?

It is for this reason that we must be very careful not to use negative names or labels.

I learned this the hard way when my son referred to himself as a 'naughty boy' during conversation one time. I had called him a naughty boy weeks beforehand and this is the impression he had held off himself since then.

Of course this was wrong. I was wrong. There is no such thing as a 'naughty' child. Children are just children. They do what comes natural to them.

So be careful to criticise the behaviour, but never the child. And do it in the context of the family unit so they know that the standard of behaviour you're demanding from them is the same standard that you apply to yourself and others in your home.

'We do not throw stones at the cat in our family!' is good.

'Throwing stones at the cat is naughty!' is passable.

'You naughty girl! Don't throw stones at the cat!' is not acceptable.

Your child may call you names from time to time. This is a natural part of them testing their boundaries. Don't stand for it, but don't retaliate either, especially in the heat of anger.

You are the lighthouse, not the sea. You are mature enough to know that she doesn't mean it and that she will apologise when she's cooled down.

The same does not go for her.

Even when she's an adult she won't be able to process or reconcile negative names or labels that you, her father, put on her. She certainly won't be able to do so as a child.

So ban all negative labels or names, no matter how funny or accurate you think they are.

I have a beautiful and intelligent friend whose nickname in her family is 'fatty' due to her size as a baby. She had long ago lost the baby fat, but she hadn't managed to lose the nickname, which dug into her as she agreed and left her scarred for life. She will always see herself as 'fat'. All because of a label she never should have worn.

Don't be Intimidated by Your Child

The title to this section may sound a bit ridiculous, but it's not. Dads are intimidated by their kids all the time.

Often we ask ourselves whenever it's worth it before disciplining our children or before asking them to do something.

Is it really worth the song and dance that she's going to put on? Maybe I should just pretend I didn't notice her misbehaving? Maybe I should just pick up after her myself?

Yes it is worth the song and dance and no you shouldn't cower.

To do so will only give your child power over you that neither you nor she wants her to have.

She will recognise this new-found power immediately and you bet she will use it against you.

It will give her licence to misbehave even more and/or to resist doing what you ask, knowing that the greater the stink that she puts up the more likely it is that you will back down.

She doesn't *want* this power as, although she will instinctively use it, she also knows instinctively that it's wrong.

She wants to comply and she prefers your attention and praise over having power over you.

So don't give her that power. Don't be Intimidated by your child.

If she misbehaves then correct it using the techniques described below. If you ask her to do something then it must be done - your word is final.

Reward Positive Behaviour

You should spend more time rewarding your child's good behaviour than disciplining her for poor behaviour.

If you're not then it's your problem, not hers.

She shouldn't have to bake you a pavlova to earn your praise... make a point of telling her what a good job she did of something, how nicely she spoke to someone else, how she used her manners, that type of thing. Reinforce the positive, especially if other children in the house are misbehaving.

It's important that your child feels like she is rewarded for doing well. It's miserable for a child to only receive negative feedback, or to mainly receive negative feedback, so make sure she gets lots of positive reinforcement.

Your other children will take notice too, particularly if they are misbehaving. This can be extremely powerful. Not only is the misbehaving child being ignored, but one of her siblings is getting positive attention *at the same time.* It creates a very strong incentive for her to stop misbehaving, start behaving and get some of that attention too.

Ignore Bad Behaviour

One of the fundamental problems with the disciplinarian approach that my parents, and many baby boomer parents, used is that it was based on the concept of punishment, rather than correcting bad behaviour.

This approach can be ineffective as it focuses too much on what the child *shouldn't do*, rather than recognising and rewarding good behaviours.

The first step to addressing this issue is to ignore bad behaviour. If your child yells or screams or throws her toys then don't reward her with your attention. This only encourages her to do the same thing the next time she wants you to notice her.

Instead, if the infraction is minor then simply turn away from her and show her that her course of action will not get her what she wants.

This is actually harder to do than you might think.

This is because we feel compelled to always have the last word. Our boomer parents would not have tolerated outbursts without a response, so it follows that we find it hard to ignore our kids when they act out too. We were trained from an early age that misbehaviour deserves rebuke. It can feel weak if we don't respond to bad behaviour, almost as if we're encouraging it by ignoring it.

But the opposite is true. By engaging with a misbehaving child we are rewarding her with the thing she wants more than any other - our attention. This might not be what she was seeking - her misbehaviour might have started for other reasons, but she'll happily take some of your attention, thanks very much.

Your love and attention is powerful and it should be showered upon her. Except when she misbehaves.

If she misbehaves then turn away. Don't say anything to her and don't respond when she asks you why you're ignoring her.

She may cry out or act out in protest. Unless she's at risk of hurting herself or someone around her then ignore her. Show her that her misbehaviour will only result in her losing the thing she values the most - your attention.

Be careful that this doesn't turn into a habit of giving your child the cold shoulder. Don't start using your attention as a weapon - you shouldn't withdraw attention as punishment or as retribution for past transgressions. You should only ever ignore bad behaviour, not the child herself.

As soon as the bad behaviour stops give her your attention again.

For younger children you should make a big deal about it. As soon as she stops misbehaving smile at her, congratulate her in a high pitched voice (e.g. 'Oh, you've stopped yelling, great!') and give her lots of attention.

This will be your most powerful parenting technique throughout her childhood and through to adulthood.

But you must remember to use it consistently.

If you reward negative behaviour by responding to your child, even if it's to chastise her, then you're reinforcing the message that she just has to be naughty enough for long enough to get a rise out of you.

In effect you're teaching her to misbehave.

But hang on... doesn't ignoring bad behaviour contradict the section above about not being Intimidated by your child?

Not at all. It's just up to you to differentiate between misbehaviour that is minor (and can be ignored) and more serious (and requires correction).

Timeouts

Coming in a close second to ignoring bad behaviour in the effectiveness stakes, timeouts are also an incredibly effective and important tool for disciplining your misbehaving child.

I have to admit that when I first heard of timeouts I thought the concept sounded weak and ineffective. Sending a child to their room isn't a punishment - if I was a kid I'd laugh at the concept!

But I was wrong.

Timeouts are effective. More effective than yelling at or smacking your children. More effective than withholding pocket money, pudding or whatever other punishments you can think of.

Why is this?

It's because timeouts remove from the child not only *your* attention, but everyone else's as well.

Your child might be totally happy in her room on her own when it's her choice to be there, but when she's on a timeout?

That's a whole different story.

The concept of a timeout is completely simple, so don't over-complicate it.

If your child misbehaves and it's too serious to be ignored then give her a warning. If she ignores the warning (or the misbehaviour is more serious) then she gets sent on a timeout to her room (or to some other predetermined **safe** area).

While she is on a timeout she is ignored. If she comes out of the timeout area or if she yells out (including if she yells out 'can I come back now?') then her timeout is extended.

And that's it.

Timeout tips and tricks

- The length of the timeout should always be the same. I usually go with a minute for every year of their age. Use a timer (such as a countdown timer on your smartphone) if you have trouble keeping track of time - it's important that you take your child off her timeout at the end of the interval.
- Don't increase the length of the timeout based on the severity of the offence - doing so is pointless and it smacks of retribution.
- If your child comes out of the timeout area and/or calls out to you then extend her timeout period. You may or may not want to say something like 'your timeout starts when you're quiet' or 'your timeout starts again when you're back in your room'. Don't penalise her for talking or playing in her room - ignore her unless she calls out or comes out. Also, don't actually start the clock again - just add a minute or two. This will be effective enough.
- Only issue a warning when you're prepared to go through with it. When you tell your child she is going on a timeout then she

must go on a timeout. If you don't follow through then you will undermine the entire regime and make it much less effective.
- If your child refuses to go on a timeout once you've told her to then simply count to three, slowly. Pause your counting when she is making an actual effort to get herself there. Keep counting as long as she refuses. Each time you get to three, add one minute to her timeout and then start counting again. Even the most stubborn child won't usually let you add more than a few minutes to her timeout before complying. If she's extra stubborn then do a quiet fist pump (there will be no drop-kick boyfriend taking advantage of her in later years!) and then consider upping the stakes. After adding 5 minutes or so, for example, try 'if I get to 10 minutes extra you're going to bed early as well.'

  Again, don't count down too quickly - she has to have time to consider her options and to decide to comply. But also don't undermine the countdown by pausing if she's not making a genuine effort to do so (and no 'two and three quarters!')
- Never, ever, manhandle your child or carry her to timeout. You can do this when she's younger, but before long this just turns into a form of physical punishment. At some stage it will also turn into an ugly competition of strength - even when you win you will lose.

  As long as she knows that you mean business and that her timeout is getting longer and longer she will comply. Be consistent and before long she'll just need to hear 'three!' before scurrying off to her timeout area.
- Don't let your child escalate the situation. You are the lighthouse, she is the sea. Ignore and extend. Don't engage.
- Don't give the timeout area a name, such as the 'naughty spot' or similar. You'll only create a label by association. 'You're on a timeout - go to your room' is fine.
- Kids soon learn if mum or dad are too embarrassed to send them on a timeout in public, so don't be. Kids should be *better behaved* in public than they are at home, not worse. Issue the

warning and, if it's ignored, send them on a timeout.

If you're in the car this may mean telling them they can't talk for the length of their timeout. Otherwise stop the car, take them out onto the side of the road (where it's safe, of course) and stand there quietly while they serve their sentence. If you're in a busy supermarket you can find a corner to stand them in or take them out into the lobby and time them out there.

- Timeouts are punishment and they should be used as a last resort. They should always be preceded with a warning unless the infraction is severe. Don't be lazy and fall into the trap of issuing timeouts left right and centre - your child will only be left feeling bewildered and anxious about stepping out of line.

Correcting Bad Language

Kids often pick up bad language habits, such as swearing, cursing or regularly criticising others. These habits are enforced by the attention that they receive from them. Whether it's negative or positive attention that they receive, a four year old swearing is likely to get everyone's attention pretty quickly!

These habits can be difficult to correct, as a timeout can be too harsh a response, so we tell the child off, which can be ineffective. You could try implementing 'swear jar' into which a portion of their pocket money goes each time they infringe, but this punishment lacks immediacy. Very few children carry cash around in their pockets, so if you dock your child's pocket money it means you will deduct it from her next payment. This concept is quite abstract for the young mind, so this approach can also be ineffective as well as being a pain to administer.

It can be particularly annoying when the children direct their bad language at each other, as they often do so out of earshot, which can result in a 'he said/she said' situation with the children.

Who do you believe and who do you punish?

Instead of punishing them, increase the cost to them of using bad language to dissuade them from using it.

An effective way of doing this is by requiring the child to say three nice things each time she swears or criticises others.

If children talk badly to each other, then require them to say three nice things about each other. Ignore any protests of innocence - you're not interested in presiding over who was right or wrong. They just have to comply.

Let them take turns and give them 30 seconds or so to come up with three nice things. Don't let them repeat any of the complements more than once, but also don't make it too hard for them, as kids can find it difficult to come with compliments while under pressure.

Once the children have finished complementing each other then ask them to hug it out and to tell each other that they love them.

If your child refuses to comply then give her a warning and, if she still refuses, send her on a timeout. I'd recommend making this a short timeout, but when she comes back give her (or them, if there's more than one refusenik) another chance to comply before repeating the warning and timeout if necessary. Don't back down and let them out of having to say nice things and hug due to time served - doing so will encourage non-compliance in future.

This approach is effective because it increases the cost of using bad language. Your child soon learns that one swear word is going to cost her three complements and possibly a hug, which is too expensive. It's not worth it!

The compliments and the hug also replace the negative (i.e. bad language and/or conflict) with something positive. Rather than giving your child negative reinforcement ('Poppy! Stop swearing!') you are turning her infraction into something positive and friendly.

A welcome by-product of this approach is that your child will become more complimentary of others, as we're replacing bad habits with good ones.

Reward Systems

Reward systems are designed to reward your child for positive behaviour over a period of time. These can be used to correct bad habits (e.g. they earn a point for playing nicely without snatching) or to help motivate them (e.g. a point for each night they don't wet the bed).

All you need is a simple system for keeping score and an agreed reward when your little treasure meets the threshold.

You can, for example, use a sticker chart stuck to the fridge and let her put a sticker on each time he earns a point. You can get her to cross out a sticker each time she loses a point and require her to cover the crosses with new stickers as she earns them.

Another idea is to have a jar of marbles (you can also use ping pong balls or anything else tactile and not easily broken) and an empty jar. Each time your child earns a point she gets to take a marble out of one jar and put it into the other. When she loses a point the marbles go in the opposite direction. When all the marbles have moved between jars she gets her reward.

This can be a really effective approach, although I would only consider using reward systems with kids after they reach 3 - 4 years in age (depending on their emotional maturity). Any younger than this and the child can have trouble understanding the regime and/or their interest trails off too quickly, rendering the system redundant.

A few tips and tricks for running effective reward systems:

- Keep them simple and easy to understand, particularly when the child is not yet 5
- Make the rewards small and the number of points required to earn them reasonable. You and your child will soon lose interest in the system otherwise.
- Think about letting your child draw up her own reward chart if she's interested in doing so - this can improve her buy-in to the process.
- Don't lose your temper and take all of her points away. It's not

fair for her to be able to lose all of the points she's earned due to one transgression. If the transgression is serious then give her a timeout.

- Once she's earned a reward it should not be taken away. Give her the reward quickly while she's still feeling good about herself for earning it. Don't take it away once she's earned it - she shouldn't have to earn it twice.
- Taking points away can be ineffective when you're outside of the home, as she often can't comprehend the loss of points if she's not crossing them out herself. One friend of mine carries her kids' rewards charts around with her so they can cross out their own points if they misbehave on the road. Personally I prefer to use warnings and timeouts with my kids.

When They Won't Stop Fighting

As we've learned, kids are attention seeking missiles. They don't just want your attention - they want each other's' attention too.

This means that, when kids are in the zone, they'll play with and entertain each other. Ahh... there's nothing more satisfying than the sound of kids playing together happily.

When they're not in the zone (i.e. most of the time) they can resort to niggling each other to get each other's attention and to relieve boredom.

This can be infuriating. Kids needling each other, arguing and regularly appealing for mum and dad to intervene is enough to drive any parent crazy.

Shouting at them won't help - this will only result in you giving them attention too, rewarding their bad behaviour. There's also no point in being angry at them for needling each other - it's frustrating, sure, but kids will only snipe at each other if they have room in which to do so.

Think instead about helping them find something to do. It may be that you have to put down what you're doing and to give them some positive attention to break them out of the cycle of sniping at each other.

Although kids should be free to have disagreements, don't ignore the sniping - it won't go away on its own. It will likely only get worse as the kids get older and could end up damaging the sibling relationship for good.

If one child is being antisocial then warn her that she's being out of line and, if she keeps at it, give her a timeout.

When she comes out insist that she apologises to her harmed sibling and that they hug it out. If she refuses, or if the hug isn't acceptable then give her a chance to fix it before sending her back on a timeout. Don't skip this bit - it is important to demonstrate that conflict between them should always be resolved with an apology and an embrace.

Be careful about punishing just one child though - it takes two to tango and often you'll find that they're needling each other, even if it sounds like only one of them is at fault. My eldest child is expert at silently winding her siblings up. Her siblings retaliate and it almost always looks like they're the aggressor.

This is why, if you're not 100% certain that one of the children was completely innocent, you should put them both in a timeout if they ignore your warning to stop sniping (or immediately for more serious infractions such as hurting each other). Even if one child was guiltier than the other they should both receive the same punishment.

Again, when they come out they should apologise and hug it out before being allowed to disperse.

If they keep fighting then keep repeating the cycle - warn them, then send them on a timeout.

They will get the message soon enough, but don't forget to help them find distractions too - they're probably only fighting because they're bored.

Educational Development

Your child learns and develops an incredible amount during her first five years. At the age of 1 she can hardly talk, but by five she can hold conversations, develop abstract ideas and possibly even write her own name.

This is a time of firsts and of wonderment for your child and she relies heavily on you for her development during these formative years.

Everything from her language and numeracy skills to her values and temperament will be heavily influenced by you and by her mother.

Above all else she needs love and support. Study after study has shown how important this is to your child's early development.

If there is violence (emotional or physical), tension or hardship in her life then her development during this critical phase can be stunted - to the point where she *may never catch up* with her peers. Take some time to think about whether or not you're providing an environment in which she can thrive.

As long as you're providing a loving environment and the necessities of life to your child then helping her develop normally is relatively easy and, most important, lots of fun. In this section we look at some of the ways that you can help her to grow and develop and to help her prepare for school.

We've already looked at pre-schooling, so we won't focus on what she does during the day while you're at work. This section focuses on what you can do with your child during the time that you spend with her, which for most dads means time outside of working hours.

Boycott the Baby Olympics!

Your child's development up until the age of five should be focused on helping her to learn motor and verbal skills, to explore the world around her and to develop the creativity, confidence and stamina that she is going to need at school and beyond.

This is not a time for her to learn to recite the alphabet backwards or to learn long division.

As we learned in the previous chapter, many parents think of their kids as 'gifted' and there's nothing wrong with that, but this doesn't mean that they shouldn't have the opportunity to just be kids.

If your child learns to mumble, talk or even spell earlier than other kids then that's excellent. Celebrate it and tell her what a good girl she is, but don't use that as an excuse to start intensive vocabulary or spelling lessons. She won't enjoy them and, here's the kicker - they'll make *zero difference* to her ongoing development.

In fact, forcing your baby or toddler to endure lessons of just about any kind is likely to retard her development. Instead of learning how to play and socialise with others she'll either be spending time being taught to read or, worse, being told how much better she is than other children.

Worst of all, parents who try and force feed their children an education before they're ready aren't doing it for their kids. They do it for bragging rights. They do it so they can enter their child in the Baby Olympics - the saddest, most awkward Olympics of all.

No kid has ever volunteered to enter the Baby Olympics. Instead they're thrust into the role by one or more demanding parents. They're trotted out at barbeques so they can recite the alphabet, or Shakespeare or whatever they've learned by rote for the amazement of all who bear witness.

This is not what kids are for.

We *should* be amazed by every child's development, including the children of our friends and family. It's hard not to be astonished at the kid who can tie his own shoelaces while others his age are still playing with their own poo. Or at the kid who can solve arithmetic problems while others her age struggle to count past 1.

But we should not be jealous and we should certainly not be competitive.

If you want to compete with your buddies then have an arm wrestle.

When it comes to kids - let them be kids.

There's a big difference between gently helping their development along (which we discuss in this section) and forcibly training them for the Baby Olympics (which we definitely will not).

Boycott the Baby Olympics and help your child enjoy these years of wonderment.

Don't Expect Miracles

Although you'll spend most of your time marvelling at how quickly your child develops during this period, it's important not to expect miracles. In some areas your child won't develop as quickly as you might expect and that's normal.

My kids love to swim, for example, and we've been lucky enough to be able to give them all swimming lessons at a local pool since they were babies. When they were really young we took them to 'tiny tots' classes where one of us would essentially carry baby around the pool doing exercises as instructed by a teacher.

They then progressed to swimming lessons on their own and I did expect that, due to the sheer volume and duration of lessons alone, they'd be pretty advanced swimmers by the time they were approaching school age.

But this was not the case at all. Although all of them are excellent swimmers *for their age*, none of them could swim freestyle by the age of 5, despite having several years of lessons under their belt. What was even more surprising was how quickly some of their peers caught up to their abilities, sometimes exceeding them, despite starting swimming lessons years later than my kids did.

The reason for my surprise was because I was expecting miracles.

I expected that somehow my children would progress as fast as adults and that they'd be swimming lengths of the pool by the time they were five.

This was ridiculous, of course. My expectations were completely unrealistic.

I was also judging my kids' progress against the progress of others, which is the first step toward entering them into the Baby Olympics.

Luckily I caught myself before I went too far. I realised that my kids were enjoying their lessons and, most important, they had learned to be confident and safe in the water. Skills that will serve them for a lifetime.

After the age of five their swimming skills also took off like a rocket. Although progress appeared to me to be slow up until then, I've been nothing but amazed at their progress since.

Their physical strength, fitness, breathing and, most important, their discipline, matured to the point that their rate of progression increased sharply.

So don't expect miracles and don't be discouraged if your child appears not to be developing in certain areas - they're probably just not mature enough yet to do so.

Limit Screen Time

A small amount of screen time (i.e. TV, smartphone, tablet, computer time, etc.) can be beneficial for your child. It can help her to zone out and relax and, as long as the content is appropriate, it can actually be educational.

Anything more than a few hours of screen time per week, however, is likely to be detrimental to her development.

We're all guilty of putting our kids on front of the flat-screened babysitter from time to time and there's nothing wrong with that, but it is important that you keep track of, and limit, her screen time regardless.

In our house no one watches TV during the day - it stays off until dad watches the evening news, which our kids aren't interested in anyway.

The older kids get a bit more screen time for work (school work) and play (games, videos, TV, etc.), but until they were five TV was strictly limited to an hour or two in the weekends, plus the odd movie or half hour with the tablet.

Some parents argue that their kids are unable to find things to do on their own without the TV on, but this is bullshit - it's a cop out.

The longer your child has been on front of the TV the more she will complain when you turn it off, but ignore it.

Turn it off you must.

Once she realises that you're not going to turn it back on (no matter how much she complains) then she'll find something else to do.

Even better, turn off the TV and announce to the kids that you're all going for a walk - this will have the added benefit of distracting them from the loss of screen time and give you some time together.

Read to Your Child

In the previous chapter we discussed how important it is to read to your child every day. This is critical to the development of their language, comprehension and reading skills.

Make sure there is always an abundance of books in your household. If you can't afford lots of books then ask around - many parents have stockpiles of books that their kids have outgrown but that they haven't figured out what to do with yet. They may be happy for you to have them.

Yes, young children are rough with books, but you'll just have to come to terms with the fact that many of their books will be drawn on, have their covers ripped off or worse. The most important thing is that they have access to books. Always.

Let them discover the joy of reading as early as possible in their lives. Let them take those books to bed with them even before they're too young to know what the words mean.

Read to them and ask them questions about what you're reading. Ask her what bear did or said or ask her to count the number of honey pots in the picture.

Make it fun and help her find the answers if she starts getting frustrated. Be positive and reward her for her answers with your praise and encouragement.

It is truly amazing to watch your child gradually learn to read. To watch her develop from only looking at the pictures to acknowledging the presence of words on the page to knowing what those words are and what they mean.

Reading to her every day is by far the best way to help her develop this lifelong skill.

Share the Wonder of Everyday Life

Unfortunately, by the time we become parents we've pretty much forgotten how utterly amazing everyday life on our little planet, in our wee spot in the universe is.

Your child hasn't forgotten this yet - she's only just realising how incredible just about everything is.

Everything has a story.

The planets, stars and galaxies. The car that you drive. The smartphone that you have in your pocket. The natural world that is often just outside your door, but so far away from your reality.

Talk to your kids about this stuff. Figure out what they're most interested in and tell them what you know about it.

Avoid conspiracy theories and old wives tales - you want your kids to be informed, not brainwashed. There's a million things you could tell them about *right now* that are factual and that are likely to delight and amaze them.

I love to talk to my kids about space, including the history of space travel, the planets and stars, galaxies and black holes. That kind of thing. They love it - they often ask me to tell them stories about space and I'm always happy to oblige.

This results in much discussion and lots of questions - often questions that I can't answer and that we have to resort to Professor Google to answer.

This is gold.

In sharing the wonder of everyday life with our kids we are developing in them a sense of curiosity and wonderment. We are helping to build their general knowledge while also teaching them critical reasoning and analysis skills. We are giving them the confidence to ask questions without the fear of looking stupid. We are teaching them to act on their curiosity and how to do so (e.g. research using the Internet).

While they benefit we do too.

These conversations can be great fun, although you have to be careful to let everyone talk and to protect everyone from ridicule, no matter how silly their questions or opinions. Only allow positive, supportive language.

It also helps us adults to rediscover the wonder of everyday things. Of clouds. Of technology. Of nature.

Use Rote, but Only When Fun

Learning should be fun and exciting. Up until they start school it should never be a chore, but there will always be some things that have to be learned by rote.

Spelling and multiplication tables are key examples.

Kids need to know how to spell and, yes, they need to know their multiplication tables up to a factor of 12, although not necessarily by the age of 5!

I use time in the car to practice spelling and multiplication tables with my kids, plus discussions about anything else that they may be working on at school at the time.

This started before they were old enough to spell and initially comprised me asking them to point out or to name objects around us. This progressed gradually to spelling and multiplication, with a very gradual increase in difficulty.

The kids love it and it's usually them, not me, who instigate the in-car learning lessons.

I keep it fun by only ever engaging in rote learning if they're in the mood for it. In the car on the way to school is usually a good time, in the evening after school and dance classes (i.e. when they're exhausted) not so much.

I also try hard to extend them, asking increasingly difficult questions, but I never let them become frustrated. If they can't answer a question then I'll help them get to the answer. Sometimes they'll ask me not to help but I will anyway, after letting them try on their own for a while, to prevent them from frustrating themselves and getting bored of it.

I couldn't recommend this enough. It's fun and educational for you and for them.

You have to keep it light and heap on the praise even if it's only for trying.

Consider keeping such learning sessions short - I usually stop before the kids are ready to do so, meaning they're often asking me to keep going. I'd much rather do this and leave them wanting more than to turn it into a chore that they will start to resent.

Finally, don't tolerate anything but supportive comments between siblings. Older kids can discourage younger ones by mocking them for not knowing answers to questions that *they* find easy. Remind the older kids that they were once that age also.

Experiences Matter

Your child is always learning. She is a sponge, ready to soak up all that the world has to offer.

The more she can experience in her formative years the better.

This doesn't mean you have to climb Mount Kilimanjaro with her, in fact I wouldn't recommend anything quite so dangerous, but don't leave her to her own devices for days on end either.

Kids need to socialise with other kids. And with adults. They need to see things and feel things to help broaden their horizons and to get those synapses in their brains firing.

Remember that nights and weekends might be rest time for you after long days at work, but don't forget to make time to give her those experiences.

She probably won't remember many (if any) of them by the time she's a teenager, but they will become part of her nonetheless. Experiences matter and the more positive experiences you can give her during her childhood the better.

Build Gritty Kids

What's the most important thing you can teach your kids? If you had to choose just one skill that you could pass down to them what would it be?

Yes, yes, you want them to be kind and loving people, that's a given. What next?

The kindest, most loving person can't get by without real skills, so what one skill would you teach them to maximise their chances of success and happiness?

For me it's a no brainer: *GRIT*.

What is grit?

It's not actually just one skill or attribute, so I'm cheating a bit. Grit is a collection of characteristics that describe someone's perseverance and passion for long-term goals.

Gritty kids are those who:

- Have courage. They're not afraid of, or overly discouraged by, failure.
- Are conscientious. They are achievement-oriented and can motivate themselves to complete tasks or achieve goals (often that they've set themselves).
- Set long term goals and have the endurance to see them through.

- Are as resilient as a cockroach. They remain optimistic, creative and confident, even after experiencing setbacks.
- Strive for excellence. Not perfection. Excellence. They want to excel at what they do. They're competitive, sure, but more so they just don't want to be in the middle of the pact.

Why is grit important?

It's important because research, and common sense, show that no one characteristic is a better determining factor in how successful and, most important, how happy someone is going to be.

We all want our kids to be amazing at something. We all secretly fantasise about them growing up to be entrepreneurs or famous sports stars.

But what's the point of them being exceptional if they're also fragile?

What's the point of excelling in life if you're not happy in life?

There is none, so none of us should aspire to raise tortured geniuses.

We need to raise children who enjoy striving and who find inspiration in adversity.

Because, until we die, we humans never stop striving.

Even if we reach the summit of whatever mountain we're climbing there's always a taller mountain on the horizon calling our name. We never truly achieve our goals because, like a rainbow, our goals always move with us, remaining beyond our reach.

'So what the fuck has this got to do with a five year old?' I hear you saying.

It has *everything* to do with a five year old.

At five your child is unlikely to display all of these gritty characteristics. I don't think there are too many five year olds who are striving toward long term goals.

But they can be learning to be gritty if you let them.

For a truly excellent analysis of grit, including why it's important and how to build it, I thoroughly recommend Angela Duckworth's seminal (and totally enjoyable) book 'Grit'. Essential reading for anyone - not just parents.

So how do we build gritty kids and when should we start?

The 'when' part is easy - right now. You can promote gritty characteristics in your child from before she can talk.

The 'how' is pretty easy too - you start by demonstrating grit in action through your own words and actions. You'll benefit too - I can tell you this from personal experience.

Also take time to recognise and encourage gritty behaviour in her, such as:

- **Encouraging her to follow her passions**. Ok, so at this age her passions are probably Barbie and riding the dog, but one day she'll be old enough to make real, life changing choices. You need to drill into her the importance of following her passions and doing things that she finds interesting. It may take a lot of courage for her to choose to follow her dreams one day - help her to start building that courage now.
- **Teach her to enjoy the challenges in life.** Teach her that frustration is a necessary part any achievement. When she stumbles you still need to be sympathetic, but encourage her back up onto the horse. Tell her stories of people overcoming adversity. Your stories and stories of others. My children love the story of how JK Rowling overcame seemingly insurmountable odds to become one of the most celebrated (and wealthy) authors of all time.
- **Show her meaning in her work.** Sound familiar? In Chapter 1 we discussed how important it is for you to find meaning in your work. Tell your child why you find what you do meaningful - it will inspire her. Help her find meaning in what she does - the tasks may be small at this age, but that's irrelevant. What's important is that she starts developing a sense of importance in what she does.

- **Teach her that she can change and grow.** Success is the result of successive failures. The successful are those who have changed and who have grown to overcome those failures. Drill this into her from the very beginning. Tell her about your failures and how you've overcome them to get ahead in life. Explain to her that failure is a necessary part of life and that, although it's fine to stop and lick your wounds every now and then, she should never let an insignificant thing like failure get in the way of her success.

Chapter 7: Ages 5 – 13

When I was a kid I was obsessed with space travel. I sadly came along too late to be able to watch any of the Apollo missions to the moon live, but I do remember vividly the first space shuttle launch and the promise that it represented.

I used to pore over anything I could get my hands on about the space shuttle, savouring every detail I could find about this engineering marvel. It was, at the time, the most complex machine mankind had ever produced.

One particularly amazing detail was that, for 12 or 13 minutes during re-entry (i.e. when the spacecraft re-entered earth's atmosphere) mission control would completely lose contact with the shuttle. This phenomenon, called the 're-entry blackout' is a result of the amazing heat generated as the spacecraft re-enters the atmosphere.

For almost a quarter of an hour, during one of the most dangerous and difficult parts of the mission, none of NASA's earth-based systems were able to communicate with the spacecraft. This meant that no one on the ground would have any idea of what was happening on board until either the re-entry blackout was over or, as tragically happened to the Space Shuttle Columbia in 2003, until things went horribly, obviously wrong.

Can you imagine it - despite the millions of human hours of research, development, construction, testing and training, not to mention the hundreds of billions of dollars invested - during this period all NASA could do was wait and have faith that the crew, and their spacecraft, was sufficiently prepared to survive this interval on their own.

Despite the fact that the entire world was watching them, the two men on board the first space shuttle mission were completely and utterly alone. Beyond the reach of any of us on earth.

This is kind of like what happens when kids go through their teens.

For a while they slip out of radio contact. They are basically beyond our influence or control.

The teenage years can still be an enjoyable time for them and for you, but during this period you've got no choice but to have faith that you adequately prepared them for the delicate and tricky stage of their lives as they transition into adulthood.

If the re-entry of a spacecraft is too steep or too shallow it can either burn up or bounce off the atmosphere - each of which would be catastrophic.

If our kids don't get their re-entry just right they can meet with disaster or adversely affect the arc of their lives for good.

So why are we discussing this now, when we haven't even made it to the teenage section yet? Who cares what they're going to be like at 15 when you're busy looking after them at the age of 6?

We're discussing it now because this is when we start preparing them for those potentially treacherous teenage years. We're also preparing *ourselves* for this period. As we'll discuss in the next chapter, parents are as big a part of the teenage 'problem' as our teens are, so it's only natural that we should have to prepare ourselves for re-entry, sorry I mean the teenage years, too.

The period of their lives between 5 and 13, the 'school years', is your chance to instil the values and principles that they are going to need to get them through their teenage years and beyond.

This period also gives you the chance to strengthen and deepen your relationship with your child. To let the roots of that relationship grow deep and strong.

She'll not only need this strong relationship to help her survive and thrive the school years, she'll also need it to help her get through the confusion and uncertainty of her teenage years.

The school years are an amazing time in your child's life, so enjoy every second of them. This truly is their age of innocence, but it passes so fast. Too fast maybe. She enters this phase of her life a child and emerges from it a young woman.

The kind of woman she is going to become is largely up to you.

The Manual

Eat Together

The importance of eating together cannot be overstated. Eating breakfast together is great, but breakfasts are usually rushed, as everyone is trying to get themselves ready and out the door in the mornings.

Most lunches are eaten apart, so that leaves dinnertime.

You should eat together as a family, at the dining room table (or some other location where you can all see and talk to each other) *at least* three times per week. More if you can manage it. Make it a priority.

No phones.

No work.

No TV.

No distractions.

Believe me, one day you will look back fondly on your memories of breaking bread together and hearing about each other's day. You will wish you had done it more often and you'll look forward to doing it again.

You will never look back and reminisce about you all eating dinner on the couch with the TV blaring, so turn the fucking thing off and enjoy each other's' company.

This isn't just for the enjoyment factor. Researchers have shown a direct correlation between the amount of time that families spend eating dinner together and a range of benefits. These include improved cohesiveness as a family, reduced incidence of mental illness and substance abuse (particularly by the children), lower incidence of obesity and of eating disorders - the list goes on!

And all you have to do is eat together!

You don't have to have a fancy meal - it's not the food that counts. It's the time together spent doing nothing but eating and enjoying each other's company.

The Manual

A few tips and guidelines:

- Leave the stresses of your day behind. Coming to the table stressed and grumpy and ready to bite the head off of the first person who talks defeats the purpose of eating together. Have a family rule that you're allowed to talk about your problems at the table, but not take them out on each other.
- No distractions. Everyone should pitch in to help get dinner ready and to set the table. Everyone sits down at the same time and no distractions are allowed.
- Maximise time at the table. You can pre-cook meals or use services that provide meal ingredients and recipes to minimise preparation time. No one's allowed to leave the table until mealtime is over (i.e. until everyone is finished).
- Everyone uses their manners. Strike a balance between everyone being respectful to each other and not becoming the manners Nazi.
- Everyone has their turn to talk. Use open-ended questions to get everyone talking - we let everyone take turns to tell us the best and worst things that happened to them that day - kids, teenagers and adults all have a turn. While they are talking everyone else should be quiet and should listen attentively. After everyone's had a turn the conversation can flow freely again.
- No one is forced to talk. If your child doesn't want to talk then don't force her. Just say 'ok, if there's anything upsetting you then we're all here to help' and move on to the next person. Upon realising that the attention is about to shift away from them they will usually change their minds and volunteer something - if they do then give them the opportunity (the next person can wait). If they don't then wait until you've gone around the table and offer them another chance to talk.
- Tell them stories. Entertain your kids - tell them stories about their ancestors or relatives. Tell them how you and their mother met, about your wedding and all of the other things that they might not have been around to witness. Tell them

their birth stories and about how happy you were when they came into the world. Tell them about the world - my kids love to hear about space and space travel. Be careful not to dominate the discussion (they should get a chance to talk too). Ask them questions to get them involved (e.g. 'Who would you take with you if you travelled to the moon and why?')

- Look around the table. We can get so wrapped up in our day to day lives that we really do forget to stop and smell the roses. Look around the table at your loved ones and to savour them while you can. This is always an emotional experience for me - I can never believe that I'm husband to such a beautiful wife and father to four such amazing children.

Once dinner is over everyone should clear their own plates and help clear the table, stack the dishwasher, etc., but try to keep their after-dinner clean-up tasks light. When they look back on these happy times eating together you want them to remember the dinner, not dad yelling at them to clean up the kitchen afterward!

School and Education

I am not a strong believer in striving to send my kids to the 'best' schools. I've certainly never aspired to give them a private school education (I don't want them to have a superiority complex) and my observation is that the 'best' public (i.e. state-funded) schools are often overrun, victims of their own success.

I am privileged to have this opinion, however. We live in an upper-middle-class area of Auckland, New Zealand. As in most countries, the public schools in our relatively affluent area are far superior to the public schools in poorer areas.

It is one of life's great injustices that the poor, who arguably need good educations the most, typically receive lower quality educations than the more wealthy.

So while I don't believe in striving to send your kids to the 'best' schools, I do strongly recommend that you do everything in your power to not send them to the worst ones either.

It pays to do your research well before your kids reach school age, as you don't want to find out on their first day at school that the place is a dump.

The best source of advice about schools in your area is other parents. Everyone's experience and perceptions are different, so seek out lots of varying opinions before forming your own view.

Look for a school that has effectively stamped out bullying and that fosters a warm and welcoming environment for the students and teachers. This is much more important than their scholastic track record, as (unless they've got a truly poor record, in which case you'd be unlikely to be considering them) this is largely irrelevant. If your child doesn't enjoy herself and if she doesn't feel safe at her school then she's unlikely to do very well there, regardless of what the schools track record is like.

If none of the schools in your catchment area are any good then you need to do something about it. You need to find a school that is suitable and figure out how you will get her into it. Yes, this can be hard, but it's not your child's problem - neither you nor she can afford for her school years to be miserable.

Talk about school with your child in the year leading up to her starting there. This will help her to build a mental picture of what school will be like and will help reduce her natural anxiety about whether she'll fit in there.

Take your child on as many school visits as possible before she starts. Most schools will have programmes for new entrants that include familiarisation visits to the school. Take advantage of these, as they will also let her meet her new teacher, see her new classroom, etc.

First Day of School

Her first day of school is an exciting but emotional time. Your child entered the world as a defenceless baby only five short years ago and now here she is - a big girl who's off to school.

This can be a particularly emotional day for you and for her mum, as you are passing the baton - not so much to her teacher but to her personally. Up until now and your partner have been responsible for her and her wellbeing 24 hours per day, 365 days per year. From now on, for the rest of her life, that changes. From now on she's going to spend most of her waking hours away from you and your partner and this can be hard to adjust to.

One of you should escort her to her first day at school, but not both of you. A class of five year olds can quickly become overwhelmed by the presence of two additional adults. The teacher should allow you to sit in on her first couple of hours in class at least, but you should retreat to the back of the class and just offer encouraging waves and smiles as she needs them.

It's not your job to go into the class to discipline her or to help her with her schoolwork - this is what the teacher is there for. You're on the teacher's turf, so be careful not to overstep your bounds.

Make it very clear to your child that you're only going to be there for an hour or two and give her fair warning that you're going to be going soon about 10 minutes before you leave, giving her a kiss and a cuddle on the way out.

Most kids will be so enthralled by their new surroundings that they will have forgotten that you're even there by the time you get up to go. If he ignores you then don't feel bad - you should do a little fist pump to celebrate getting out of there so easily.

If he's not happy for you to go then calmly but firmly tell her that you are going to go, as you had both agreed earlier and then leave.

If he's really not happy about it then he may cry. He may even have a tantrum. Ignore it - within a couple of minutes of you leaving (once he's realised that you're not coming back) he'll be fine. If you stick around then you're just delaying the inevitable and you'll probably disrupt the teacher and the rest of the class.

Remember that the teacher has seen this all before - she knows what to do to distract your child's attention away from you leaving, but he or she can only do so if you actually go.

Whatever you do, don't cry or otherwise get emotional on front of your child on his first day at school. He will be absolutely fine on his own as long as he doesn't see his mum or dad in tears. As soon as he sees one of you crying he will become anxious and confused and he may start crying himself. After all, how scary must this new place be if it can make her mum or dad cry?

It's perfectly natural to shed a tear or two when depositing her at school for her first day. Just make sure you save those tears for when you're in the car or otherwise well out of view of your child and his classmates.

You Determine Their Success

One of the main reasons why I care so little about sending my kids to the 'best' schools is because nothing is going to be a bigger determinant of their educational success than what happens at home.

In my hometown people will pay hundreds of thousands more for homes in the right school zones just so they can send their kids to the best schools, when it's often a complete waste of money.

Your child can (and probably will) do poorly at an excellent school if they don't have sufficient support at home. Conversely she can excel at an average school as long as he's well supported at home.

You determine her success, not your postcode.

Here are some tips on how to provide an environment that is conducive to her success at school:

- Protect her from bullies and from bullying (see below).
- Demonstrate a positive attitude to education in the household. Reinforce the message that she is going to need a good education if she's going to be able to make choices in her life. She needs to hear this before she starts school - we should all *just know* how important an education is.
- Make schoolwork at home fun, but don't make it optional. If they have homework or project assignments then these should be completed before they have time for distractions. Don't become the homework Nazi, but also don't allow them to wait until the day before it's due before they complete it. See below for specific homework tips. This may mean that you have to let them off some of their chores from time to time - I'd suggest that homework should have a higher priority if it comes down to it. Your child will learn a lot more from her homework than she will from doing the dishes.
- Read to your children and encourage them to read regularly (see previous chapter). Make books available, take them to the library regularly.

- Talk to your child - bring up topics that are interesting and educational. When she asks you questions that you can't answer then encourage her to research them for herself, with your assistance if needed. These days all you have to do is pass her your smartphone and she can start researching an answer to that question *instantly*.
- Regularly ask her how things are going at school and work hard to get through the superficial 'good' you normally get when you ask them how school's going. Be supportive always - she might find it hard to tell you about things that are bothering her, so make sure you don't fly off the handle.
- Make practicing spelling and multiplication tables a game (as discussed in the previous chapter). Play this game often. Also, get them to play educational games, such as Sudoku and crosswords, which can really get them thinking.
- If your child needs specific help then make sure she gets it. Kids with sight or hearing difficulties, emotional or learning difficulties may need professional assistance to help them achieve in the classroom. Teachers won't always pick up on problems, so stay on the lookout for signs that your child might be struggling in one area or another.
- Promote gritty behaviour (see previous chapter). Encourage your child to be a self-starter and to work toward long-term goals.

It's not good enough to leave educating your kids to the schools. You have to take a hands-on approach and this does require work on your part.

Homework

As your child gets older she's likely to bring more and more homework home with her.

At my kids' school this starts with simple reading assignments at entry level (5 years of age) and progresses to a greater quantity of more advanced homework by the time they're 10.

Some schools don't believe in sending kids home with homework at all.

Ideally they shouldn't be doing more than a couple of hours of homework per week. If your child's school is consistently giving her more than that then have a chat to them about it - there may be a good reason why they're doing so. If not then ask them to consider scaling the workload back a bit - excessive amounts of homework doesn't help kids - it only discourages them.

Helping your child with her homework can be a thankless and downright painful process. If there's any time that you're likely to get attitude from your child this is it. She's likely to be tired and grumpy and frustrated that she can't solve the problems on her own. This can result in a rapid, short-term deterioration of the relationship between father and child as you get increasingly frustrated that she can't understand what you're explaining to her ('it's almost like you're ignoring me on purpose!') and she withdraws further and further into her shell.

Don't let it happen - you don't want a stalemate. It's not going to help her get her homework done and it's not going to help you to get it all over and done with.

When you're helping her with her homework, remember to always keep it light. If she gets grumpy or snaps at you then don't bite back - cut her some slack and concentrate on helping her to get through it. Remember that she'll learn absolutely *nothing* from you telling her to think harder or to try harder. It may not look like it, but she's trying - she's not sitting there frustrating herself on purpose. If she's stuck then help her out of the hole:

- Make homework a habit. A no arguments, no negotiations, 'I don't care if Mike's mother lets Mike play video games before he's done his homework' habit. This is an important habit of a lifetime.
- If she hits the wall then call it a day. Homework is usually done at night, which is the worst possible time to be doing it.

Your child will be tired after a big day at school and she may have a lot more trouble concentrating than she would do in the morning. Don't flog the dead horse - if she's obviously struggling to function then congratulate her for giving it a go and get her off to bed. I often find that my kids sometimes finish homework in minutes in the morning, despite getting nowhere with it the night before.

- Restrict time-wasting activities. Video games, TV and wasting time on the web are productivity killers. Limit the amount of time your kids can spend on them and then only allow them time on these after they've finished their homework.
- Provide an appropriate area for them to work in. It should be relatively quiet and free from distractions.

Support, Don't Undermine Teachers

Teachers do a tough job. It's appalling how underpaid and undervalued they are in our society given that we entrust them to care for and teach our precious offspring for so much of their lives.

As well as managing a classroom full of kids teachers also have to manage the demands of parents, including those who are regularly unhappy with one or more aspects of how the teacher is doing their job.

Let's be clear that no teacher is perfect and some are better than others.

Unless the teacher is *really* out of line, however, you should generally let them get on with their jobs and not undermine them.

If your child complains to you about the teacher then listen carefully, but encourage her to think about how she might sort the issue out herself. You should only intervene if she's unable to do so and if it sounds like the teacher is being really unreasonable.

Don't badmouth the teacher, to your child, to other parents or to anyone else. Even if you're upset with them, you don't want to escalate the situation. Your child still has to sit in his or her classroom, after all.

This is your opportunity to show your child how to resolve issues calmly and in a friendly manner.

Ask the teacher for a quiet chat and discuss the issue with them in a dispassionate way. Listen to what they have to say and then focus on how you can work together to solve the problem. He or she may have a different perspective on the issue than you, but that's OK. You're talking to them so you can solve the problem, not so you can win an argument.

Get Involved at School

Your kid's school is always going to need volunteers for something or another and most schools encourage parents to attend assemblies and special events.

I could never find the time needed to participate in the PTA or serve on the school's board of trustees, but I do volunteer to help with the annual school fair and I make a point of coming to at least a few other events each year, including school camp, etc. My wife volunteers for a lot more.

Try and volunteer and attend as much as you are able.

Sure it may be difficult to find time off work to attend their school camp (or whatever else is on) but these events are a great opportunity to spend time with your kids while they're in their element. It's also a great opportunity to get to know their teachers and the other parents.

Exercise

Between the ages of 5 and 12 your child should have, at minimum, an hour of exercise each and every day of the week.

An hour per day.

It is not her responsibility to ensure that she gets an hour of exercise per day - it's yours.

Unfortunately most kids in Western countries get a lot less than this and this can be catastrophic to their physical and emotional development and to their ongoing health.

Child obesity is on the rise and adult obesity is at epidemic proportions.

The single most effective thing you can do to help your child to avoid becoming part of this epidemic is to ensure that she has at least an hour of exercise per day. She may get exercise at school, but it is not her school's responsibility to make sure she does so, so don't rely on the school to meet this quota.

It couldn't be starker or simpler, but how much exercise does your child get per day? Be honest with yourself. Think through her entire week and think about was exercise she's had over each of the previous seven days.

If you're reading this and finding yourself justifying her lack of regular exercise (e.g. 'It's impossible for my child to get an hour of exercise per day - our family is too busy') then stop. There's no copping out on this. Her physical and emotional health cares nothing for your excuses.

Yes, it's true that it can be busy to fit exercise into our busy schedules, but there are opportunities *everywhere* to introduce more exercise into her, and your, routine. The previous chapter contains just a few ideas about how to get your child to exercise more - use these and your own to make sure it happens.

Diet

Your child's appetite will increase significantly as they get older - be prepared for this and make sure there's plenty of healthy food available so no one's tempted by fast food.

You need to have a steady supply of fresh fruit, vegetables seeds and nuts for them to snack on. This can be expensive, but it is important that they learn to eat fruit and vegetables as their first choice. They should never be allowed to snack on biscuits, sweets, crackers or other high-calorie, low-nutrition options.

In our house we make our own hummus, which is quick and easy. The kids love to dip carrot, celery and cucumber sticks into it - delicious and nutritious.

Be prepared for them to come home ravenous from school, particularly as they may have been too busy or too picky to eat all of their school lunch. It's not such a good idea to tell them to wait for their dinner - their concentration would likely suffer, as would their behaviour. It's better to feed them something nutritious and spoiling their dinner just a little bit than to leave them gnawing at their belts until dinner time.

If your kids have after school activities (and won't come straight home after school) then consider taking plenty of food with you when you pick them up from school. If someone else is picking them up then pack something they can carry in their schoolbags for eating after school - they'll get a lot more out of their activity if they're not starving.

School Lunches

Ahh... school lunches. Probably the only meal that your little treasure regularly eats without you, meaning they can be as picky as they like.

Your child should be making her own lunch from about the age of 7. You can step in to help on particularly stressed mornings, but she should make her own lunch on other days. If you have more than one child then they should take turns at making lunches for each other (i.e. one child makes everyone's lunches each day).

This is really important - it teaches them about time management, nutrition and working in the kitchen.

Although they are responsible for making lunches from an early age, you remain responsible for making sure they have a nutritious lunch every day - right through childhood and into their teenage years.

Yes, into their teens.

You may be able to trust your teen to look after her younger siblings, but she may not be trusted to pack a healthy lunch each day.

For our kids a healthy lunch comprises a sandwich and fresh fruit, with occasional nuts, raisins, yoghurt or carrot sticks. They have excellent compartmentalised plastic lunchboxes that can be used to keep all of the components of their lunch separate. They even put hummus into them sometimes.

Thankfully their primary (elementary) school does not have a tuck shop (kiwi for 'school cafeteria'), so there was no pressure for us to allow them to buy lunch at school between the years of 5 and 11.

But isn't it mean to not let them buy lunch?

Absolutely not. They eat enough junk food and treats outside of school. My kids are hardly deprived, and hopefully neither are yours.

If your kids' school has a tuck shop then you may decide to allow them to buy their lunch once per week, but no more than that.

Here's another shocker - they *don't need treats* in their lunchboxes either! No muesli bars, fruit bars or other confectionary that's packaged and marketed as if it's health food. We get pressure from our kids to give them as many treats as their friends get (or supposedly get), but we resist - we explain how important it is for them to limit their intake of junk food (including junk food that's marketed as 'healthy') and over time they have taken this to heart.

If you want to give them a treat then why not bake something for them to take with them? At least then you can choose a recipe that's at least a little nutritious and they can help you make it.

Bliss balls are a particular favourite in our household. They're raw and full of healthy ingredients, but they look and taste like treats. They are high in calories, but they're really nutritious and filling.

Yes, you will have more trouble getting your kids to eat healthy options. It goes without saying that they'd rather eat sweets and cakes than sandwiches and carrot sticks. But this does not mean you should start cramming their lunchboxes with junk food to ensure they'll eat *something*.

Our kids' primary school does not allow kids to throw anything out at lunchtime - all of their rubbish has to go back into their lunchbox to be brought home after school. This means they're unable to throw out uneaten food at school and we can see exactly what they have and haven't eaten when they get home.

If they've given it a good effort and have eaten most of their lunch then they're allowed to throw the rest out when they get home and they're allowed healthy snacks. Otherwise they have to finish their lunch before they're allowed anything else.

This is an effective way of reducing food waste but, more important, it also sends our kids the strong message that they will eventually eat their lunch - whether it's at school or at home.

This encourages them to eat what they have at school, even if they'd rather something else.

Discipline

Between the ages of 5 and 12 your approach to discipline should pretty much be a continuation of what we learned in the previous chapter, although as they get older you need to be ready to give them more and more responsibility and leeway.

By the time they are in their teens your child will be too old for timeouts and other such corrective techniques. A teenager is a young adult and, although she will still have a lot of maturing to do at 13, you don't humiliate an adult by sending her on a timeout.

During this period, therefore, you will gradually phase out the corrective techniques that have served you so well in the past and replace them with something even more powerful: adult expectations.

In this section we move beyond sticker charts and similar reward schemes that are better suited to younger children (up until the age of 7 or so) to using techniques that are more appropriate for them as they approach their teenage years.

Give Them Your Time

Remember that your child needs food, sleep and your time. If you find that she's getting on your nerves and may very well drive you crazy then ask yourself 'is the problem her, or me?'

If you've not given her enough of your time then it's the latter.

Remember that your time and attention is her birth right, not a privilege that she can lose for misbehaving.

Parents Back Each Other Up

It is vitally important that you and your partner back each other up and that you are both consistent with rules and your general approach to discipline.

You should **never undermine each other**. It's often tempting to rush in and be the 'good guy' when one of your kids is in trouble (i.e. in trouble with your partner) or vice versa. This does not help your child, in fact it's guaranteed to make matters worse. Examples of undermining your partner can include:

- Stepping in to protect your child when she's being reprimanded or punished by your partner. This excludes scenarios where your partner is becoming abusive, which of course you'd step in to prevent.
- Criticising your partner on front of your child, particularly when she's disciplining your child. Even cracking wisecracks (e.g. 'yeah, like that's going to stop her from misbehaving...') can be really harmful.
- Developing an 'exclusive' relationship with your child, for example casting knowing looks at each other, sighing and rolling your eyes when your partner says something or anything else designed to invalidate your partner in the eyes of your child.
- Going behind your partner's' back to console your child when she's on a timeout or after being reprimanded. This is not a time for either of you to step in - let her serve her time and/or cool off. If your child wants to talk about it afterward then encourage her to do so, but make sure your partner is in the room also so you're not undermining her.
- Saying 'yes' when your partner has already said 'no' (or vice versa). If you don't agree with your partner then ask her if you can discuss it with her privately. Come to an agreement and then let your child know. If you've jointly decided to overturn the decision then your partner should tell your child so it's clear that *she* (your partner) has changed her mind. Otherwise you should tell your child that the decision stands so it's clear that you're backing your partner up.

Undermining each other creates tension between you and your partner. Your child will feel this acutely. She will instinctively feel as if she's the cause of the conflict - she will feel responsible and this will be stressful for her. It will make her feel like she has to pick sides. It can also make your child resentful at one of you if she feels that one parent is stricter than the other.

It will also cause confusion and uncertainty about what the rules are. Although she may be chuffed to get one over mum or dad when the other parent leaps to her defence, it is going to leave her uncertain of what the rules are in the long term, creating anxiety that she may break the rules and find herself at trouble at any time.

When you undermine each other you also alienate yourself from your partner and, by extension, from your child. At very least this will leave one or both of you feeling hurt and betrayed. It's also likely to create a simmering resentment between the two of you.

You end up blaming each other for this tension while your child continues to blame herself. Everyone can end up resenting everyone else, even if this isn't verbalised.

So don't do it. Don't undermine each other. Support each other in a positive and friendly way. *Even if you're divorced and/or estranged.* You might hate each other's guts (I hope not), but that's no excuse for your child to be stuck in the middle.

Don't Be Sorry for their Misbehaviour

You should never be reluctant to apologise to your child if you've done something wrong. Let's say you ate the chocolate she was saving (I've been there), stepped on her favourite toy and broke it (done that too) or even forgot to pick her up from school (guilty as charged - the school office rang with all four of them standing there waiting for their dad to come and get them).

It doesn't undermine our authority by apologising to our children if we've done something wrong. It teaches our kids that, just because you're an adult, it doesn't mean you don't make mistakes. It shows them that we're not afraid to acknowledge our mistakes and to make amends for them.

What we should never apologise for, however, is our child's misbehaviour.

Don't apologise if you send her on a timeout (or dispense some other form of punishment) and don't apologise when she returns. You don't need to tell her you still love her - this will only send mixed messages. You tell her you love her several times a day (right?!?) - she knows it. Yelling out 'I still love you' when she's off for a timeout is just apologising in a more insipid way.

She was punished because she misbehaved. She will have received a warning or (if the transgression was more serious) she would have known very well that what she was doing was going to get her into trouble.

You don't need to explain yourself or make amends as a result. If she pouts after being punished then *ignore it* and she will soon learn that pouting gets her nowhere.

If you feel you must explain why she was punished then don't start the sentence with an apology (e.g. 'I'm sorry that I had to send you on a timeout, but...') As soon as you apologise you are assuming the guilt for her transgression. Suddenly it's not your child who's done wrong - it's her mean dad who put her on a timeout for no valid reason.

When you apologise for punishing her fairly then you are absolving her of responsibility for her actions and you're undermining your own authority.

There is one exception here - if you lose your cool and/or you punish your child too harshly then it is entirely appropriate that you acknowledge this with her and, if appropriate, apologise.

If you've blown your top and you're still angry then that is **not** the time to apologise. Both of you should have time apart until you've both had time to calm down and to regain some perspective. Remember that it is never, never ok to abuse your children, no matter how angry you're feeling, so diffuse the situation if you find yourself getting angry in the first place.

If you've acted unfairly then wait until everyone is cool and calm again. Take your child aside and talk to her eye to eye. Kneel down if you need to so you're not standing over her - you don't want to intimidate her while you're apologising.

Explain that you don't condone her behaviour but that you lost your temper and that you shouldn't have done what you did (e.g. shout, swear, whatever). Tell her that you're very sorry and that you won't do it again. Tell her you love her and ask her if you can have a hug (don't force her - she may need to get over it herself).

Finish by asking her how she feels, but don't let it turn into another argument - her feelings are valid no matter if you agree with them or not (they are *hers*, after all).

Punish Only Some of the Time

We have a range of options at our disposal for punishing bad behaviour. For instant punishment the timeout should be our go-to. Other punishments can include early bedtimes, reduction (or full loss of) pocket money, loss of screen time privileges or, for particularly bad behaviour, being grounded completely (i.e. all of the above!)

Punishment should be the exception, however, and not the rule. This is the hardest lesson that I've had to learn as a parent - and I'm still learning it.

We shouldn't punish our kids (or threaten punishment) every time we're displeased which, let's face it, can be often. We also shouldn't be overly strict, which is my ongoing challenge.

Punishment should only be used as a last resort and/or when bad behaviour is intentional and needs to be corrected. Punishment should not be used to suppress your child's childlike behaviour - she still needs to be a child.

Your child should get her pocket money *most weeks*. She should only be sent to bed early a small percentage of the time. She should only be grounded on very rare occasions. You get the picture.

I can tell you this from experience - it is too easy to slip into the habit of being overly strict, as we often don't realise we've been too hard on them until much, much later. Often too late to do anything about it.

Here are some pointers to help you be firm but fair (and friendly):

- Don't get in the habit of using your 'grumpy dad' voice excessively. I sometimes do this without realising - I'll come home and start barking out orders and talking way too loud. I often only realise when one of the kids asks me why I'm so grumpy at them.
- Find opportunities for them to 'earn it back'. Remember your primary goal is to promote good behaviour, so look for opportunities to relax or even reverse every punishment. This will encourage them to correct their own behaviour over time - if they know they can earn their punishment back they are much more likely to try to do so.
- Don't make a point of punishing your kids for show. Some dads tend to be stricter on their children in public to demonstrate their alpha maleness. This is lame and just makes everyone awkward. Don't be one of those dads.
- Remember to praise more than to punish. Don't fall into the habit of only recognising them when they annoy you or soon that's all they'll be doing.
- Don't make punishments ridiculous. Taking away pocket money for a week is **just as effective** as taking it away for a year. A timeout can be even more effective under the right circumstances, as it's instant and direct. Don't compound punishments - it's ineffective.

Rewards and Bribes

As your child gets older you need to think more and more about how to motivate her with rewards (for doing well) rather than punishment for not meeting expectations of behaviour.

This is not to say that you should feel compelled to offer a reward for everything that she is asked to do. This won't work - the last thing you want is for her to ask 'what will I get if I do this?' each time you ask her to do something.

Here lies the important distinction between *rewards* and *bribes*.

Rewards are discretionary and are awarded for good behaviour or for excelling at a given task. The most common type of reward is, of course, your praise and appreciation - you should never underestimate the value and importance of this. This type of intangible reward should be dispensed regularly and liberally.

Rewards are generally awarded after the fact, or at least after they've started doing whatever it is you'd like to reward them for.

For example, if she tidied her room without being asked, did her homework without complaining or otherwise did something exceptional then you can offer her a reward after completion. If she undertakes something more significant then you might want to offer her a reward, awardable upon completion, to help motivate her to complete it.

One day one of my daughters decided she was going to work through a book of math problems, just for the fun of it. It was a big book - it was covered entire school syllabus for the year ahead of her (she was in year 3, this book covered year 4) and, although it was designed for self-study, it was a major undertaking.

Wanting to encourage and reward this behaviour I offered her $50 to spend on anything she likes (except food - more on this later) upon completion.

I didn't truly believe she'd finish it, but she did. She hacked away at it off and on for months, even returning to fix mistakes along the way (I marked it as she went).

It was the best $50 I ever spent. Would she have finished the book if I hadn't offered her the reward? Possibly. I'll never know. What was important, however, was that she started doing something exceptional of her own volition *and managed to complete it.*

The most common reward you should give your children is your praise. It's too easy to only notice and comment on bad behaviour sometimes. Remember to praise your child when she's being good, *especially* if your other children are not behaving themselves. Instead of rewarding the misbehaving child with your attention, heap praise on the child who is behaving herself - the others will notice and will quickly emulate her behaviour in attempt to earn your praise also.

When they start behaving better then praise them too, but don't forget about the child who was behaving in the first place.

Bribes are different to rewards. They comprise cash or other desirable items that you offer your child to do something, or to stop doing something. For example 'I'll give you these lollies if you clean your room' or 'I'll give you a dollar if you stop annoying your brother'.

We don't offer or pay bribes. Not ever.

Excessive Sulking

In this section we refer to sulking is the practice of feigning sadness, sickness or injury to elicit the sympathy of others. It's often used to avoid participation in a group activity, such as sports.

It's insipid and, frankly, unattractive. It's the antithesis to grit.

Before we go any further, remember that your child can be genuinely upset about something. There's a fine line between them being sad and them sulking - be careful to make the distinction.

Adults, particularly the adults responsible for the group activity, feel responsible for the 'sulk'. They shower the sulk with attention and of course they allow the child to sit out the activity. The child gets to chill out while her peers engage in the activity. As an added bonus, they're rewarded with loads of attention.

Don't let your child be the sulk.

It's a form of tantrum and unless the behaviour is corrected, it takes hold and becomes an ongoing issue.

Minor cases of sulking can be addressed by simply ignoring the behaviour. When they sulk simply exclude them from the activity and continue having fun. Praise the children who aren't sulking and comment on what fun you're having with them. The sulk will usually get the message pretty quickly and will return to the activity. Welcome them in immediately - there should be no punishment for sulking, just congratulations for getting over it and re-joining the group.

In all cases they should be required to join in with the activity or sit it out quietly on their own with nothing else to occupy their time. Don't give a sulking child anything to eat or your cell phone to play with while other kids are engaged in the activity - they should be required to join in or nothing.

If sulking becomes an ongoing issue then it indicates that your child is getting the attention she desires by sulking. Think about your behaviour and what you can do to correct this.

If your child becomes a persistent sulker then don't get worked up about it, but you will need to intervene to put a stop to it. The next time they sulk, just casually ask them where it hurts, give them a hug and tell them they can either participate in the activity or go home to bed.

If they choose the latter then call their bluff. Take them home to bed. Even if it's the middle of the day.

Tell them that, if they feel so bad then they need to go home for a lie down. Take them home and give them one.

Don't argue with your child about whether they are injured/unwell or not - this just gives them the drama they are seeking. By taking her home and putting her to bed you are demonstrating that sulking will result in a negative outcome for her.

It should never get to this - if a child is faced with the choice of re-joining the group or going home to bed then she will usually choose to re-join the group. In this case you may need to use this technique on several different occasions to make it clear that sulking will result in her being taken home to bed. As long as you're consistent she should get the message pretty quickly.

Remember that, once you've told her what the outcome will be if she continues to sulk (i.e. going home to bed) you need to be ready to follow through with it.

It can also pay to set out your expectations prior to the event. If you're taking your child to dance practice then before you arrive tell her that you expect her to get through the class without crying or having to stop. Explain that minor injuries are part of any physical activity and that, if she gets one, she needs to suck it up and get on with it, just like everyone else. Condition her to be gritty.

Do be careful not to ignore real injuries for obvious reasons. Also, there's no point in telling your child to suck it up while they're sulking - doing so is only likely to create more drama as they try to convince you of the unbearable pain of their unseen injury.

Finally, recognise sulking for what it is, but never call your child a 'sulk' or refer to their behaviour as 'sulking' - the connotations are too negative.

Bullies

Dealing with bullies and with bullying behaviour is a real problem. Your child has every right to enjoy their school years, not to mention their lives, without being harassed, intimidated or humiliated by bullies.

But dealing with bullies can be so darn difficult.

Often your children won't tell you about bullying behaviour at school. This may be because they're embarrassed by it, or they may be afraid of what the bully will do to them in retaliation for dobbing them in.

As a parent it can be difficult to know when and how to intervene. You don't want to have to swoop in and solve all of your child's problems, after all. Also, you might not be completely confident that you're getting the full story about what's going on.

Bullies usually use their superior size or strength to intimidate and/or to harm others, but bullies aren't always bigger than your child. In fact, it can be difficult to even identify bullies at school, as they could be smaller and sometimes even younger than those they're bullying.

Bullying doesn't always have to have an element of physical threat or physical violence. Emotional harassment can be just as bad, if not worse, and can be dished out by bullies who are smaller and weaker than those they're bullying.

These days most schools do an excellent job of identifying and stamping out bullying, but it can be difficult to stamp it out entirely. Also, not all bullying happens at school - your child may be bullied at their sports club or even by their own friends.

Unfortunately we tend to leave our kids woefully unprepared for dealing with bullies. We tell them that the best response to bullies is to 'walk away', but this is bollocks. If your child is being bullied then walking away from the situation only encourages the bully to keep tormenting her. It provides positive reinforcement to the bully that their campaign of intimidation is working and that they can continue to make your child's life a misery without having to worry about the consequences.

So what do we do? Do we do anything? Isn't being bullied part of life - don't we all need a bit of bullying to harden us up?

No, bullying isn't an acceptable part of life and it does not 'harden us up'. In fact, quite the opposite.

Bullying is extremely detrimental to both the bullied **and** the bully. In fact, the bully usually suffers worse psychological damage as a result of bullying as his or her victims.

Bullying should not be tolerated and it doesn't need to be. To know how to deal with it, first we have to understand a bit more about bullies.

You see, although not all bullies share common physical characteristics, they all have one key trait in common - all bullies are cowards.

Think about it - bullies will only *ever* pick on kids who they see as weaker as they are. No bully in his or her right mind is going to walk up to a much larger/older child and try and push them around. They'd get their arses handed to them and they know it. Bullies will only ever pick on kids who they think are weak.

So the first step to preventing your child from being bullied is to remind them how strong they are. Prepare them for the fact that they are going to encounter bullies from time to time (and not just at school), but that they have nothing to fear, as all bullies are cowards. Explain this to them often - drill it into them until they know it to be true.

Explain that bullies only ever pick on those who they think are weaker and that they should always stand up to bullies. Explain that standing up to bullies does not mean fighting with them - she should use her words and her actions to show the bully that she is not to be trifled with.

If a bully tries to intimidate your child then she should scream at him, *scream*, that he's a bully and that she's going to tell the teacher and her dad and that the bully has to stay away from her. By this stage the bully is already regretting his decision to mess with your offspring, but it's only going to get worse for him. She should then go straight to a teacher and report the behaviour. She should also report it to you and you should ask the school what they are doing to address the situation (remember to be supportive of the school - it's not just your child who they have to look after).

This alone is probably enough to stop your child from being bullied. Explain this to your child before she needs to use this technique. Increase her confidence and increase the likelihood that she'll actually use this technique if the time comes.

But shouldn't your child worry about retribution? Thankfully, no.

Remember that bullies are cowards. Once her bully has had his fingers burnt from messing with your child, he won't want to go back there in a hurry. If he does then she should repeat the technique above and this time you probably need to see the school taking a harder stand with the child in question.

The beauty of this approach is that not only will this bully not mess with your little princess again - the rest of the bullies at school (cowards all) will recognise her as someone not to be messed with and they will stay well away from her.

But she shouldn't stop there. She should also use this technique to help others.

You see bullies can only be bullies when everyone around them enables their behaviour.

In the schoolyard this means that kids often ignore the fact that others are being bullied. Usually this is out of fear for their own safety and it means that the bully can intimidate others without fear of being caught. To make matters worse, other kids will often find it entertaining when other kids are being bullied, so not only will they not do anything to prevent it, they'll cheer the bully along, adding to the bullied child's humiliation.

This is where your kids come in. They should not only stand up for *themselves* when bullied, but they should also stand up for others, regardless of whether they know them or not. Your child should use the exact same technique as above - including the shouting, telling a teacher and telling you. She should make it loud and obvious, for the same reasons that she should make it loud and obvious when she's being targeted herself.

This will help some other child avoid being bullied, which is great, but that's not the only reason why you're going to teach her to do this.

By standing up to those bullying others your child is not only demonstrating that she is not to be messed with, she is demonstrating that no one in her *vicinity* is to be messed with either.

The psychology of this is very powerful. By protecting those around her she is protecting herself. She is breaking the illusion that all of the other bystanders are, by virtue of their inaction, supporting the actions of the bully. As a result the bully's power over the assembled, the power of intimidation and silence, will crumble.

She is, in effect, building a safe zone around herself that bullies will be much too cowardly to breach.

Notes on bullies and bullying:

- Your child can be a bully too. Explain to her from an early age what bullying is and how important it is that she doesn't bully others. Proactively monitor for signs of her bullying others and don't tolerate this behaviour if you find it.
- From their pre-teens, kids can go through cycles where one or more members find themselves ostracised from their group of friends for some perceived infraction or another. This is usually short lived, but it is hurtful and if is a form of bullying. Prepare your child for this - encourage her to have the confidence to defy the mob and to remain friends with the ostracised one. Tell her that it may happen to her someday too and that it's not a reflection of her and she shouldn't let herself be bothered by it. The best way to handle it is to ignore it completely - starve the mob of drama and conflict and it will soon find some other poor sod to target.

- Teach your kids to befriend others who are being bullied **as well as the bully himself**. The bully is a person, after all, and his behaviour is likely to be the manifestation of problems that he has elsewhere, such as in the home. Teach your child to be the bigger person and that they should always seek to move on from conflict as quickly as possible.
- Teach your children self-defence. Not so they can use it, but so they have the confidence that they could protect themselves if they had to and so they are less intimidated by larger/stronger bullies. Self-defence lessons are a great way to stay fit while learning skills that will last a lifetime. My children all do Kung Fu and this makes them *less* likely to engage in physical violence than other kids their age.

Putting Them to Work!

Other parents usually scoff when I tell them this, but it is my firm belief that all kids *want* to work.

Not work in a sweatshop making shoes or that kind of thing - they all want to be useful around the house. They want to contribute.

Often we discourage them from helping or from offering to help. We may be busy emptying the dishwasher or cooking dinner when they ask if they can help, but we say 'no' because we're too busy. Too busy for them to help!

When they're younger this 'help' is often anything but. They can slow you down, make a mess and basically just get in the way of whatever busywork we're doing. On the other hand, we also often avoid asking them for help because they're likely to object and we convince ourselves that there's less work involved in just doing it ourselves.

These are mistakes, as all kids want to contribute, even if they complain about it at the time. They want to participate in running the household, not to be a guest in it.

Although, initially, their efforts at helping often cause us more work than they save us, this isn't the case for long. Kids are more capable than you might think and they're keen studies. Be careful not to set unrealistic expectations, however - your child is probably not going to complete tasks to your own personal standards, no matter how many times you explain how you like something done.

So if your kids ask if they can help then try and let them. It gives them an opportunity to spend time with you and to feel useful. Praise their efforts and be really appreciative - before you know it you'll have other volunteers lining up to get in on the action.

Giving Them Jobs

As well as allowing your kids to help when they ask, you should also give them light duties around the house that are suitable to their age and abilities. These should be regular tasks that are not optional.

The Manual

They're otherwise known as 'chores', but I prefer to use the word 'jobs' when talking to the kids, as 'chores' has such negative connotations.

From about four years of age your child is capable of making her bed and tidying her room each day, as well as dressing herself and at least trying to brush her hair on her own.

When it comes to tasks like tidying her room she can quickly feel overwhelmed and find the task too difficult to complete (or even to start). Avoid a stalemate - help her if she gets stuck, but only if she's helping too. Try and keep it light and make it fun - you don't want her jobs to become miserable.

By the time she's five she should be able to feed the pets and make her own breakfast, although she may need a bit of help at first, or if handling the microwave, etc. Teach her how to stay safe around the kitchen, including how to use the toaster, which cutlery and other utensils she's able to use, etc. Give her increasing autonomy in preparing her breakfast - as long as she's had proper instruction (and the odd reminder about being safe) she can be trusted.

By the time she's seven she should be able to make her own lunch and empty the dishwasher.

Be careful not to overload them with work in the mornings, but each child should have one or two jobs to do, as well as getting themselves ready, each morning before school. These jobs should be automatic and should become part of their morning routine (see below). There should be no discussion about whether they're doing them each day and no ambiguity about who's doing what. It's a good idea to put up a roster if they have different jobs each day so there's no confusion.

You're likely to be pleasantly surprised at how capable your kids are and how helpful to you their participation is. More important, you are teaching them skills that will last them a lifetime - not just the practical skills (like how to prepare food, look after animals, empty the dishwasher, etc.) but they're also learning to *not be lazy*.

Too many kids grow up not doing jobs around the house and this continues into adulthood. They end up moving out of home without the skills they need to look after themselves or to participate in the running of their household.

You should be careful not to become a tyrant - you may need to jump in and help them some mornings or let them off their jobs altogether (particularly if they have homework to do or something else that consumes their time). Jobs should also be fun - if they complain about doing them then don't browbeat them with tales of how bad you had it as a child (and how soft they have it now). Crack jokes with them and offer to help them (if they agree to laugh at your jokes, of course).

Refusal to perform their jobs shouldn't be an option for them and as long as you're consistent you won't find too much resistance on a daily basis.

Paying Them to Work

You have every right to expect your child to do her regular jobs, plus any small ad-hoc tasks you ask her to do from time to time, without payment. You should provide all children over the age of five with pocket money, as we discuss later in this chapter. But pocket money is not payment for doing her jobs around the house - we all do jobs to keep the household running for each other.

It is also completely acceptable to pay them for doing large or difficult jobs.

If your child wants you to buy them something then tell them that they must save up for it and give them a list of exceptional jobs that they can do to earn money

Don't expect perfection - their effort will vary based on their age. My 9 year old son cleaned every window of our house once - it took him hours and he did it with a bucket of water and a rag. By the time he was finished the windows were a cloudy mess, but it didn't matter.

I didn't expect him to learn how to properly clean the windows. What he learned was how to do a really big job from beginning to end on his own. Afterward, as he surveyed the windows in horror to see that they were all worse than when he started, he also learned something about cleaning windows. The next time he did it with a squeegee and the end result was a lot better.

But isn't paying your kids to do jobs like this inviting them to put their hands out every time you need them to do something?

Not really. I ask my kids to perform small tasks around the house all the time without the expectation of payment. They are genuinely useful and I make sure I thank and praise them when they do.

For larger tasks I believe they deserve a reward, so I give it to them. Most important, they are learning about working toward a goal and about doing hard work.

As with pocket money, all of the money they earn goes into their bank accounts, as we want to help them save toward their goal. Before a certain age kids can't be trusted with cash - it either burns a hole in their pockets (i.e. they end up blowing it on junk) or they lose it.

Morning Routine

It is vitally important that you have a structured, well understood morning routine.

Without a routine mornings are that much more stressful, you run a greater risk of being late to work and the kids can become miserable. No one wants to start the day yelling at their kids or being yelled at!

For a start either you or your partner need to be up early enough to make sure everything runs smoothly. You need to have enough slack in your morning routine that you can help the kids to finish their jobs, find their socks and do whatever else they need help with in the mornings. Every morning they throw you a new challenge - it's amazing what they come up with!

Next, lay down some ground rules that will help them get themselves ready on time and without forgetting anything. Here are some suggestions for weekday morning routine rules:

- Everyone has to be up by a certain time (in our house it's 7am).
- No screen time in the mornings. This will only distract them from getting ready. If they're ready early then they have to find something to do that doesn't involve a screen, as we don't want them distracting each other. Also, they're fresher and more vibrant in the mornings without screen time.
- They have to make breakfast as soon as they get up. My kids can be really hangry (hungry to the point of grumpiness) when they get up. Also, eating straight away gets their routine started on a good note.
- Nothing other than the routine until they're ready for school. Even homework has to wait until they're ready to go, including all jobs done.
- Everyone has to kiss mum and dad and say 'I love you' before they leave (or when they're dropped off at school). This is non-negotiable. We want this to be the last thing that we've all

said to each other before we go our separate ways for the day.

The morning routine works really well in our house - it's like a well-oiled machine. We can have rough mornings like everyone else, however, particularly if one or more of the kids is tired.

You have to use a mixture of toughness and tenderness on these tough mornings. If your child is having trouble finding her shoes, refusing to cooperate and the tears are flowing then take a moment to give her a hug, help her find those shoes and remind her that, if she's not ready on time you'll be sending her to bed early.

Avoid stalemates and confrontations - they'll just make your blood boil. Count her down once or twice and, if she fails to comply, reduce her bed time by 10 minutes each time. This should get her moving. If not then try waiting her out if you have time.

Otherwise you'll have to swallow your pride, help her get ready and get her into the car. Send her to bed early that night as promised - show her that her behaviour will have consequences. She will remember this the next time.

Kids should be in their routine well before their teens, including doing their jobs. You're likely to face much greater resistance from your teenagers when it comes to jobs (along with just about everything else), so make sure doing them is habit well ahead of time.

Celebrate Their Achievements

If you want to help your kids to be successful, if you want them to become gritty strivers, then you need to recognise and celebrate their achievements.

Every time they win 'player of the day', receive a certificate at school or even when they try extra hard at swimming practice - celebrate with them.

Make a big deal about it. Tell them how proud you are of them and *why* you're proud. Bring it up again at dinner and let the whole family join in the celebration of this latest achievement.

Always remember that the biggest reward that they can get is your approval and your delight in their achievements, so give them your time and attention!

I was once dismayed to see a fellow dad fail to even acknowledge his son when he proudly announced that he had won 'player of the day' at Saturday morning soccer. His father didn't even look up from his smartphone but mumbled something about 'every kid on the team gets that in turns - it just happens to be your turn this week' or something to that effect.

Don't be that dad. Yes, it is true that the kids on her soccer team may have turns in getting player of the day. They may also have turns at getting a certificate for achievement in class, but that is completely irrelevant.

They are there and they are trying and they deserve recognition for it.

The reason they have turns at getting 'player of the day' is because this motivates them to work harder.

It's a fact.

Even the kids who *know* that they take turns to win player of the day (there's always one who keeps track of who's won it so far and who's yet to win it) still want to win it desperately. They still want the recognition of their coach and peers and, most important, of their parents.

Some parents see this as celebrating mediocrity and believe that rewards should only be awarded for truly exceptional performance, such as scoring a hat trick, winning a race or coming first in a test, but this is complete and utter bullshit.

How many kids score a hat trick or win a race on any given day? When these kids do deliver a truly exceptional performance did they simply pull it out of the hat? Did they turn up to the game (or to class) and just decide they were going to be sublime?

Of course not. Every exceptional performance is the result of hard work. It's the product of countless mediocre performances before that.

Every kid started somewhere and, despite all of their hard work, not all of them are going to be able to excel in all areas, so don't wait for them to meet some ridiculous definition of excellence before rewarding them with your congratulations.

If they deliver a middling performance then don't let it pass, but don't be discouraging either. Let's say they were goofing off during a game or they were told off for messing around during class. Talk to them about it, but do so in the context of what they are doing well.

Statements like this:

'I really liked the way you were trying hard when you were paying attention, but there were times when you weren't paying attention and you need to work on that.'

Are much more motivating than statements like this:

'You weren't paying attention and you let the whole team down. It was a waste of my time coming to watch!'

So even when there is an element of 'bad' you need to celebrate the 'good'.

Although it's fine to take them out for an ice cream or for dinner to celebrate one achievement or another, be careful not to associate food or other tangible rewards with such achievements. This can be unhealthy from a dietary perspective, but more important it can substitute what they want most (recognition and validation from you and the rest of the family) with something that is less satisfying.

As an example, when my children were younger all four of them played soccer on Saturday mornings at the same club, so it was quite often that we'd be bringing at least one 'player of the day' certificate home after a morning on the mud. Those certificates all have a tear-off voucher for a free cheeseburger at McDonalds, but not one of them has ever been used.

This wasn't the result of a conscious decision on our part – my wife and I always agree to take the kids to McDonalds so they can redeem their vouchers, but it's never been important enough to them to even rip the vouchers off, let alone asking mum or dad to take them to redeem them.

When they win 'player of the day' the whole family congratulates them and me and my wife make a special effort to commend them on their performance - not just on this day, but on the days leading up to it. We focus on recognising their hard work over individual achievements. We focus on how they overcame adversity, such as how they were hurt but managed to play on, and other such 'gritty' behaviour.

When we get home the certificate goes on our 'achievement wall' where all of us can admire it.

Create an Achievement Wall

When your kids are awarded a certificate or some other form of recognition then this needs to be displayed prominently in your house for the whole family to see.

It's no good to celebrate their achievement only to then let the certificate get lost in a pile of papers somewhere, as this sends the message that it's not really that important after all. It's just a piece of paper.

In our house we have an Achievement Wall in our kitchen. There's no sign to designate it as such - just drywall that's been completely decimated over the years by drawing pins.

Every year, at the beginning of the year, we remove everything from the Achievement Wall and store it all away. From then on, whenever one of the kids comes home with a certificate or anything else that's noteworthy they are allowed to pin it to the wall (with our help if necessary to keep everything spaced out correctly) and we all congratulate them on a job well done.

This is an excellent idea for helping to maximise the sense of achievement that they derive from these awards - if they're hanging around in the kitchen they'll often admire their certificates and each other's and this helps motivate them to continue to work hard and do well.

Somewhere along the line they started pinning up school photos, team photos and the like. This happened organically and without prompting from me or my wife. At first we resisted, as the Achievement Wall was for achievements only, but we soon saw that they were as proud of the photos as they were of the certificates. We were celebrating their active participation, after all, and here they were in their photos, beaming smiles and bursting with pride - they're there and they're giving it a go. The photos stayed.

Pornography

Access to pornography and other objectionable content is a huge problem facing children and parents.

Objectionable content has been accessible via the internet since its inception, although until the advent of the smartphone it was relatively straightforward to prevent children from accessing it.

Prior to the smartphone the only practical method children had to access the internet was via PC's at home or at school. These machines are relatively easy to secure - there are lots of software programs available that can be used to block access to objectionable material.

The smartphone changed all that.

They can be used to access almost anything online, including the worst that the web has to offer. And, increasingly, everyone has one.

By the time your child reaches 13 most of her friends will have a smartphone, which creates huge pressure on you to get her one also.

Cost is no longer so much the issue - you can pick up a decent new smartphone for less than a hundred bucks these days. Mobile data plans are cheaper and free Wi-Fi can be found just about anywhere in urban areas.

Content, namely their access to content, is the issue.

Much of this content is hard-core and even violent. It's not harmless - exposure to it can be incredibly damaging to a young mind.

When kids view porn they aren't able to process what they're seeing. They become confused by it. It disturbs them. They can become embarrassed and even ashamed by what they've seen. It's not fair for them to be exposed to this kind of material and, prior to their teens, they can't be held responsible for doing so - they're too young to make informed decisions on whether it's safe to do so.

Hard-core pornography also has incredibly damaging effects to the development of your child's sexuality, how they see their bodies and their expectations around sex.

Often your child's school won't be of much help. Many of them don't want to deal with the complexities of children using, losing and stealing smartphones at school, so they ban them outright. At very least they take a 'your phone, your responsibility' stance, meaning that no effective smartphone policy exists at most schools.

You can install software onto all of the devices in the house to prevent them from accessing objectionable content and you must certainly should do so.

This will not prevent them being exposed to such content from devices belonging to others, however.

You can encourage other parents to install filtering apps onto their children's devices too - this can be effective if everyone participates, but some parents may choose not to (thinking that there's no way *their* precious child would ever engage in such behaviour). It can also be difficult to maintain the blanket of protection over time, as devices are replaced, kids find workarounds, etc.

The best defence against this type of objectionable content is education and empowerment.

Your child is going to be curious about anything that is forbidden or taboo. They will experience peer pressure to view content exposed to them by others and they may even show objectionable material to others for the notoriety and attention that it will bring them.

Preparation is key. Explain to your child early that there is lots of 'bad stuff' on the Internet that kids should not be looking at. Reassure her that it's unlikely that she will come across this kind of material during her normal use of the Internet and emphasise that she should never feel pressured to look at things that are inappropriate, even when her friends find it amusing (using language she'll understand, of course).

It is also worth explaining to your child that much of the objectionable content on the internet is the result of exploitation of people, usually the people in the images or clips themselves.

Yes, this is heavier, more serious subject matter than you'd otherwise like to discuss with your child and you'll need to be careful to get the timing right (i.e. time it for as late as possible, but before she becomes at risk of being exposed to objectionable content). Unfortunately the decision of whether we want to address this with our children has been made for us - they are going to be exposed to this material whether we like it or not. It's only a matter of time.

If they can empathise with the people on screen, however, then they are less likely to trivialise what they've seen. If they know that many actors are forced into prostitution and the creation of pornography by virtue of their situation then they are less likely to engage in laughing about it or sharing it.

Peer pressure is very strong in these situations and it only takes one child to object to what's being distributed to put an end to it.

Notes on reducing the risk of pornography and other objectionable material:

- Don't legitimise this type of material by being caught by your children with it. If you want to view porn then that's your prerogative, but they don't need to know about it and they certainly should never find it.
- Encourage them to be honest without fear of punishment. They're more likely to open up to you if they don't fear the outcome. Remember that their safety and the safety of the any other children who might come into contact with this type of material is paramount. They're too young to know better, so be cool about the situation and take it easy on them.
- Don't over-dramatise the situation. If your child or one of her friends is caught with objectionable material then take it seriously - discuss it with your child and other parents, etc., but don't make a big deal about it. Doing so will only increase the mystique and sensationalism around the event while stigmatising the offending child. That child deserves

protection too, no matter the circumstances of the event.
- Just about anything with a screen poses a risk. Including smartphones, web-enabled televisions, game consoles (including handheld game consoles). Think carefully about what you have around the house that could be used and consider how you'll keep your kids safe.
- Utilise technology. Use devices with parental controls, including controls already built in or using software that you install. Consider buying an Internet router that can filter traffic as it enters your home.
- Keep devices in well trafficked areas around the house. This not only reduces the likelihood of them accessing objectionable material, but also of them developing inappropriate relationships online (see below).
- When kids go to bed insist that their devices be deposited somewhere they can't use them (somewhere you can see them).
- Most important, demonstrate trust and remind them that you trust them to do the right thing. This may sound a bit rich after all this talk of preventing them from having the capability to access inappropriate content, but the fact is sooner or later they're going to see something that they're too young to be exposed to. Trust them to do the right thing and avoid watching them too closely.

Device Safety

By the age of 12 your child is likely to either have a smartphone or she soon will. With a smartphone comes new and varied threats to her safety.

As with other safety-related issues at this age, the best defence is a solid offence. You should start training your child for owning a smartphone (or other devices) well before she does so. The following safety rules (plus any that you may come up with) should be drummed into your child for at least a couple of years before she owns such a device.

Keep discussions about these rules light and friendly and invite your child to ask questions and to share her opinion, but remember to share this advice with her regularly so she's prepared for the responsibility that owning such a device brings.

- No risqué photos. Drum it into your children that they should never, ever take risqué or revealing photos of themselves or of others and they should certainly never share such photos. Explain that even adults fall into the trap of sending revealing photos to each other only to have those photos come back to haunt them when the relationship turns sour (or the recipient's phone is stolen, etc.)
Explain that, with the advent of digital photography and the Internet, photos are forever and they should protect themselves and their friends from harm by never allowing intimate photos to be created in the first place. Reassure them that if a member of the opposite sex (or anyone else) pressures them into taking and sharing intimate photos then that person, not your child, is in the wrong. She should be confident enough to flat-out refuse such a request and to cut communication the creep if he keeps pressuring her about it.
- No communication with adults. Notwithstanding trusted relatives, no adult should be communicating with your child except through you. Explain to your child that it is inherently

unsafe for any child to communicate with an adult who isn't a relative without a parent present.
- Encourage your child to be open and honest about their communication. Assure her that you will be open minded and not too inflexible (you'll need to back this up with action). Explain that communication is not something that should be covered up and that she should be suspicious of anyone who asks her to keep communication secret.
- Positively identify people before communicating with them. Explain that people aren't always who they claim to be when communicating via electronic mediums, such as SMS text messages, social media, etc. Explain the importance of positively identifying everyone she comes into contact with.
- Devices should be kept out of view when in public. They can invite muggings and harassment.

When preparing your child to be safe with devices it pays to relate this advice back to what we do as adults. Most of us would never dream of sending a dick pick to someone, as we know the embarrassment this would likely cause.

If your child understands that these aren't just rules for kids, bur are in fact rules that you follow yourself, then they are a lot less likely to reject them out of hand.

Storing Devices at Night

As recommended earlier in this section, everyone under the age of 16 should be required to turn their devices off and store them in a central location (e.g.in the kitchen where everyone can see them) each night.

Although you should offer leeway when mistakes have genuinely been made (e.g. phone left in car or school bag overnight) you should consider confiscating devices (for a day or so) that make their way into bedrooms at night.

Kids often lack the self-control to moderate their own smartphone use, particularly at night when they should be sleeping. There is also a higher risk of adverse encounters (such as discussions with older

Ben Gannon

boys) late at night.

Puberty

Like it or not your child is going to go through puberty. In girls this usually starts around the age of 11 and in boys around the age of 12, but it can start earlier or later for boys or girls.

Coming to terms with puberty can be hard for dads, as in some ways we want them to remain children forever. Although the onset of puberty isn't quite the end of innocence, it is a reminder that, before long, our little boys and girls will be all grown up.

Puberty affects all children differently and it can be a confusing and even worrying process for your child.

She (or he) will constantly compare her development with that of her peers. She may become anxious about whether her development is faster or slower than that of other girls her age.

Your child might be unlikely to talk openly about her questions or concerns with you out of fear of embarrassment.

She could be mortified at the thought of someone talking about or joking about her developing body, even if she appears to go along with the jokes. Children can be really cruel and it may be that she's getting teased at school (particularly if she's developing differently to her peers at the time).

So be sensitive.

But how do we avoid such subjects becoming taboo? The last thing we want is for everyone in the house to be too scared to talk about it. This will only increase your child's sense of embarrassment and discomfort about the ongoing changes to her body.

The trick is to desensitise the issue before puberty starts.

You should talk regularly with your prepubescent children about puberty and what they can expect. If you're bashful talking about breasts, pubic hair, etc. then get over it - your embarrassment will show and it will send your child the message that puberty is something to be embarrassed by.

Don't just tell her about how the human body changes and why, but also that everybody is different. Reassure her that her body is perfect and just the way it should be, no matter what stage of puberty she might be at.

Take time to talk about some of the more unfortunate aspects of puberty, such as acne, and how they affect everyone to varying degrees. Tell them (male and female children) about the human menstrual cycle and how women have periods.

Tell her that kids do tease each other about their changing bodies, but that this is a defence mechanism to hide their own insecurities (which it normally is). Encourage your kids to respond to such jokes with statements like 'actually, my body is just perfect the way it is and so is everyone else's'. She should not engage in tit for tat insults and you should encourage her to refrain from teasing others about their bodies or how they're developing.

Even better, encourage her to stand up for others who are being teased. This will not only help them avoid embarrassment, it will reduce the likelihood that she will be teased herself.

Once your child's body starts changing you should refrain from making comments on particular body parts unless she asks you about them or mentions them herself. If you suddenly notice that your child is developing breasts then resist the urge to point at them and say 'Look! You're growing boobies!' This will only cause her acute embarrassment. Instead wait a few minutes and try something like 'Wow, you're blooming into a beautiful young woman. You're getting so big and I bet your body is going through a lot of changes - how are you feeling about it all?'

If she doesn't want to talk about it then respect that.

If she does talk to your partner about her body but doesn't want to talk to you about it then learn to deal with it.

You can still be supportive and you can still ask her how she's doing from to time, but it's up to her how much or how little she wants to talk about it.

If she does mention a problem or ask you or your partner for help then give her your attention, assure her that whatever it is that she's having a problem with that it's perfectly normal and help her solve the problem.

When she starts developing breasts then either you or your partner should take her shopping for training bras.

Before she has her first period one of you should take her shopping for sanitary products.

Neither of you should be embarrassed about buying such products - if you are then it might be a good opportunity to get over yourself. You want to normalise the process of buying and using these products as much as possible. You want to let her choose the products - you may be paying, but she should be empowered enough to do the choosing. Just make sure you're ready to provide advice on products that she's unlikely to ever have used before - you need to know the difference between pads and tampons and what they're likely to want to use under various circumstances. She's also unlikely to want to use 'super heavy duty' tampons, but she might not know that yet.

Yes, she is much more likely to ask her mum for help with her period, but you still need to be prepared for the eventuality that she asks you. Mum might be away on business at the time, after all.

You don't need to be an expert in women's products, but if you have daughters then you need to make sure you have at least a basic knowledge of them. You can buy several different products and let her try them out at home, but you don't want to end up buying incontinence pads by mistake (which is what one particularly clueless friend of mine once did).

Also, remember that children aren't the best at planning ahead or replenishing things when they're finished. My kids couldn't change a toilet roll between the four of them!

It's up to you and your partner, therefore, to make sure she has a good supply of sanitary products. I recommend buying a couple of spare packets and hiding them away somewhere she doesn't know about (i.e. so she can't grab them without telling you). This is her emergency supply - just don't forget to replenish it after use!

Attention from Older Members of the Opposite Sex

Note - this section focuses on younger girls receiving romantic attention from older boys, as this is the most common scenario that we, as parents, are likely to be faced with. It is, of course, just as worrisome and dangerous if younger boys receive romantic attention from older girls, so the following advice should apply to all of your kids, male or female.

For a father of daughters, nature's decision to allow girls to blossom into adult form years before boys is particularly unhelpful. When you see a bunch of 12 - 14 year old girls and boys playing together you will see what I mean - the girls look significantly more advanced physically than boys their own age. In short, the girls are becoming women, while the boys still look like kids.

The girls are often no more emotionally mature than the boys - they just look more mature.

This is unhelpful, because it means that the girls increasingly attract the attention of older boys. Sometimes much older. This can cause discomfort for dads when the boys are a couple of years older. It can cause downright horror when they're older still.

This is also a problem for the parents of boys, as it is not fun to find out that your 16 - 17 year old (or older) boy is showing romantic interest in 12 year old girls (for example). By this age it's often too late to stop them.

To make matters worse, girls often notice how under-developed boys are at their age. Older boys seem more mature and worldlier. They certainly can seem more physically attractive.

Why is this important?

It's important because older boys are *much more* likely to pressure younger girls into sex than boys their same age. Girls in this situation may comply, even when they really don't want to, for fear of appearing to be immature or uncool. Even if they do want to, it's not healthy (or sometimes even legal) for either the boy or the girl in this situation.

In our house, until the kids are 18 we have a '+/-2 year' rule. No one in our house is allowed to have a boyfriend that is more than two years older than younger than them.

We're careful to explain to our kids that, until they're adults, romantic attention from older people (i.e. more than two years age difference) is unsafe. It's no good waiting until your child is 13 to tell her that it's unsafe for her to be romantically involved with an 18 year old boy.

You have to prepare her for this situation much earlier.

Prepare her for the fact that older boys will show an interest and that, while she should be flattered, older boys should really be interested in girls their own age. Explain that the law protects younger teens from adults for a reason and that she should be wary of anyone older than her who encourages her to be secretive about their relationship.

Preparing them for the Teenage Years

First, let's be honest. Nothing truly prepares you or your children for the teenage years.

Who knows what the fuck happened during human evolution to bring us the angst of teenagers. Whatever it was, it at least shows that Mother Nature has a sense of humour.

By the time you child is twelve the fires of teenage rebellion will already be lit and may even already be a raging inferno. Lucky you!

We look at strategies for parenting teenagers in the next chapter, but one of the secrets to parenting teens effectively is to start preparing them well in advance of them entering this turbulent stage of their lives.

Just like preparing her for puberty, preparing your child to be a teenager won't eliminate the confusion and angst of being a teenager, but it will help. A lot.

You were a teenager once. You know what it was like.

Start by telling your child about your experiences as a teenager and how your world view changed from childhood, into your teenage years and then into adulthood.

Tell her about how teenagers feel the need to rebel and how their raging hormones make them act fairly extreme a lot of the time.

No, this won't inspire her to rebel herself. If anything it will reduce the likelihood. What it will do is to help her understand what teenagers go through and it will give her perspective on her own feelings as she approaches her teenage years.

This **does not** mean that you should start regaling your child with tales of the crazy things you did or the drugs you took as a teenager. Save these stories for when they're adults and they can't throw them back in your face. This is no joke - try telling a teenager not to smoke dope after telling them that you did as a teen. Spoiler alert - it won't work.

Before she becomes a teenager explain that the physical, hormonal and psychological changes that teenagers go through can make her feel alienated from her family. She could end up feeling angry at her parents, despite still being reliant on them.

Tell her that no matter how bad or lonely or angry she ends up feeling it is normal and it will pass. Remind her that you will always love her and care about her, no matter what.

Remind her that you will always love her. This is so important.

Plant the seeds early and you'll make her path, and your path, through the turbulent teenage years that much easier.

Chapter 8: The Teenage Years - Ages 13 – 18

I'd like to start this chapter with a story that affected me profoundly - one that will stay with me for the rest of my life.

Some years ago, when I had already experienced being a guardian to two troubled teenagers (my niece and nephew, who we fostered) and had four kids under 6 years of age, I struck up a conversation with my neighbour, let's call him Bill, about what I thought was a remarkable situation under his roof.

Bill is a fairly hard man, son of a police officer and the kind of dad who you'd expect to brandish a shotgun when boys came sniffing around his teenage daughter.

What amazed me was that Bill's teenage daughter (she was 15) not only had a boyfriend who was older (he was 17), but Bill let the two of them live together in his home.

I was amazed by this and I couldn't help but ask him about it - how in the world did it come to pass that this *man* had come to shack up with his schoolgirl daughter under his own roof?

Bill admitted that, initially, it was difficult to accept the presence of this interloper. It was hard to come to terms with the fact that his daughter was having sex with someone who was older. And they were doing it in his house!

He said, however, that this boy was kind and gentle to his daughter and that they loved each other very much.

His daughter was 14 when she started the relationship with this boy and he said that he was faced with a choice - he could either forbid the relationship, which would only drive his daughter away, or be supportive of her and her choice of boyfriend.

On reflection he realised that by forbidding the relationship not only would he damage his relationship with his daughter, but he'd also force the two young lovers to continue their romance behind his back. Worse, he might actually succeed in driving away this nice kid, this kid that his daughter loved and who he liked, and he might be replaced with someone older and who doesn't treat his daughter with the same respect.

Instead he decided to be supportive of his daughter. Bill decided that it was better to be the lighthouse than to be the sea.

He negotiated with his daughter and they came up with a set of rules that they could all live with. This helped ensure her safety and that she would stay in school.

Over time the boyfriend stayed more and more at Bill's house and he came to treat him like a son. When Bill's daughter asked if the boyfriend could move in with them it was a no-brainer.

This story shocked and amazed me. This wasn't how fathers were supposed to behave.

I thought of myself as open minded and easy-going, but even I saw it as my job to protect my daughters from boys. Especially older boys.

After all, it's only once you've lived inside the mind of a teenage boy that you realise how depraved they can be.

But I could see in an instant that Bill had it right.

He wasn't crazy. The world was crazy and, on this issue at least, his was the only sane voice I had heard.

It was a beautiful, elegant compromise that this hard man had made for the love of his teenage daughter.

And it paid off big time. The young lovers were happy (they're still together, living in their own place, 8 years later) and Bill and his wife were happy.

Everyone followed the rules that they had agreed to and his daughter ended up with a good education (at time of writing she's studying to be a teacher).

This is now my gold standard for how to deal with teenagers. It shows how important it is for us to meet our children in the middle. It shows how important it is for us to start recognising our children as adults, possibly well before we're comfortable in doing so.

In this chapter we're going to look at what can be a really challenging period as a parent - those crazy teenage years.

I say 'can be' challenging, as no two teens are the same. Some teens can be a nightmare, while some can be a breeze.

We'll look at strategies for minimising the turbulence of these years and for maximising the chances of maintaining a warm and loving relationship with your teen.

Remember, however, that there's only so much you can control during this period of their lives. There's only so much you can influence.

They begin this phase of their lives a child and they end it an adult.

After all of your hard work raising him your teen will still make his own decisions.

All we can do in the end is set a good example and hope he makes good ones.

Keeping Them Safe

It's a fact that the parts of the brain that assess risk are some of the slowest to mature.

This is one of the main reasons why teens do things that are stupid. They develop the bodies and the desires of an adult, but they can be hopeless at assessing risk and their judgement can be appalling as a result.

Things that you and I would look at and think 'hmmm...not sure about this, might be worth avoiding it' can have the teen brain thinking 'this looks like fun... wonder if I'll get laid if I do this?'

All jokes aside, teens are a hazard - to themselves and to those around them. Not only are their brains poor at judging risk, the turmoil of being a teenager can cause mental illness, meaning that teenagers are at higher risk of suicide than the general population.

In most countries the leading causes of death amongst teenagers are suicide and accident (primarily motor vehicle accidents).

So how do you keep teenagers safe?

For a start we can't wrap them in cotton wool. This is only likely to result in greater rebellion (as they rage to break away) and even higher risk.

As we learned in the last chapter, often the best way to communicate with the teenage brain is to get to it before it becomes a teenage brain.

Talk to your child before he becomes a teenager:

- Talk about how the teenage brain develops the way it does and why this makes teenagers terrible at assessing risk
- Talk openly about suicide and how badly it affects those that the dead person leaves behind.
- Tell him how glad those who are saved from suicide are to be saved (this is true) and point out what a tragedy it would have been if they had succeeded in killing themselves.
- Ask your child to read news reports out loud about young

people who have killed themselves or others on the road. This is extremely powerful, as it forces to picture themselves in the tragic circumstances that they're reading about. Point out that all of the young people involved in these accidents thought they were skilled enough and sober enough to get themselves and their passengers home that day, but that they were wrong.

- Emphasise that his life is important and that, no matter how bad we sometimes feel, the bad times never last. Life is good and he is destined to live a happy life.
- Discuss depression and mental illness and how such illnesses are as normal and are as treatable as physical injuries. Explain that you can't simply tell someone to 'get over' depression any more than you can tell them to 'get over' a sprained ankle - all injuries and illnesses need time and treatment.
Remove the stigma around mental illness and encourage them to be supportive, not dismissive, of friends that suffer from mental illness, regardless of how minor it may be.
- Ask for his promise that if he, or anyone around him, is having thoughts of harming himself that he will ask for help. In return, promise that he would always receive help in these circumstances and that there is no shame in leaning on others when we need their support.

You should have these conversations often. From before, during and after his teenage years.

If you introduce these topics into conversation when he's already a teenager then you're more likely to encounter resistance - he may just see it as an attempt to over-dramatise and to control him. He will be more receptive when he is younger and this will in turn make him more receptive when he's a teenager.

If he already *knows* that he should never get into a car with a drunk driver by the time he becomes a teenager then he's going to put up less resistance when you attempt to talk to him about it during his teenage years.

Offer Amnesty

When your teenager really fucks something up what do you think he's going to say?

When he makes that massive error in judgement that we all make as teenagers will he say 'I need my dad's help!' or will he say 'My dad is going to KILL me!'?

This is a serious question to consider. If he finds himself in a dangerous situation will he ask for your help? If not he's likely to remain in danger.

In this chapter we're using male personal pronouns, but this issue is particularly important for female teens, who can be at a greater risk of physical and/or sexual assault in some circumstances.

For example, if your teenager sneaks out and gets himself blind drunk, vomits all over himself and gets left in a dark alley by his 'friends', what will he do? Will he call you for help, or will he avoid doing so out of fear of your reaction?

When he gets himself into trouble your first and only priority should be his safety.

He should know that, no matter when or where the problem is, he should be able to give you a call and that you'll help. No exceptions.

This is not the same as giving him a licence to do whatever he wants - quite the opposite.

Explain to him that there will always be ramifications of any stupid action or decision, but that if you're called on to help you will and that all lectures, punishments, etc. will be withheld, at least until the following day.

Once you've offered amnesty you need to be ready to back this up with action. This may be more difficult than it sounds, as it's natural to become upset when your teen (or one of his friends) does something particularly stupid, but if ever there was a time to be the lighthouse, this is it.

You want your teen to know that they can always trust you in these circumstances and this will make them *more* responsible, not less.

This may sound counterintuitive, as you might expect a teen to be more reckless when he knows that dad will be there to bail him out of whatever mischief he might find himself in, but this is not the case.

When he knows that you're there to rescue him, when he trusts that you'll prioritise his safety over everything else, he will think harder before doing things that are stupid. This is essentially because he won't want to let you down by getting himself into situations where he has to ask for help in the first place.

This isn't to say he won't do things that are stupid - sometimes I wonder how teenagers make it into adulthood at all - but he should at least be thinking more seriously about risk and about how to keep himself out of trouble.

This amnesty should extend to his friends, too, as you may be called on to save their bacon from time to time also. If so then wear this as a badge of honour - it's not only your teen who trusts you, but his friends too.

Safety Training

Safety training is an easy and effective way to help your teen say safe in a variety of situations. Best of all - it's inexpensive: You can teach your teen basic, common sense safety techniques for free.

As mentioned in the previous chapter, I strongly recommend enrolling your kids in martial arts training well before they become teenagers. They will not only learn useful self-defence techniques, but will also learn how to avoid and how to diffuse conflict.

You may not be able to teach your teen martial arts yourself, but you can teach him some common sense techniques for identifying and for avoiding risk and what to do if he gets himself into trouble.

This type of safety training can make a real difference. To demonstrate this, consider that those who take a note of the fire exits when entering an enclosed space are many times more likely to survive a fire (or other such emergency) than those who do not. People who actually listen to the pre-departure safety briefing on airplanes are much more likely to leave the plane safely in an emergency, meaning they're much more likely to survive a variety of disaster scenarios than those who don't.

The psychology behind this is amazing and it boils down to this - if we have even a vague plan of action in our minds when an emergency occurs then we're much more likely to do *something* in an emergency. If we don't have a plan of action in mind then it's very likely that we'll do *nothing* in an emergency.

This doesn't just apply to large-scale emergencies, either. If we find ourselves in a threatening situation, if we're being intimidated by someone, for example, then we can freeze, suddenly finding ourselves unable to talk or to move.

This is the absolute worst thing to do. You need to train your teen on how to both avoid these situations and how to handle them when they do come up.

You don't have to conduct safety training in a classroom setting (your teen is unlikely to comply anyway). It can be just as effective to drop advice into conversation.

Focus on practical advice for keeping himself safe in real-world situations.

He's got more chance of choking to death on a chicken nugget than he does of being killed in a terrorist attack, so offering advice on surviving a terrorist attack is probably a waste of time.

Instead focus on simple things like:

- Staying in a group when they're out, particularly if they're intoxicated
- Assessing situations before he gets into them and getting into

- the habit of discussing safety with his friends before deciding to enter (or stay at) a particular location
- Grabbing his friends and leaving an environment if anyone feels unsafe
- Diffusing confrontational situations and getting away from them
- Not allowing himself or his friends to reach a level of intoxication where they become incapacitated
- Looking after friends who are intoxicated - getting them home safely or even to hospital if they need it

There are lots of excellent resources that you can use for advice and inspiration. Check your local police departments' web site - they often have advice on keeping safe, including advice tailored to teens. There are also books on the subject that are full of practical and useful advice.

Driving

In my home country of New Zealand teens can apply for a learner driver's licence from the age of 15 and can be driving unsupervised from as young as 16. Although some countries require people to wait until they're slightly older before they can drive, it's fair to say that we licence teens to drive well before they've developed the maturity required to do so safely.

This is evidenced by the fact that vehicle insurance in most Western countries is so much more expensive for teenagers - in New Zealand it's only once you reach 25 that you start paying the same as other adults for vehicle insurance.

In short, driving is extremely dangerous for your teen and for everyone around him. He's a menace. A ticking time bomb.

Hopefully by the time he's old enough to drive you've already conditioned him for the responsibility. This should have him thinking seriously before getting into cars with drunk drivers and hopefully at least thinking about moderating his speed.

If you really want to reduce this risk of him being behind the wheel, however, you have to maximise the number of hours he spends behind the wheel as quickly as possible.

Nothing beats experience, so you need to make sure your teen has as much experience as possible before he starts driving without you on a regular basis.

You should start by setting a good example. You cannot expect your teen to be responsible behind the wheel if you are not. You cannot expect him to remain calm and to respect other drivers if you do not. Think about this from when they are quite young, as they pick up on a lot more than you'd probably expect.

Next, teach your child to drive as soon as you are legally allowed to. This can be stressful, so think carefully about how you will keep it light and fun. Driving lessons should not result in a shouting match - if things are getting stressful then take a break or agree to postpone the lesson until you've both calmed down a bit.

Help your teen to get his licence as soon as possible and let him drive you around whenever you have the opportunity.

This is really important. Many dads teach their teens to drive but, once they have their licence, they don't often let their teen drive the family car. This means that your teens' formative driving experiences (i.e. where driving becomes an ingrained skill) are spent either driving alone or with his teenage friends.

When he drives you around he should drive safely and courteously. He should not speed, nor should he take undue risks.

This will help build his driving experience and confidence. Most important, it will mean that his formative experience is spent driving safely, which will maximise the likelihood of this safe driving becoming a habit.

If you have the financial means, you should also consider buying your teens a car. It should remain *your* car, but they are given unrestricted use of it *if certain conditions are met.*

If you buy your teen a car then he is much less likely to buy one for himself. This gives you greater control over the safety of the vehicle (preventing a situation where he buys some clapped out death trap) and over how the vehicle is used.

You shouldn't require him to ask to use the vehicle each time, as this could become a bit demeaning and it defeats the purpose of giving him a car to use.

You can, however, insist that he abides by certain rules when he does drive it, such as:

- Any use has to be in accordance with his driver's licence conditions
- No alcohol or drugs
- The car must be licensed and roadworthy at all times. Possibly you could go halves with him on the on-road costs
- No speeding
- No reckless driving

You could also require him to use one of the many driving monitoring apps on the market. These apps, which typically install onto his smartphone, can be used to track and monitor driving behaviour. Personally I prefer to rely on trust - he may not always reflect that trust in the quality of his driving, but I prefer this approach to being big brother watching over him all of the time.

Accepting Your Teen

As your child grows into a teenager, and then into an adult, you will find out things about them that you didn't know. They will be finding out things about themselves that *they* didn't know.

Some of these things may be challenging to you and maybe even to him.

Your teen may be passionate about something that you don't understand. He may choose to pursue a career that he's truly passionate about, but that doesn't fit with your hopes and ambitions for him.

He may be gay.

I can't tell you how your teen will be but I can tell you one thing - he will be exactly as he *should* be.

It can be hard if he doesn't fit with your perceived ideals, but it is not your job to define who he is. This is his job and his alone.

So be ready to accept him as a child. Be ready to accept him as a teen. Be ready to accept him as an adult.

Happiness is not about following the dreams of your parents. Happiness is about being who you are and what you are and it's about following *your own* dreams.

He doesn't *need* your approval to be happy, but it will make it a lot easier for him to be happy when he knows that his dad's love is unconditional. He will be happier when he knows, deep in his soul, that his dad accepts him for who he is and that you admire him for it.

Believe me when I tell you that there's nothing more fulfilling in life to see your children happy. So be accepting of who he is not just for his sake, but for your own.

Giving Them a Path to Adulthood

When we talk about teenagers we tend to focus on the huge transformation that they go through and the problems that this transformation causes. What we often ignore is the transformation that we must go through as parents and how much this can contribute to the 'problems' of raising teenagers.

By the time your teen is 18 he's an adult. He's your peer. He's your equal.

Ok, he might still only change his underwear once a week and he might constantly be asking you for money, but he's still an adult.

But ask yourself this - how likely is it that you'll treat him like an adult?

Almost all dads that I talk to claim to treat their adult offspring as adults, but many actually don't.

As fathers we can find it difficult to let go of the tools and practices that we used when they were children, even when they're grown up and have children of their own. This is why most of us would struggle to live under our patents roofs for more than a couple of days, yours truly included.

We feel like kids again. We feel smothered. We feel marginalised. Even when our parents are accommodating, which they normally are, we still feel like we're being treated like, well, children.

In response we often resort to acting like children.

If this is how we feel after only a couple of days under our parents' roof then how do you think our teenagers feel living permanently under ours? If we fail to give them a path from childhood to adulthood at home they can end up feeling isolated, alienated and frustrated. They can become defiant and uncooperative as they grapple to find their identity as an adult.

This isn't their problem - it's our problem.

If we fail to give them a path to adulthood then the relationship between us and our teen can become strained to breaking point. This often results in the teen moving out before he is, or we are, ready in an attempt to find independence.

Just to be clear - they are going to become adults whether we 'give' them a path to adulthood or not. The only difference is whether we start treating them like adults at the appropriate time or not. We're not giving them their adulthood but we *are* giving them something important. We are recognising them as adults and treating them as such.

This can be harder than it sounds, particularly as we want so hard to stop our young, impressionable teens to avoid making the same mistakes we did. They still need our help, of course, but it has to be on their terms, not ours.

So how do you give your teen a path to adulthood?

First, remember that it isn't something he has to earn. Becoming an adult is a birth right, not something you get to bestow upon him. His path to adulthood can't be conditional - he's going to become an adult whether you're happy with his behaviour or not.

Sit down with your partner and think about what you can do each year, from ages 13 to 18, to progressively give your teen the freedom and the respect that he deserves. Write the plan down and discuss it with friends. It's likely that you'll need to give them more freedom at each juncture than you're happy with, because this is an uncomfortable process.

Then sit down with your teen and ask him for his views. You need to listen carefully to what he has to say and you need to be ready to have this discussion more than once. As he gets older his perception will change, as will yours. You will need to be ready to renegotiate the plan on a regular basis - this is normal and it should not become adversarial. The more mature he becomes the more eloquently he will state his case for greater freedom.

Listen carefully and put yourself in his shoes. He deserves your trust and respect. Yes, he will betray that trust from time to time by doing stupid things, but he will learn more from having an open, honest, trusting relationship with his parents than he would with an acrimonious, distrusting one.

There is no 'one size fits all' for his path to parenthood. This path will vary for every young adult, particularly as some will want their independence faster than others. Remember that, by the time they reach the age of 16 or so, your job is not to prevent them from obtaining their independence, but to help them achieve it safely.

It's not just about giving him freedom, either. As your teen starts approaching adulthood you also need to start treating him like an adult. Here are some ideas for how to do so authentically:

- Ask him for advice. This can be thrilling for him - after a lifetime of you being the font of all knowledge, here is his dad asking *him* for advice. His dad wants *his* opinion. This can be on matters that are trivial (e.g. 'what do you think of this shirt with these pants') but try and find opportunities to ask about matters that are more substantive. You may be surprised at how insightful and useful his advice can be.
- Engage in banter, just like you do with your friends. This is the ultimate sign that you are peers and that one does not hold power over the other. Engage in playful banter, but keep it clean and don't let it become overly aggressive or personal.
- Let him drive. You should be doing so anyway - he can use the practice.
- Take him out with you and your mates. If going out with your friends doesn't appeal then just take him out with you. Getting blind drunk and making a fool of yourself is not recommended (not quite the example you should be setting), but plan an adults night out without any of his younger siblings in tow.
- Make him pay his own way. This shouldn't be optional. If he works then require him to contribute financially to the running of the household. Regardless of whether he works or not require him to help cook and clean. This is what adults do -

your young adult should be no different.
- Most important, let go of the power struggle. Stop expecting him to do things *when you ask him*. Stop expecting him to share your opinion. Yes, you can still expect him to contribute to the running of the household, but he should have the freedom to do so on his terms

Your House/Their House

When you were growing up, did your parents ever refer to what you would and wouldn't do in 'their house' or under 'their roof'?

Mine did and I hated it. The subtext to statements like 'while you're under my roof you will [insert demand here]' is 'this is my house, not your house and if I don't like your behaviour you'll be kicked out of it'.

What a terrible message to send your kids, let alone your teens.

Of course it is your house. But it is also *their* house.

You may be responsible for paying the mortgage or the rent, but they have just as much right to be there as you do.

There should be no underlying threat, spoken or unspoken, that they're likely to be tossed out on their ear if they don't comply with your rules.

While we're at it, avoid patronising your teen with statements like 'you wanted to be treated like an adult, so I'm treating you like an adult..."when they protest about having to contribute around the house.

Of course they want to be an adult, but that's not something that needs to be thrown back in their faces.

This isn't to say that your teen gets to abuse his position as an adult in your household. He still need to pull his weight and he doesn't have licence to throw wild parties in your lounge.

Instead of issuing ultimatums, however, work together to discuss and agree what you expect from each other.

He needs to be ready to respect the feelings of others in the house, including of you and your partner. He should agree to keep his space clean and tidy and to help around the house. You might even put a roster together - it's likely to be what he faces in a flatting situation, so it would be good practice for him.

In return you need to listen to his wants and needs and only object if there is a reasonable and demonstrable reason for doing so, not simply because you're not entirely happy about it.

He may want his girlfriend to sleep over, for example, but you have younger children in the house.

Rather than telling him 'Not in my house!' consider a compromise that protects the innocence of the children while respecting his rights as a member of the household. Such a compromise might, for example, include that only long-term girlfriends are allowed to stay over (no one night stands) and that they need to maintain a certain amount of privacy around the house.

In situations like this, when I'm negotiating, I take a deep breath and ask myself what Bill my neighbour would have done. Maybe you should too.

Be Ready for 'I Hate You!'

Although many parents like to think that *their* precious child would never say such a thing, unfortunately we all get to hear our kids tell us that they hate us at least once or twice while they grow up.

If you're the father of three highly spirited girls like I am, then you get to hear it a lot more than this. And I didn't have to wait for them to become teenagers, either.

To an unprepared parent hearing this can be utterly devastating.

My child hates me! How did this happen? Where did I go wrong?!?

First, let's get one thing straight: Your child doesn't hate you. These words have *no meaning*.

All teens say that they hate their parents from time to time because they don't have the tools to articulate how they feel. Sometimes they blurt it out in a stressful situation as a test to make sure you're still there and that you still care. It may not even be you that they're upset at - they may just be lashing out blindly as a result of stress or frustration.

So be prepared to hear those three words that all parents dread.

When you hear them then for goodness sakes don't return fire. No matter how angry or upset you are, you must never tell your child that you hate him too. Nor should your partner.

You are the lighthouse. You know that your teen doesn't actually hate you. Your teen, however, is the sea. If he hears you say 'I hate you too' then he'll be left devastated. He will instantly forget that he said it first. All he'll hear, and all he'll remember, is that his dad does hate him after all!

Don't do it. Don't lose your cool. Don't return fire.

If your teen says he hates you, either directly or indirectly, then either ignore it or tell him that 'we don't talk about each other in our family'.

If he says it to your partner then you should leap to her defence, but only to tell him that that's not the way you talk to each other and asking him to apologise. By standing up for each other you're showing that your family really doesn't tolerate that kind of language.

Once he's apologised then ask for a hug, tell him you love him and then **leave it at that**.

That's it. No more.

Don't tell him how hurt you were, lecture him or otherwise go on about it.

He will already feel guilty about it, you don't need to lay it on thick.

This isn't to say that it won't happen again - the teenage mind us rash and impulsive, so it very well may happen again. Each time it happens just treat it the same way. Eventually he will grow out of the habit, but he will always remember how his dad never returned fire when he told him he hated you.

'Man, my dad really must love me a lot.'

Don't Expect Rationality

Teens can't be expected to be rational all of the time.

Come to think of it, I don't think any of us can be expected to be rational all of the time, but for teens things can be much worse.

The rapid developmental changes that he is going through can cause mood swings, angst and confusion, particularly in stressful situations.

Don't let yourself get caught up in this.

If another adult lashes out at you then it would be natural to be alarmed and upset. You might become defensive and you might even retaliate.

It's different when your teen lashes out at you or otherwise has a meltdown.

Yes, he may be an adult, but he doesn't yet possess a mature adult brain.

It's a fact that he feels emotions more powerfully than you. He finds it easier to get worked up and harder to calm himself down again. He's easily confused and, let's be honest, just a bit pissed off at everything.

Don't expect rationality. Be pleased when he's rational, but don't be surprised when he's not.

When he is irrational then just don't engage with him. If he's upset and accuses you of ruining his life (or whatever it is that he's aggrieved about) then simply tell him that you're not prepared to talk to him until he's calmed down and then just ignore him.

Don't try and convince him that you haven't in fact ruined his life - it's a waste of time. If he's not seeing things rationally then you're unlikely to do annoying more than wind him up further.

What's the point?

Set some ground rules about what will and will not be tolerated.

Abusive behaviour certainly should not be tolerated. If he becomes abusive then ask him to leave the house until he's calmed down *and ready to apologise*. If he won't leave then don't have a showdown with him - either walk away or call the police. Do not fight fire with fire - see the section below on dealing with abusive teens.

Also, make it clear that any damage to any property caused by an angry teenager will be paid for, post haste, by said teenager.

It may sound shocking, but almost all of us break at least *something* in a fit of rage while we're teenagers.

If it's minor (such as a foot through drywall) then ignore it at the time, but make sure they're made to pay for the repair or replacement. Every cent. They don't have money for anything else until it's paid for.

You'd be amazed at how much more careful they will be the next time they're in a rage - the pain of having to pay for damage they caused will be seared into their consciousness.

If it's more serious then call the police. It's normal for your teen to lose his cool and to lash out at an inanimate object in frustration. Anything more serious, such as a sustained attack on property or any kind of assault against people or animals. Is criminal and the police should be involved.

But it should never get to this. Remember that it is normal for your teen to be irrational and this will mean that you sometimes get the blame for things. Ignore it and don't let it bother you and his behaviour shouldn't escalate into something more serious.

Loving, But Not Friends

If you're one of those cool dads who is more like a friend than a parent to your teen and his friends then I have bad news for you.

You're not his friend. You're his father.

You can be friendly and have a deep, loving relationship, of course, but if you're expecting him to consider you as 'one of the boys' then you're bound to be disappointed.

Just like the coach is never part of the team, the dad can never be one of the teens and you shouldn't try.

Your teen should have friends his own age and so should you.

He should have secrets from you - ones that he will share with his friends but not with you. He's also going to lie to you from time to time. This doesn't make him a bad person - it just makes him normal.

How are you, as his 'best mate', going to feel when you find out that you've been left out or lied to?

You'll feel hurt and resentful, but you shouldn't. You're the lighthouse, not the sea.

Also, how are you going to discipline him if you're his mate rather than his dad? You can't and parents who fool themselves into thinking that they're friends to their teens (rather than parents) usually allow discipline to slide. They're too cool to discipline their teens, after all.

Your teen still needs your guidance and discipline. He needs you to be the lighthouse now more than ever.

He doesn't need the pressure of a dad who expects to be part of his group of friends.

This doesn't mean that you can't be close to your teen. Far from it - stay as close as you can for as long as you can. You can still horse around with him and his friends. You can still spend time with him.

But remember that he needs space to exist apart from his family, just like everyone else.

The Manual

Tell Them They're Beautiful

It's really important that you tell your teen that he's handsome (or that she's beautiful) often.

Teens are still forming an opinion of themselves. Their self-esteem is very delicate.

They're also likely to be experimenting with different fashions, slang, etc. as they try and find their place in their peer groups.

In short, they're very impressionable.

If you don't find your teen handsome or beautiful during this period of their lives then that's your problem, not theirs. If so then take a long, hard look in the mirror, as something needs to change in you, not in them.

If your teen comes home with a Mohawk and a staple in his ear then don't criticise him. You can be shocked, sure. You can ask him about it. But as soon as you criticise him you knock a chunk out of his self-esteem that will be very hard to grow back. No matter how he presents himself he still wants to know that he looks good.

You may not approve of what they have done, but if they've already done it then it's too late for them to go back, so embrace it.

He's expressing himself and no matter what he does to his appearance he's going to feel unsure about it.

You can help avoid situations like this by encouraging him to wait until he's older before getting tattoos or other permanent changes.

With girls you can prepare them for the teenage years by explaining, when they're still young, how clothes don't have to be skimpy for them to feel beautiful.

If he comes home with a look that shocks you then stop and wait for the shock to subside before you say anything. He's still your beautiful child and, no matter how he looks, people are going to be attracted to his charm and character more than his looks. So don't attack his character!

Here are some examples of the careless, throwaway comments that dads can make that can make our kids feel terrible about themselves:

- 'You look like a slut, you can't go out in that!' Usually followed by 'I didn't call you a slut, I said you looked like one!' Of course he called her a slut and he probably broke her heart at the same time.
- 'What the hell are you wearing? You look like a freak!'
- 'Look at your messy, greasy hair - when are you going to get a haircut?'

What we forget is that, by the time they are teenagers, we may be helping to fund their sense of style, but that doesn't give us the right to try and dictate it to them.

It is not our job to tell teenagers what they should or shouldn't wear, do with their hair, etc.

Of course, you can and should prevent your thirteen year old from getting a body piercing or a tattoo, but this is unlikely to be an issue, as he's unlikely to find anyone who will perform such a procedure on a minor.

Our job is to tell our kids, our teens and our adult children that they look amazing.

It is our job to admire them and tell them how proud we are of them and how great they look in whatever they're wearing.

It our job to build them up, not to tear them down.

Social Events

You should encourage your teen to organise and to participate in social events. They're great for helping them build up their social connections while learning social and organisational skills.

But how can you be sure they'll behave themselves? How do you know they'll be where they say they'll be?

Can I trust them?

Until they're 16 trust shouldn't come into it - you're legally obliged to know where they are and that they're safe at all times (check what the legal age is for responsibility in your home country).

So you should encourage them to organise and to attend social events, but you should set rules and guidelines that they have to abide by. The more carefully they follow the rules, the more freedom they should get. If they break the rules you curtail their freedom. Easy.

Sit down with your teen on a regular basis and review 'the rules'. Seek his input and listen carefully to what he has to say. Your objective is not to clip their wings. Your objective is to give them their freedom as quickly as they can responsibly handle it while remaining safe.

Tell them this. Make your objective known to them. Your objectives are aligned - you both want him to have more freedom.

Listen to what he says - if he asks for more freedom then try and find a compromise that gives it to him, while being careful to keep him safe. If he asks for more freedom then it means he feels he's earned it.

If you don't agree then tell him why and set out what he needs to do to get there. He may have to get six months older, or it might be that he has to show that he can be home by curfew for two months. That kind of thing.

Remember that you are going to have to actually give him more freedom no matter what. You can avoid relaxing restrictions for a while here and there, but you'll need to play catch up later.

If you get behind he will find himself without the freedoms that are appropriate for someone of his age. His peers will have more freedom than him and he will feel this acutely. You don't want to find yourself in this position, as he is likely to start defying your rules in an effort to *take* his freedom.

Some tips:

- Always, always talk to other parents whenever they organise anything. If your teen is staying at his friends place, or vice versa, then make it conditional on you talking to a parent first. No matter how pedestrian the event is, at least text the other parent to confirm the details of the arrangement. On the few occasions that my wife and I let this rule slide we ended up regretting it, as our teen conspired with her friends to be somewhere she wasn't supposed to be.
- Get to know all of your teen's friends' parents. You may even find that some of them become your friends too. You need to be careful that you don't stifle your teen - he still needs his privacy and it's not reasonable to track his every movement, but by working with other parents you can reduce the risk of being taken advantage of by your teen.
- If your teen wants to do something then let him organise it. Much of the time he will find it all a bit too difficult and will give up. If he actually does the organising then it's good experience for him and you don't want to get stuck organising it for him.
- Don't just set a curfew, ask your teen how he plans to get back on time.
- Enforce curfews, but give him a grace period. Don't allow yourself to be taken advantage of, but remain reasonable.
- Make sure he always has a way of getting home. There are no lessons to be learned from being stuck in the middle of nowhere in the dark. Make sure his cell phone is charged and that he has credit so he can contact you in case of an emergency. You can also use apps such as Uber to give your

teen a virtual voucher to get home if he doesn't have any money. This isn't just important for his safety - it also removes one of the most common excuses for him getting home late (i.e. no transport).

Drugs and Alcohol

Drugs and alcohol and intoxication in general can be a really tricky subject that you need to approach with caution and forethought.

You could preach total abstinence, but I believe this is completely ineffective, if not damaging.

If you ban your teen from drinking until they're an adult then you're likely to encourage them to defy you and to drink alcohol behind your back. You're also not going to have the chance to teach your kids how to drink responsibly, which is really important.

Drugs are even trickier. Most of us have taken recreational drugs and they are becoming more and more commonplace in our society. When I lived in the UK around the turn of the century it was cheaper to buy an ecstasy pill from some dodgy guy at a bar than it was to buy a pint of beer. I hadn't even had kids by that stage, but even then I was worried about how you'd keep kids safe from drugs when ecstasy was only a few pounds per pill.

The problem with illicit drugs, however, is that they remain exactly that - *illicit*. They can also be severely damaging to the young mind, as even by the age of 18 the human brain hasn't fully developed, making it more susceptible to damage from psychoactive substances.

As with alcohol, if you teach abstinence when it comes to drugs then you may simply force your teen to use drugs behind your back.

My advice is to use a slightly more sophisticated approach that focuses on teaching your teen about drugs and alcohol to maximise their chances of making smart decisions when temptation (or peer pressure) arises.

The most important thing is that you set a good example. This means:

- No smoking. Yes, it can be hard to give up, but you should have done so *before* you decided to have kids. If you smoke then you're going to need to stop, as children of smokers are more than twice as likely to pick the habit up themselves.

Quit. Quit now.
- Drinking in moderation. This doesn't mean that you can't get drunk, but you can only get drunk in socially acceptable settings (no, sitting on your own in the dark on front of the telly does not count) and no getting shitfaced. Drink infrequently. Make sure you remain a happy drinker.
- Not taking illicit drugs and not telling your impressionable kids about your drug taking. If you want to take drugs then do it when the kids are with their grandparents for the weekend or when they otherwise **won't find out about it**. Never keep drugs in the house and don't tell your kids about your drug taking exploits - you'll have lots of time to boast about what a party animal you were once he's an adult, not when he's a teen,

Now that you're setting a good example you should:

- Discourage your teen from smoking. Don't wait until he's a teen - drum it into him from childhood. Reiterate how smoking is expensive, it makes you stink and how horrible smoking-related illnesses usually are.
- Let him have a drink. Teach him how to drink responsibly. Demystify alcohol and, while you're at it, teach him about the harm that alcohol can cause. We let our kids have a sip or two of beer or wine from the age of 10 - from 14 or so they can have a glass of beer or wine on occasion and by the age of 16 they can drink as much as they like if they're in our company.

  We regularly talk about the dangers of binge drinking (getting paralytic) and of alcoholism. We teach them how to respect alcohol and how to moderate their intake. As long as their parents are ok with it, we also let their friends drink in our company and we subtly teach all of them about drinking in moderation and looking out for each other.
- Prohibit drugs, but focus on education rather than demonisation. Kids are informed enough now to realise that they're not in mortal danger from most illicit drugs. When I

was a kid we were essentially taught that drugs would turn you into a junkie and ruin your life, yet we could plainly see that this wasn't the case. Lots of people I knew took drugs and, although some of them were listless stoners, none of them became junkies.

Drugs are still illegal however and they are particularly harmful to the young brain. So instead of teaching moderation, I recommend teaching your teen about drugs and their effects. Instead of demonising drugs, which isn't going to work, why not educate them about the real harm that illicit drugs can do to their young brains and encourage them to wait until they're older before deciding whether they will take illicit drugs.

But won't educating my kids about drugs and alcohol normalise them and make it more likely that they'll drink or take drugs? Actually, exactly the opposite.

Your teen will still encounter peer pressure around drugs and alcohol, but the more he knows about them, and the less mysterious they are to him, the better equipped he will be to deal with it.

When it comes to alcohol, the biggest short term risk is that he or one of his friends drinks to the point that they put themselves in danger. Help mitigate this risk by playing on the same peer pressure that some of his friends will exploit to encourage him to drink.

Talk about how embarrassing it is to get blind drunk, act the fool, puke all over yourself and maybe even to piss yourself in social settings. Explain how it can take a while to feel intoxicated and help him to develop strategies for monitoring and controlling his level of intoxication.

It's also important that he and his friends feel responsible for each other in social settings, particularly where alcohol is involved, and that they all look out for each other. This not only means they help their drunk mates get home, but also that they help each other to moderate their alcohol intake and prevent the embarrassment of having to look after a paralytic mate.

When it comes to drugs it's important that you don't disclose to your teen that you've taken drugs in the past. This can create a difficult situation for the majority of us who have taken drugs at least once, as we don't want to lie to our children, but we certainly don't want to undermine the 'abstinence' message by telling them that we've dabbled in the past. Often teens will see the fact that you have taken drugs as validation that they can too and that any advice you give them about abstinence is hypocritical.

In a way this is right. The situation is hypocritical. So avoid it completely.

Of course we don't want to lie to our teens either.

So what do we say when our kids ask us if we've taken drugs before?

Here's what I say:

'That's a difficult question. On the one hand, if I tell you that I haven't taken drugs before then you'll think I don't know what I'm talking about when I teach you about the dangers of drugs. On the other hand, if I tell you that I have taken drugs before then you might see this as a sign that drugs aren't dangerous, but they can be.

Instead what I will tell you is what I know about drugs and their dangers and I hope you will make the right decision of you ever get tempted. When you and your siblings are old enough I promise I'll answer your questions fully, but until then our priority is to keep you safe.

To do that you must remember that, until you are in your twenties, your brain is still developing and any kind of illicit drugs can be dangerous, so you should avoid them.

Most important, you should always feel comfortable discussing drugs with me and asking me questions about them.'

If might look like a mouthful, but it's not really - this message is usually delivered in conversation, not as a monologue, so it flows naturally.

I do still find this dissatisfying and you may too. This is because my natural desire is to be open and honest with my children, but on the topic of drugs I don't believe it is safe to do so. Not until they're well past their teens.

When You Find Drugs

So what do you do if you catch your teen smoking a joint with his friends? Or maybe you find drugs in his room?

First, don't freak out and overreact. You have every right to be upset, but losing your cool won't help either of you. If he's intoxicated then it may be a complete waste of time anyway.

Think about it for a moment - your number one objective is likely to be to discourage him from abusing drugs, right? Yelling isn't going to help you achieve that goal.

If anything it will be counter-productive, as yelling will simply alienate him and push the behaviour underground.

Instead take him home (if not already) and let him sleep it off while you think the situation over. Avoid making threats or lecturing him - you simply need to tell him that you'll be discussing it with him in the morning.

While he sleeps it off take some time to calmly think about how you will handle the situation.

My advice is to treat the ensuing discussion as a learning experience for both of you.

He's been caught doing something he shouldn't, so you should be able to expect an explanation. Don't force a stalemate, however - if he won't give you any details then there's no point trying to force him.

Let him talk first and be patient - the quieter you are the more he's likely to say.

Call him out on any bullshit, but don't resort to foul language or insults. Tell him when you think he's lying, but do so without calling him a liar. It's much better to say 'come on, that can't be right' and to wait for an answer than to become aggressive.

Your learning opportunity comes from hearing what he has to say and how he's feeling about it. Is he using drugs regularly, or (more likely) are they experimenting? Is he feeling peer pressure to take drugs, or is he a willing participant?

If you're thinking 'there's no way my kid would tell me any of this' then you're wrong. They *want* to share this kind of information with you and they *want* your advice and guidance.

If you're non-judgemental and if you give him plenty of time to talk then you'd be surprised what comes up.

Your response from there will depend greatly on his age. If he's 17 then, like it or not, you can only influence him. You can't make demands or issue ultimatums - he'll only ignore them and it will drive a wedge between the two of you. If you focus on fact-based education, avoiding sensationalism and exaggeration, then you've got the best chance of getting through to him.

If you want to communicate effectively with your teen in this type of situation then your best bet is to be authentic. If you tell him he will end up a drug-addicted junkie if he keeps smoking dope then don't be surprised if he ignores you completely. If you take a more realistic approach, telling him that smoking dope could affect his performance at sports and at school and that (due to randomised drug testing) he could lose his job then he's more likely to listen and take notice.

If he's younger (up to the age of 16, although you'll need to use your judgement) then you can, and probably should, take more of an interventionist approach. It's simply not safe for a younger teen to be abusing drugs. You should still reason with him and try and educate him, avoiding hyperbole. But in this case you should also take steps to ensure that the behaviour will stop.

Try talking to your teen and seeking assurances that he will stop. Find out who he has been getting drugs from and/or taking drugs with and talk to them and their parents (involve the parents before talking to the teen).

Avoid confrontation - relationships will quickly break down if you lose your cool. Explain to all parties that your son is too young to be experimenting with drugs and that you want assurances that it will stop.

Ask for specifics. Press your teen and his friends for details on how they plan to stop and why you and their parents should trust them.

Then you have to trust them a bit, but don't be naive. In most situations they'll stop. Regardless you don't want to hound them.

If it becomes an ongoing issue, however, then buy some drug testing kits. They're inexpensive and easy to use. Use this as an absolute last resort and only when the safety of your teen is at stake, as this is a truly invasive parenting technique.

If you do resort to extreme measures then remember that they should be relaxed as his behaviour improves and as he gets older.

Keep Them Working

From the day your child goes to school until the day they leave home they should be working. People are like sharks - we have to be swimming to stay alive. If we stand still for too long we stagnate. We become listless and unmotivated.

This is particularly an issue for teens, where physical and hormonal changes combined with the gradual change in their responsibilities (i.e. as they become more and more responsible for their own motivation and schedule) can create real motivational issues if they're left to their own devices.

So keep them working.

Whether it's at school, sports, part-time work or even volunteering - the important thing is that they're doing *something.*

This may seem like it conflicts with the rationale behind giving your teen more responsibly and freedom - if I'm giving him more responsibility then isn't it up to him to decide whether he does anything or not?

I think it would conflict with this approach except for one significant detail - if he is a member of the household then he must contribute to the household.

If he's 16 or older (in NZ this is the legal age when teens are allowed to leave school and move out of the parental home) then he may move out on his own and you truly have no right to demand he keeps working unless you're supporting him.

If you are still supporting him (i.e. if he lives with you and does not pay market rent, etc., or if you're supporting him outside of the house) then you do have the right to expect him to keep working.

You shouldn't confuse this with having the right to tell him what to do - as above, as he gets older he should have more and more responsibility to decide what he wants to do. By the time he's 16 it should be his full responsibility to decide his future.

But, no matter what he decides, he should still be made to live in the real world.

And this means working.

Come to an agreement with your teen about what 'working' means and revise this each year - as he reaches adulthood (i.e. 18 years of age, more or less) he should be working just like a normal adult.

Of course, we want them to continue their studies for as long as possible, so we want to devise a plan that encourages academic work over manual labour. Here's what I recommend you do (remember - this should be the result of a negotiation with your teen, not a decree from you to him):

- Figure out what the 'market' rate is for someone to live with you in your house. This should include financial contributions (i.e. rent, bills, shopping, etc.) and physical exertions (helping keep the place clean, helping with gardening, etc.) If your teen is working full-time then this is what they will contribute in terms of money and time.
- Figure out how much you are willing to subsidise him based on his circumstances (i.e. whether he is in full time education, full time employment or somewhere in-between).
- Implement the system and revise annually, but monitor weekly. The objective should always be to incentivise the right behaviour in your teen, not to raise money from him. If he stays at school (or engages in tertiary education) but lazes about the rest of the time then it might be time to adjust the formula so he has to go out and get a job to contribute more (or for his spending money). If he's working all hours after he finishes his studies so he can pay rent then it may be time to subsidise him more.

This is a great method for keeping your teen working and for preparing him for the real world. A few suggestions and pointers:

- Don't cop out - make him pay his share, either financially and/or by staying at school. You are not helping him by

treating him like a 'man baby'.
- You can still be generous, but rather than subsidising him, think about contributing toward his non-essential expenses by buying him clothes, helping pay for vehicle expenses, etc. This means he'll still need to work to earn his keep.
- He should still have to help around the house, just like everyone else. Don't tolerate any 'but that's not my mess' nonsense either - it's a home, not a hotel.
- Give him credit for positive activities, such as sports, lessons, etc. If he can reduce his rent by playing sports or learning new skills then that's a win/win.
- Your teen has to be making a good go of his studies if he's still at school. Think about a penalty arrangement if he's not working hard enough, but make sure it's something simple that you can both agree on in advance.

Managing Angry or Abusive Teens

Sadly, despite your best efforts, the relationship between you and your teen can break down and can become acrimonious.

This section isn't about the minor outbursts that all teens have from time to time. These should be expected and promptly ignored. Talk to your teen about them, have a laugh together about them (no teasing) and expect an apology if they have spoken badly to you, but don't make them into a big deal.

This section is about when the relationship becomes truly acrimonious and your teen retreats into a dark fog beyond your reach.

This can be heart-breaking for any parent - a few short years ago they thought the world of you. Now it seems like they hate your guts.

If you find yourself in this situation then you're not alone and you're not the first parents that this has happened to. There are two things that you must always remember:

1. The safety of you and your family should be your number one priority. You should not tolerate violence (emotional or physical) and you **must not** resort to violence. If you or your teen ever find yourself losing your cool then you should both **walk away** from the situation and let yourselves cool down.
2. This phase of his life does not last forever, so don't let it get to you. Always remember that you are the lighthouse and he is the sea. If you let his behaviour get to you, if you become the sea too, then you can end up crashing into each other and can damage your relationship irreparably.

As with so many aspects of raising a teen, preparation is the best defence against future problems, so start conditioning your teen early - well before he reaches his teenage years (see the end of the previous chapter).

It's no use telling him when he's angry or frustrated that 'this is just your hormones talking' - that will only make him angrier and more frustrated. By preparing him beforehand it will give him a greater perspective on his thoughts, feelings and actions.

You also need to maintain a loving but firm relationship with him.

If he tells you that he hates you when he's 12 and gets away with it, for example, he will keep resorting to this kind of behaviour and it will escalate over time.

Don't settle for it and don't expect him to either.

If he's 16 and he tells you to fuck yourself then you can hardly send him on a timeout, but you can still tell him that 'this is not how we talk to each other in this family' and ask him to leave the room.

Regardless of whether he does or not, don't let the situation escalate. Neither of you will benefit.

Wait until the situation has diffused and sit him down, preferably with your partner present and tell him you're unhappy with his behaviour, that you deserve an apology. Then wait to see what he has to say.

Wait.

You have the advantage of patience and experience.

Don't contradict him or talk over the top of him. You have every right to be upset about his behaviour, but give him a chance to talk about what is bothering him.

It may be that something has been stewing for a while. It may just be that he was feeling irritable and that he lashed out for no real reason.

Ask short, probing questions, but let him talk until he's told you all he has to say.

The very act of talking and listening will help bring you both back together. You can't hate what's right on front of you. You can't seethe while you're spilling your guts. Pressure can't continue to build when the outlet is open.

Then think carefully about what he's said. Put yourself in the shoes of a teenager. What he's saying might not sound correct or important to you, but it may be important to him, even if fleetingly.

Then it's your turn to talk. Always start by acknowledging what he has said, but addressing his behaviour.

Use phrases like 'I understand what you're saying and I need a few seconds to process this, but this still doesn't justify you swearing at me. That's no way to communicate if you have a problem.'

Wait for him to think about it and respond. Avoid guilt trips - trying to intentionally make each other feel guilty is not how mature adults communicate.

Then discuss how you are going to work together to address the issues that he's raised. You can't solve his problems for him, but you are his dad, so you can certainly help.

If he has issues with your behaviour then, instead of getting defensive, be ready to meet him halfway.

Tell him you're prepared to meet him halfway.

It's not unreasonable for you to expect him to meet you there. Use conciliatory language - tell him that, even while you might not agree fully with what he's saying, you can tell that he's genuinely bothered by the issue, so you are prepared to meet him halfway to resolve it, but that he's going to have to do the same. Also, make everything conditional on you being respectful *to each other*. Yes, he was the aggressor in this instance, but instead of just focusing on his behaviour (which can put him on the defensive) relate your expectations back to how you treat each other in your family.

You should find this an effective way of resolving the situation whenever your teen becomes aggressive or abusive. Here are some other tips and techniques for avoiding the breakdown in the relationship with your teen and for mending bridges when the relationship does break down:

- **Give him your time**. He still needs time with his mum and dad, even when it doesn't seem like it. When someone's behaviour is vile then the last thing we want to do is to spend time with them, but that's exactly what you need to do. Insist on one on one time. Make it fun. Don't discuss anything too heavy and don't fight. Just enjoy each other's company and tell him you love him.

- **Remember that teens don't share the same perspective that you do.** They feel emotions more powerfully than we do - both positive and negative. They can also have trouble seeing beyond how they're feeling right now and they can react more strongly to situations than you or I do. The best antidote is to be calm.
- **Criticise the behaviour, not the individual.** When we become flabbergasted with our teens it's too easy to criticise them, saying things like 'you're always so morose!' or 'why are you so horrible?' These may sound like throwaway comments to an adult, but they can be cutting to your teen.
Criticise his behaviour and do so in the context of how the family behaves (e.g. 'You're being rude - if you're feeling grumpy then that's one thing, but we don't talk to each other like that in this family.')
- **Don't blame them for things outside of their control**. For example "Now you've ruined the whole day!" or "We're all depressed because of your behaviour!" Your day and your feelings are your responsibility, not his. By blaming him for things outside of his control you are creating an insurmountable behavioural issue that he has no chance of being able to address.
- **Tell him he's handsome, special, amazing.** Do it often. Do it every day. As above, if you don't see him that way then that's *your* problem, not his. Teens, particularly troubled teens, often only hear negative language from their parents - imagine how this would make you feel if you were in his shoes.
- **Tell him you love him at least once per day.** We all need to hear it from those we love. His behaviour may create a distance between the two of you that may make it difficult to even want to tell him you love him. Find a way. Don't fall into

the trap of telling yourself that 'he's not said it to me so I'm not saying it to him' - he's a teenager, so he has an excuse to act immature. You're an adult.

- **If the relationship truly deteriorates then get help.** Find an experienced, completely independent relationship counsellor who can help. Seek out one who specialises in helping families in your situation if possible. You would be amazed at how effective relationship counselling can be - you may have to drag your teen along kicking and screaming, but remind him that it's a chance for each of you to hear and to be heard. Don't leave it until it's too late - there is no shame in seeing a relationship counsellor and a good one can help you to completely reboot and revitalise the relationship with your teen.

When Anger Becomes Abuse

If you continue to work hard to maintain a positive but firm relationship with your teen then things should never degrade to the point where ultimatums are necessary or to where abuse creeps into the relationship.

In a small minority of cases, however, your teen is going to slide 'off the rails' no matter what you do.

This may be because they are unable to overcome the emotional turmoil that goes with being a teenager, particularly if they are haunted by a traumatic event from their past. This can be particularly distressing for adoptive or foster parents who do their best to help their charges to overcome a troubled past, but sometimes are simply unable to do so.

It may be because they have fallen in with the wrong crowd or a range of other possible causes.

Whatever the reason, it can come to a point where your teenager starts abusing his position in the family unit and you are unable to modify this behaviour. This can escalate to the point where he actually becomes abusive to you and/or other family members. This can include emotional or physical abuse.

How you deal with this differs based on his age.

First, let's talk about abusive behaviour.

Parents can be the last to recognise when their teenager has become abusive toward them, as you want to see the best in him, as you should. Seeing the best in him is one thing, but turning a blind eye to abuse is something altogether different.

Abuse is not ok and you should not tolerate it.

Abuse doesn't always have to comprise actions. In fact, with teens, abuse is most likely to take the form of threats - threats to you and/or your property. These threats can escalate into actions over time, so don't ignore them.

If you ever feel unsafe then withdraw and call the police. This is really important - not only for your safety, but for his. If your teen attacks you or a member family then it is likely that you will defend yourself and in many cases the teen is more likely to be hurt than you are.

If you don't feel like you are in imminent danger then it's important that you respond to abuse firmly.

If the situation is heated then withdraw and let things cool down.

Once you've both had a chance to let off steam then tell your teen that abuse is unacceptable, that it makes you and your family feel unsafe in your own home and that, if it doesn't stop immediately then you will call the police.

If it doesn't stop then call the police.

What they will do will vary from place to place, but any good police department will be trained in how to deal with this kind of situation and they will take it seriously.

Remember that, once you have called the police, you may lose control of the situation to a certain extent. If the police decide to arrest your teen, for example, then you may not be able to prevent this from happening, but this is his problem - not yours.

You may be thinking to yourself 'that's a bit extreme - I don't want my teen to be arrested' or something to that effect, but this is wrong. If you were abusive to your family then you would hope that they'd call the police. No one should accept abuse in their lives, including you or your family members.

It can be hard to make that call, but you have to - it's not going to help you or him if you chicken out.

The very fact that you have called the police will send a strong message to your teen that you and your family won't accept abusive behaviour from him. This alone will be enough to shock most teens into stopping the abuse.

The police department should send police around to at least talk to you and your teen and they may or may not arrest him depending on his age and the severity of the offence.

No matter what happens, it's important that you talk to your teen about the event after the fact, once everyone has calmed down. Don't accept any deflection of blame. It's not your fault that the police were called - it's his. The most important thing is that he realises that abuse will not be tolerated and that he needs to find another way of dealing with his anger.

Whether or not you resort to calling the police, you should also seek help from social services if you think your teen is becoming abusive. The support you receive can be variable depending on how good (or bad) social services are in your area, but it is worth a try. If they are good then they may offer assistance and support to help you manage the relationship with your teen and to address his abusive behaviour.

If the abusive behaviour doesn't stop then keep involving the police.

If it doesn't stop then you're also going to be left with no choice but to ask your teen to leave.

Where will he go?

That's his problem. If he has become abusive then you have to put your family's safety first.

This will be a hard call for any dad to make, but you won't be helping him by avoiding it. You have to make it very clear that the family, like the world in general, won't tolerate abusive behaviour and that abusive people will find themselves marginalised.

If he finds himself kicked out of the family home then that's a choice that he's made, not you.

It's one he'll have to live with.

Sexuality and Sex Education

Ahh... sex. Is there any more awkward subject to discuss with your teens?

If there is then I'm not sure what it is.

Most dads find this subject matter uncomfortable, which unfortunately means that many dads avoid the subject altogether. This is unfortunate because teens *need* sex education and the best place to get it is from their parents.

Yes, they will get some form of sex education at school, but schools are very limited in what they can teach your kids. Schools walk a very fine line when teaching sex ed due to the widely varying views and beliefs of their students and their parents.

So you are going to have to bite the bullet and have that uncomfortable discussion with your kids. Like it or not, it is your job to educate them about sex. As we learned above, if you don't then they will educate themselves, and their primary source of education will be porn and other undesirable sources. This is not the kind of sex education that you want your kids to have.

Although I'm just as awkward as the next dad when it comes to discussing sex and sexuality with my kids, I have found that there are a few techniques that we can use to make it less daunting and more effective.

For a start, don't wait until they're old enough to have sex to talk to them about sex. By this stage it's probably too late. They may not have had sex, but they will have formed their own opinions about it and it will be really difficult to bring up.

If you haven't spoken to your teen about sex for the first 16 years of their lives then you can pretty much guarantee that they'll be mortified when you finally summon the courage to bring the subject up. You can imagine how much more awkward this is going to make you feel.

So don't wait 16 years - start educating them about sex from an early age.

Before we go any further let's get something straight: educating your kids about sex *will not* increase the chances of them being promiscuous, getting an STD or being a teenage parent.

In fact the opposite is true. If you really want to maximise your child's chances of him having an *unhealthy* sex life then teach him nothing but abstinence. Study after study shows how foolish teaching abstinence is. It almost always simultaneously involves teaching your kids nothing about sex and results in much higher incidences of sexual dysfunction, teenage pregnancies, STD's and other undesirable outcomes.

So when your child asks where he came from (and he will) don't use euphemisms or folklore. Don't tell him that a stork delivered him or other such fairy tales.

Tell him in your own words how you and his mother love each other very much and how you made a baby: how you made *him*. You probably don't want to be overly graphic when he's at a young age, but you also shouldn't be afraid to use words like 'penis' and 'vagina'.

As he gets older make these discussions more detailed. Initiate these discussions with him, but don't make a big deal about it. You don't have to sit him down and tell him it's time to talk about the 'birds and the bees' like some 1950's movie.

I find the best place to talk about subjects like this is in the car, where you can maintain each other's attention, but you don't have to make eye contact with each other while discussing such delicate subject matter.

It's very important that any discussion about sex and about sexuality revolves around safety and consent.

Make it very clear to him from an early age that his body is **his body** and he decides who touches it. Describe 'yes' feelings (warm hugs, pats on the head, etc.) and 'NO' feelings (*anything* that he finds inappropriate) and how he should react whenever he has a NO feeling.

How should he react? Easy: if he has a NO feeling then he should say NO! He should run to an adult and tell that adult that he didn't like what happened, regardless of what it was or who made him feel that way.

You need to make it clear that you will always listen to and believe him if he tells you he's had a NO feeling and that he doesn't need any more justification than it made him feel 'NO!'

Children can be curious and this can result in unfortunate situations as they experiment on themselves and on each other. Tell him that he shouldn't be touching other people's 'privates', as doing so is likely to create a NO feeling in others.

As he gets older these messages can become more sophisticated, but this is a discussion that you need to have often for the message to be effective.

As he gets older, introduce messages about respecting others and about consent.

It is so important that your teen fully understands and appreciates the concept of consent before he becomes sexually active, particularly given the influence of pornography on teenagers. He should not only seek consent from his sexual partners, but he should also look out for others who may not have consented to sexual behaviour also.

Parties are a particular risk area for teens, as they can become inebriated and they can be taken advantage of.

Explain to your teen that someone can appear to consent to sex when they're paralytic, but can be devastated to find out they've been taken advantage of when they wake up the next day. This can ruin lives - one partner can feel violated while the other can become stigmatised. In serious cases one party could be accused of, and may be guilty of, rape.

To be safe he and his friends should have a rule that sex is only allowed with those who are not completely shitfaced. Encourage him to make this a rule for life - not just while he's a teen. If his sexual partner has been drinking then he should ask for consent, and receive a clear approval to proceed, before engaging in sexual activity. He should continue to ask questions, such as 'is this ok', 'do you want to continue' to be absolutely sure - these don't necessarily have to be a passion killer if handled sensitively.

Just to be clear, you don't have to talk about sex with your teen all the time - this wouldn't just be awkward, it would be weird if not inappropriate. But you should broach the subject from time to time.

Simply saying 'if there's anything you need to know about sex you can ask me anytime' is not enough. You may feel like 'dad of the year' for telling them that your door is always open, but this won't make saying so effective. You've chickened out and your teen will too - it's very unlikely that he'll summon the courage to ask you questions regardless of your invitation.

If the subject doesn't come up naturally for a while then try asking your teen questions about sex and sexuality. Think about what you will ask before you talk to check that it's both appropriate and that it will minimise discomfort or embarrassment. You might want to try relating it back to your experience by saying something along the lines of 'Things have changed a lot since I was your age - we had very little sex education growing up, which was a problem. They are a lot better at it now in schools, what do they teach you about...'

Again, it's important that you use your own words, but an approach like this sets the discussion up as a conversation, rather than a lecture. You have shared a little information about your experiences, which will pique their curiosity and you have intentionally lowered your guard.

A few tips for having effective conversations with your teen about sex:

- Encourage your teen to have the courage to wait. Explain that peer pressure can make teens engage in sexual activity

before they're ready and that no one ever looks back and is glad that they rushed in. Lots of people are, however, glad to look back and say that they waited.
- He should never, ever, allow himself to be pressured into sex, even with someone he's had sex with previously. This is a particularly sensitive issue for girls, especially when older boys are involved. Condition them to be repulsed by such pressure and that they should reject partners who put undue pressure on them.
- Focus on messages of love and mutual respect, tenderness and kindness. Talk about the importance of discretion and how he should not betray the trust of his sexual partners by discussing intimate details that they might not want him to discuss.
- Assure him that, as long as they do not involve harming others, his sexual thoughts and desires are normal, no matter what. We're all different and we all want different things. The teenage mind can be a dark and mysterious place, but he shouldn't be ashamed of the thoughts that he's having.
- Talk about contraception and drum it into them that they should use a condom for *every* sexual encounter until they have a steady, long-term, monogamous relationship. Even then they should consider using one. If this goes against your religion then I suggest you reassess your priorities, as your child's sexual health is important. Make condoms available - figure out a system for doing so that minimises embarrassment for all parties.
- Talk about abortion. Teens can have an overly simplistic view of abortion - one that can make it sound a lot less traumatic than it can be. Keep the discussion factual, not ideological.
- Talk about STD's, how to avoid them and what to do if they get one, including notifying recent sexual partners.
- Drum it into your teen that they should never, ever take nude or risqué photos of themselves, allow such photos (or video) to be taken of them or to take photos of others.

- Be brave enough to talk about foreplay, masturbation and sexual intercourse. Explain that there is nothing wrong with masturbation and that he should never be ashamed of it, but that he should always be careful to not let porn and masturbation take the place of a healthy sex life.

Pornography

We covered pornography in the last chapter, but we're going to cover it again here, as considerations around porn change as kids get older.

You can't reasonably monitor your 16 year olds surfing habits, so your focus has to shift away from prevention and toward further education.

For a majority of teenagers their main source of sex education is porn and this can be really damaging as it:

- Distorts their attitudes and expectations around sex and consent
- Harms their perceptions of women, resulting in increased harassment, discrimination and abuse toward women
- Encourages the self-creation of porn, including everything from naked selfies to homemade pornographic videos

It is important that you continue to talk to your teen about pornography as he matures. You must continue to emphasise the importance of respect, consent and good old fashioned romance.

You probably won't be able to talk him into avoiding porn, but at very least you may be able to help him maintain a healthy perspective on what he's seeing.

With your help he will realise that what he's seeing on screen is not the same as reality.

You Don't Choose Their Friends

It can be particularly galling when your teen, who you have invested so much time and energy into raising 'right' comes home with a friend or girlfriend who is obnoxious or otherwise undesirable.

What does it say about your son if this is the type of person that he hangs around with? Worse, what does it say about you as a parent?

How his choice of friends reflects on him or on you is irrelevant and it probably reflects on both of you a lot less than you think.

He has the right to choose his own friends and, as long as they're of an appropriate age and as long as there are no safety issues to contend with, there's nothing much you can do about it. Not after the fact, at least.

If you want to minimise the chances of your teen becoming a 'shit magnet' then you have to start early.

From when he's a child he should hear about the importance of surrounding himself with the right people. He should value friendship, loyalty and integrity over looks, money and race. You should encourage him to help friends when they are in need of help, but also how important it is for him to exclude negative influences from his life.

He should know the difference between being *generous* and being *taken advantage of* and the importance of being the former and not the latter.

Also focus on *his* self-esteem. If your teen has low self-esteem then he's more likely to surround himself with negative influences.

By the time he's a teenager he should be a relatively good judge of character, so trust him to make his own decisions about who he associates with. Bear in mind that we can make unkind initial assessments of teenagers (excluding our beloved angels, of course) simply because they are teenagers. Even if your son's friends (or girlfriends) are genuinely nice people, they may not appear to you that way at first.

Regardless of how you feel about his friends, they are his friends and you should do more than tolerate their presence. Your teen has chosen to associate with these people, so don't embarrass him by being rude or disrespectful to them. Doing so will only leave your teen feeling conflicted and torn between you and his friends.

You may think that being rude to friends you don't like might discourage your teen from hanging out with them, but often the opposite is true. By being rude to his friends or by disparaging them to your teen you're probably just driving a wedge between the two of you.

If you're right, and if his friends are not people that he should be hanging around with, then these undesirables are likely to exploit this split, helping to drive the wedge further between the two of you.

Instead, be kind to his friends, even the ones you don't like.

Get to know them. Get to know their parents.

Let them stay at your house (which is also your teen's house, don't forget) and let them eat at your table.

Once you get to know them you can call them out about behaviour you don't like. If they are obnoxious then have them up about it - explain the standards of behaviour that your family expects and that they will need to abide by these standards while in the family home (note - the family home, not *your* home).

If elements of his friends behaviour bothers you then talk to your teen about it while his friends are not around, but remember to criticise the *behaviour*, not the person. You can try serving up what's called a shit sandwich to prevent getting your teen's back up (and thereby provoking a backlash). A shit sandwich comprises a compliment (the first slice of bread), the message (the shit) and another complement (the second slide of bread). Here's an example:

'I like Michael, he's really funny. You know, it does bother me how he talks about his girlfriend - he can be really cruel and disrespectful when he talks about her. Still, you've chosen him as a friend, so I'm sure he must nice and that this he's maybe just showing off a bit around his mates.'

Be careful not to lay it on too often or too thick. You don't need to criticise everything his friends do - save your comments for the things that really bother you and that you think could be harmful to others. You need to avoid becoming a constant whisper in his ear - he won't appreciate it and it wouldn't be fair for you to do so.

Otherwise you should be positive and supportive about his choice of friends.

Stay Out of Their Disputes

Don't get involved in your teen's disputes unless there are genuine safety issues for you to be concerned with. There are likely to be many minor disputes over his teenage years - they should all be minor and relatively brief. Many dads make the mistake of getting involved in these disputes out of loyalty to their teen, but this is a mistake.

Remember that disputes between teens are typically a lot shorter in duration than disputes between grown adults. They can also seem a lot more acrimonious than they really are.

Teens can be overly emotional and they can react strongly to conflict. They can say things to each other, and about each other, that can leave you feeling alarmed and as if you need to step in to defend your teen, or maybe even help him inflict damage on the other party.

Don't do it.

For a start, it's completely inappropriate for a grown adult to be caught up in such a conflict. It won't help your teen (who will miss out on the opportunity to learn about conflict resolution) and it certainly won't help the person he's feuding with (who will feel ganged up on). In the worst case scenario, your involvement will cause other parents to become involved and before you know it a minor spat between teens has become a major diplomatic incident.

Also, teens are likely to make up, and may even become best buddies again, before you know it. One minute they want to kill each other, the next they want to stay over at each other's houses.

Where does that leave you if you've told your teen that you always hated his friend anyway and that you're glad that he's no longer friends with him (or worse)?

This is not a position you want to be in. You've instantly created a wedge between you and your teen. You can start pretending to like his friend again, but you've already let the cat out of the bag - your teen (and soon his friend) will know that you hate the friend's guts.

When your teen is engaged in conflict your job is to listen and to be supportive.

Encourage them to see the problem from both sides and to always put himself in the other person's' shoes.

If a group is ganging up on an individual, which can happen often, then encourage your teen to be brave enough to defy the peer group and to support the person being victimised. It doesn't matter how odious the person's alleged behaviour is, no one deserves to have an entire group gang up on them.

Encourage him to moderate his behaviour and to turn the other cheek when he feels that he's been aggrieved. This will help him to minimise both the amount of drama and the duration of the conflict.

Chapter 9: Into Adulthood

In case it's not clear, references to 'children' in this section refer to your adult children.

It's a strange and wonderful transition as your offspring become adults in their own right.

It's strange, as your child no longer relies on you for life's necessities.

It's wonderful as she still needs you and wants you in her life regardless.

This is a parenting manual, so we won't dwell on adulthood for too long. But it is worth remembering that you'll be dad to her as an adult for longer than you were dad to her as a child. It takes her only 18 years or so to become an adult, but hopefully you'll have another 50 years or more with her in your life after that.

The trajectory of her adult life will be influenced greatly by the childhood that you've given her.

Now that she is an adult you have to stop trying to influence this trajectory and trust that your daughter will make it on her own.

You still need to be there to support her. Emotionally, logistically and possibly even financially.

But now it must be on her terms.

Many parents lose sight of this fact and they struggle to relinquish control of their children's lives. This causes friction, as the child can feel suffocated and resentment can quickly breed.

Looking in on our adult children's lives we often think we know better than they do about what they should and shouldn't do. This is particularly the case of we watch them make the same mistakes that we did.

But we are wrong. We don't know better than they do.

We started this book by discussing how there was no better parent for your child than you. We end it by discussing how there's no one more qualified to live your adult child's life than her.

She is the only one qualified, in fact, so you have to take a back seat.

This is not to say that we can't be strong and supportive fathers to our adult children. They should expect nothing less.

But supportive and meddling are two different things entirely. We have to learn how to be the former without becoming the latter.

Successful But Unhappy

To demonstrate the importance of giving your children room to find and pursue their own passions, let me share the story of Chang (not his real name), a successful accountant in a big firm in Auckland, my hometown.

I met Chang, who is about my age, at an industry event for early stage companies (commonly referred to as 'start-ups'). I and the other attendees assumed that Chang was there to scout for business - it is common for accountants, lawyers and investors to attend these events on the lookout for business opportunities.

It was only later when I started talking to Chang that I found out that the real reason he was there was because he hated his job and he yearned for something different.

He had excelled at school and at work and was in the path to becoming partner at his firm, but he told me that he hated every minute of it.

By now he thought it was too late to make a career change, as he had a big mortgage and kids in an expensive private school. He yearned to do something else, but he felt trapped by his own success.

I asked him why he chose a career in accounting if he disliked it so much.

'Because that's what his parents wanted me to do.' was his answer.

He didn't put up a fight - he knew how hard his parents had toiled to give him the education that they didn't have and he figured he'd come to like working in an industry that, at the time, held no interest for him at all.

By the time he was old enough to realise he'd never come to enjoy being an accountant he felt like he was trapped there.

The surprising thing about Chang's story isn't so much that he would find himself in this position, but rather the number of people who do. It never ceases to amaze me how many people I come across in my professional and private lives who are successful but unhappy.

Of course, the blame for this cannot be laid at the feet of their parents. We are talking about adults, after all.

Chang *feels* trapped but of course he's not trapped at all. He's choosing to stay where he is. He has the luxury of being able to choose to do so - there's nothing stopping him from selling his expensive house and putting his kids into a public school so he could quit his job and pursue his dreams.

But it is true that most of us are conditioned to measure our worth in terms of our financial success. It is drummed into us from an early age: Money = Success = Happiness.

But in reality, as we discovered in the first chapter, there's no correlation between wealth and happiness. And what is success if we're not happy? Surely it's impossible to be simultaneously successful and unhappy? We may excel in our careers, but if we're not happy then what's the point?

So forget about trying to 'make' your adult children successful, as one day you may succeed, just like Chang's parents did. His parents didn't make Chang successful but unhappy, but they certainly created the conditions for this to happen.

Instead support your children in their quest for happiness.

Don't judge their actions, their decisions or their associations unless safety issues arise that leave you no choice.

Your progeny might end up living hand to mouth, but if they are truly happy and contented then what more could any parent wish for?

Supporting Their Decisions

Being supportive of your adult child starts with supporting her decisions without criticism. You can ask questions, of course. You can even ask 'have you thought carefully about this?' or 'are you sure that this is a good idea?', but these need to be genuine questions, rather than criticisms dressed up as questions.

You can provide advice, but it has to be advice that she wants to hear. This doesn't mean that she has to agree with your advice - just that she wants you to dispense it in the first place.

Establishing this is so easy - all you have to do is ask 'do you want my advice on this, or do you just need me to listen?'

That's all there is to it. But how often have your parents asked this simple question?

If she says yes then offer your advice in a reasoned and dispassionate way that doesn't criticise her, even if you're cautioning her against her idea.

If she doesn't want your advice then *just listen*. That's what she needs you to do. She may figure it out as she's verbalising it to you. She may even ask you for your advice at the end.

But if she doesn't then just drop it. You don't need to keep reminding her that your opinion is either readily available, or that it was available after the fact.

Regardless of whether she listens to your advice or not, she may end up making a decision that you don't agree with. You need to be prepared for this and, most important, you need to find a way to support her, even if you don't agree with her.

Again, so many parents get this wrong and they choose to attack the decision, even after it's been made. This doesn't help their child, it hurts them.

We value and respect the opinions of our parents and we *all* seek their approval, whether we acknowledge it or not. We value our own independence more, however. If we didn't then we wouldn't be able to make any decisions on our own.

Your child still wants your approval. If you withhold it then you're likely to leave her feeling conflicted and upset.

So if she makes a decision that you don't agree with then take a second to get over yourself and then support her regardless. This doesn't mean that you have to be dishonest with her, you can still make your opinion known, but in a way that is supportive rather than discouraging.

For example, you can say something like 'Well, that's not the choice that I would have made, but I know you'll find a way to make this work. Is there anything I can do to help?'

From that point on there is *no need* to remind her that you disagreed with her approach. If she falls flat on her face then the last thing in the world she will need is for you to say 'I told you so'. Instead try something like 'Well, you were brave for trying. I'm proud of you for giving it a go, what are you going to try next?'

Better Said than Unsaid

I once read an article that claimed that one of the most common regrets of the dying is that they didn't reconcile with their children sooner. Now I don't know how much science there was behind this claim or how accurate it is, but it did fascinate with me nonetheless.

How can the most sacred relationship between parent and child become so calcified that reconciliation is required, let alone so difficult that we wait until we're dying before contemplating doing anything about it?

Of course, I know the answer to this question. Well, one answer, anyway. I never did reconcile fully with my alcoholic mother before she died suddenly one day. She had long before disappeared into the fog of alcoholism, which made me feel like any meaningful communication was impossible, let alone reconciliation and redemption.

I cannot tell you what will come between you and your children over time. I cannot tell you what disputes you will have with each other or how you should go about resolving them.

All I can tell you is that you should resolve them. And fast.

Instead of allowing what is 'unsaid' to linger like the proverbial elephant in the room, *say it*. If you are upset enough about something that it warrants action then tell your child about it. Talk to her openly and honestly and expect the same from her.

It is important to remember that, once she is an adult, she is your equal and she needs to be treated as such.

She doesn't owe you anything and you don't owe her anything. Just focus on discussing the issue at hand.

If you are discussing a difficult subject, such as something you are unhappy about, then avoid generalisations or historic grievances. Any sentence that starts with 'You always...', 'You never...' or 'Why do you always...' should be avoided.

If you sense that your child is growing resentful about something then talk to her about it. Be ready to listen and to work with her to resolve the problem, whatever it is. Life is too short to let issues fester between the two of you.

Give Them Independence, Whether They Want It or Not

Every adult should be able to stand on her own two feet. We covered this in the last chapter, but as they move from teen to adult it is important that they become truly independent.

When should this happen?

Every situation is different. If your progeny is doing a PhD or some other form of long-term study then you will probably want to cut her some slack. There's also nothing wrong with supporting your child for a year or two if she wants to let loose a bit after finishing her studies.

Otherwise she needs to be gently but firmly pushed out of the nest and able to fly on her own.

You will do her no favours by mollycoddling her.

You can still be generous to your adult children, but be careful to be generous in ways that are not going to spoil them.

If you have the financial means to help her then, rather than subsidising her lifestyle while she's younger, consider saving some or all of it away so you can help her with a deposit on a house or an investment in a business in future. Not only will your contribution have a much more significant and longer-term impact on her quality of life, you'll also reduce the risk of her becoming overly dependent on you (which will stunt her independence).

Tell Them You Love Them

Your child still needs to hear that you love her, even when she's an adult. Sometimes especially now that she's an adult.

We all need to know that someone, somewhere is thinking about us and that they'd notice if we were gone.

We have so many communication options at our disposal these days that there are simply no excuses for not talking to your child often and, of course, for letting her know that you love her.

Over time she may form a family of her own and you need to tell them you love them too.

If you're really lucky you'll hear 'I love you too'.

Made in the USA
Middletown, DE
22 May 2018